ITALY'S WORLD OF WINES

Italy's World of Wines

INCLUDING WINE INDEX AND COMMENTARIES

◆

Arturo Barone

RENAISSANCE BOOKS
FOLKESTONE, KENT

ITALY'S WORLD OF WINES
INCLUDING WINE INDEX AND COMMENTARIES
by Arturo Barone

First published 2008 by
Renaissance Books

Renaissance Books is an imprint of
Global Books Ltd
PO Box 219, Folkestone, Kent CT20 2WP, UK

© Arturo Barone 2008

ISBN 978-1-898823-60-5

British Library Cataloguing in Publication Data
A CIP catalogue entry for this book is available
from the British Library

Set in Garamond 11.5 on 13pt by Bookman, Slough, Berkshire
Printed in England by Athenaeum Press Ltd., Gateshead, Tyne & Wear.

To my family

CONTENTS

ACKNOWLEDGEMENTS

A number of individuals and firms, much too numerous to mention all by name, have been of help to me in compiling this guide to Italian wines. Nevertheless, I should express my thanks to Aldo Vajra for clarifying the applications of the barrique, to Barry Walker for his unfailing encouragement, to my old friend Gerald Rothman for correcting some aspects of my idiosyncratic use of the English language, to my doctor of over thirty years standing, Stephen Cohen, for his enthusiasm and support, and to Alessandra Bottaro of the Italian Institute for Foreign Trade in London for ensuring that my rather judgemental approach to wine tasting should not become too irritating.

At the end of the day, I accept full responsibility for my inevitable mistakes.

Lastly, I acknowledge a great debt to my publisher, Paul Norbury, for his inspiration to write this book in the first place, and subsequently for his patient revisions and tidying up without which this work would never have seen the light of day.

PREFACE

This is not a textbook on Italian wines but merely a simple guide which I felt might be useful given their increasing popularity. This growth in the market is largely thanks to the enterprising spirit of a few exporters and many importers, together with the efforts of the Italian authorities, and the decision by the supermarket chains to promote Italian wines (initially prompted no doubt by the comparative cheapness of the product rather than for any cultural reasons).

One outcome of this 'discovery' of Italian wines is the publication of a number of books on the subject. Most of them are comprehensive and, in my view, probably too detailed for the layman who is in need of simpler information that will enable him to determine why he might choose a Barolo rather than a Chianti, a Lugana rather than a Soave. Indeed, I am tempted to suggest that an Italian Wine Appreciation Society is called for!

As far as this volume is concerned, I have tried to approach the subject-matter in a relaxed and accessible way, avoiding technical language as far as possible, allowing the reader to dip in and out of the text to suit time and inclination, and thus become a handy work of reference.

Until recently, Italy was the greatest producer of wines in the world. During the five-year period, 1986-90, Italy's average annual wine production was 65m hectolitres, as compared with France's 64m hectolitres. Between 1991 and 1996, however, Italy's production fell but so did that of France, and Italy was still ahead in terms of average annual output (60m and 52m hectolitres respectively). In 1997, this difference began to be reduced and for the first time, in 1999, France beat Italy by producing 60,435,000 hectolitres, Italy dropping substantially to 56,454,000 hectolitres. Spain came third with 41,692,000 hectolitres, a major increase on previous years. I mention these three countries at the outset because they play a primary role in wine production. Not so far behind was the United States, with a yield of 32.13m hectolitres.

Quantities produced elsewhere are not comparable. For example, Germany comes fifth, with a mere 9,852,000 hectolitres, Portugal sixth with 6,694,000 hectolitres and, almost at the bottom of the scale, Luxembourg with 132,000 hectolitres. Surprisingly, the United Kingdom was not quite last. It produced 14,000 hectolitres (1,000 more than in the previous year) and the country with the smallest output, understandably because of its size, was Belgium with 2,000 hectolitres, which is negligible. (Figures supplied by the Office International de le Vigne et du Vin (OIV) in Paris as at 31 December 2000.) For the reader who is interested in statistics, a small up-dated league table is provided at the back of this book (App 4). That apart, the reader might like to have before him the figures relating to the production of wine in the United Kingdom for 2005: white wines 10,427 hectolitres equivalent to 1,390,267 bottles, red wines 2,379 hectalitres equivalent to 317,000 bottles. The area under production in 2005 was 722 hectares out of a total dedicated area of 793 hectares. (Figures provided by the English Wine Producers Association.)

As a general up-date, I provide the estimated wine yield for the two principal wine-producing countries: production in France in 2004 has remained fairly constant at about 57m hectolitres; that for Italy is said to be 52m hectolitres, which is the equivalent of 11.55m gallons.

The reader may also like to know that the European Union wine production for 2003 was the lowest in ten years, because of high temperatures and drought. It is not expected to increase significantly in the short term, not least because wine consumption generally is decreasing in the three principal production countries, namely France, Italy and Spain.

Another statistic worth mentioning here relates to exports. In 2003, the worldwide share of the export market was as follows:

France 22%
Italy 20%
Spain 17%
Australia 8%
Chile 6%
United States 5%
Portugal 4%

Germany 4%
South Africa 3%
Argentina 2%
Others 9%

Three further statistical items are of interest:

1. It has been calculated that in Italy at least two out of ten square metres of cultivated soil are dedicated to the vine.
2. Italy produces 21% of total world production of wine and 33% of that of the European Community.
3. The Italian wine export trade represents 20% in value of Italy's total exports.

The area in Italy planted with vines is 908,000 hectares (over 1.5m hectares, or 2.9m acres). There are more than 3,800 *types* of wine produced, in varying quantities and, obviously, of differing quality. There are said to be 50,000 wineries and 18,000 different wines in Italy. One of the Italian 'Bibles' on wine production[†] claims that in 2006 its inspectors sampled 15,476 wines of more than 2,126 producers (equivalent figures for 2007 are 2,206 producers and 16,000 wines). One of its competitors, the *Espresso Wine Guide*, stated in 2004 that its inspectors had tasted over 14,000 wines, had reviewed 8,200 wines and had commented on 1,668 producers!; although neither can compete with the 2005 Hachette *Guide des Vins* whose experts claim to have tasted 'blind' 32,000 wines! (the number of wines for the 2007 version of the Hachette guide is 10,800). Understandably, because of lower production, the number of Spanish wines reviewed in the *Guia Pēnin* for 2006 only amounted to 11,745.

There are over 150 *officially recognized* varieties of grape growing in the territory of the Italian Republic; another 250 are to be found scattered in various localities and some writers maintain that the real total number of Italian vines approaches 1,000. In wine terms, they are Italy's real, unique wealth. It follows that it would be almost impossible, in an introductory guide such as the present one, to list all the wines and the detail of all the grape varieties. Furthermore, the number of Italian grape growers is said to exceed 900,000. Given

† *Vini d'Italia* published by Gambero Rosso/Slow Food, now in its twentieth year, is updated every year and contains approximately 800 pages; the English edition is entitled *Italian Wines*

that many will be converting at least some of their harvest into wine
in their own garages, one could boast that the number of producers
must comfortably exceed half a million!

In view of these awe-inspiring statistics, I have confined
identification and comments to DOCG, DOC, IGT (as subsequently
defined) and a few other wines available for purchase outside Italy.
Most table wines (and there are hundreds) could not possibly be dealt
with individually here.

Since not all producers are named, I shall not mention any of the
outlets where the wines that are reviewed can be found. Nor shall I
make any comparative observations as to quality: I have no desire to
advertise for anyone. The readers who want to know, for example,
where they can buy a Falanghina from Campania (and elsewhere),
can contact the Italian Trade Commission in their country, who will
no doubt offer help and advice.

Alternatively, reference can be made to the following websites:
www.italianmade.com, www.agriline.it, www.milioni.com, and
www.vqprd.it (Feder.doc Wines). The individual wine producers
also have, in most cases, their own websites. A better, more objective
source of information, however, are the websites of the individual
regions of Italy (e.g. www.umbriadoc.com). A list of the principal
Italian (indigenous) vines can be found in Appendix 1.

As far as the UK is concerned, its principal wine imports come
from Australia with 2,519m hectolitres. Next comes France with
2,376m hectolitres, third the USA with 1,504m, fourth Germany
with 1,285m and fifth Italy with 1,219m (figures as at 31 December
2004).

Most wine labelling or descriptive matter for Italian wines
invariably offers brief advice on suitable food-matching combinations. Unfortunately, these suggestions are, perhaps traditionally, only
of the 'serve at 18°/or serve at room temperature; suitable for red
meats, game and cheese' variety. As I shall endeavour to show when
considering food and wine (Chapter 7), so much food/wine pairing
is entirely subjective and indeed depends on either the cooking
method itself or the sauce that is used. Accordingly, I have chosen to
ignore any automatically 'recommended foods' suggestions for the
wines that will be discussed, except where there is a traditional or
totally persuasive marriage; preferably a marriage made in heaven,
like *Biscotti* and Vin Santo, perhaps. (It has now become very
fashionable in Italian restaurants in the UK, at least, to offer at the

end of a meal *Cantuccini* with Vin Santo. Cantucci/or Cantuccini are almond-based biscuits, originally of Tuscan origin, which one dips in sweet wine and, of course, cappuccino.)

Yet, though I am prepared to be humble regarding my personal views as to wine and food combinations, I have no such inhibitions when expressing opinions about the wines themselves. In this, I claim no personal merit, but given my age and experience, I feel that I have a contribution to make. Not always speaking with one consistent voice I shall throughout be motivated by a love of wine in general, of Italian wine in particular and, above all, by a desire to help and encourage as many people as possible to appreciate its manifold delights.

In conclusion, may I offer the following guidelines to non-linguists regarding pronunciation. Most Italian wines are masculine in gender, regardless of the particular ending of the word, so you have *il Frascati* or *il Marsala*. All masculine Italian wines take the masculine definite articles, so you say *il Montepulciano* or *lo Sfursat*. Similarly, most Italian wines which are masculine end in 'o', but as you will have gathered from Frascati, some end in 'i'. (see also Chianti) and others even end in consonants (see Pinot, Sfursat, Picolit).

To confuse matters, however, many Italian wines end in 'a': for example, Barbera and Marsala. Of these, most are feminine but some are masculine: thus, believe it or not, you say *la Vernaccia* (whether of San Gimignano or of Sardinia), or *la Spanna*, but, as already noted, *il Marsala*. Others are either masculine or feminine, depending on the speaker. So there is an argument among purists as to whether you should say *il Barbera* or *la Barbera*, *il Freisa* or *la Freisa*, *il Valpolicella* or *la Valpolicella*, *il Lugana* or *la Lugana*. . . . . Sorry! (In a sense, to explain away this oddity, the Italian researcher Arturo Marescalchi described *Barbera* as having 'the body and strength of a man and the amiability of a woman'. Perhaps sexist, but quite apt, really, as any reader might find out having sampled it!)

So much for the record. Obviously, nothing turns on such fine linguistic points as far as the appreciation of the wines themselves goes. If you like a Barbera, it will be a matter of complete indifference to you whether, in Italian, it should be called *il Barbera* (implying that one omitted to use the word *vino* so that the full description would be *il vino Barbera*), or *la Barbera* (implying that one meant to say '*l'uva Barbera*', referring to a well-known Italian variety of grape). I mention the matter solely in case you are ever struck by the different usages.

A note of warning by reference to the names of Italian wines. As a result of the very great number of available grape/vine varieties, there is no uniformity in the description of Italian wines which, broadly speaking, can be said to fall into three categories. In the first are those wines which take their names from the villages or areas in which they are produced; for example, 'Barolo' (a charming small village), 'Chianti' (a region), 'Marsala' (a port), 'Soave' (a delightful small town), 'Velletri' (a city).

Others are named solely after the grape from which they originate. Hence, for example, 'Albana', 'Dolcetto', 'Greco', 'Trebbiano', 'Vermentino'. The names of the wines derived from grapes in this second group can be further qualified depending on where they originate, i.e. where the vine itself grows. Hence you get a *Barbera d'Asti* to distinguish it from the *Barbera d'Alba* or *Greco di Tufo* as distinct from that, say, of Calabria. *Vermentino di Gallura* as distinct from wines made with 'Vermentino' grapes but originating elsewhere.

The third category comprises those names which combine that of the grape and of the town, hence *Brunello di Montalcino*, *Moscato d'Asti*, *Nero d'Avola*, *Vernaccia di San Gimignano*.

The reader should not be put off by this slight complication: it is initially confusing, it must be admitted, but with practice and, above all, through drinking the wines themselves it all slots nicely into place!

EXPLORING
PRONUNCIATION

I have no desire to be pedantic but it might be helpful to remind readers of a few basic rules of pronunciation in the Italian language so that they may avoid making unnecessary, clumsy mistakes when asking for Italian wines, whether in Italy or elsewhere.

The most common mishaps occur in the pronunciation of the consonants 'c' and 'g'. Here are a few essential rules. The letter 'c' is pronounced with the same sound as the English 'k' when it appears in words in front of the vowels 'a', 'o' and 'u' or when it is followed by an 'h'. Accordingly, one would say 'Karignano', 'Kortese', 'Tokai', or 'Kianti'.

When the letter 'c' is followed by the vowels 'e' or 'i' it is pronounced like the English 'ch', i.e. with the same sound as you would find in 'chair', hence 'Cherasuolo', 'Chesanese', 'Rechioto', 'Saliche', Valpolichella' and 'Vernachia'. Please do not be tempted to call it 'Vernakia'. . . . .

The same rule applies to the letter 'g', which is pronounced like the English 'j'; hence 'Valjella' or 'Torjano' before an 'e' or an 'i', but as an ordinary, *hard* 'g' before 'a', 'o' and 'u', hence 'Gavi; and so on. If 'g' is followed by an 'h', it is also pronounced hard, as in 'Ghemme'.

The Twenty Regions of the Republic of Italy

Valle d'Aosta

Trentino-Alto Adige

Lombardia

Veneto

Friuli-Venezia Giulia

Piemonte

Emilia-Romagna

Liguria

Toscana

Marche

Umbria

Abruzzo

Lazio

Molise

Puglia

Campania

Basilicata

Sardegna

Calabria

Sicilia

PART I

THE WORLD OF WINE

CHAPTER 1

THINKING ABOUT WINE

Wine is the fermented juice of the grape; this is its scientific definition. A number of others have been given and, perhaps affected by having imbibed too much, scientists and individuals have waxed lyrical about wine; this is understandable, of course, because of its mood-enhancing qualities, which had already been noted back in the twelfth century by the Salerno School of Medicine.

The Salerno School of Medicine, in fact, was the first of its kind in the Western world, having been licensed by Frederick II of Sicily in 1224. But it had been in existence long before that date, given that it was considered as 'ancient' three centuries earlier.

The patients who flocked there from all parts of Europe were given a *vade mecum* before leaving; that is to say, an 'aide memoire', or guidelines, of how to live. This is not the place to consider the *vade mecum* in detail, save to say that one very often discovers in it what modern medicine has confirmed. A classic rule in the context of wine drinking is that, if one has had too much to drink the previous night, a drop of the same stuff first thing in the morning will redress one's natural balance and biorhythms, which I believe is true and which, in any event, has a broader application insofar as a number of cures for allergies would appear to acknowledge this principle.

The following extract from the Salerno *vade mecum* will give the reader some sense of its contents and approach:

> The better the wine, the better the moods that it produces; but should the patient find that red wine makes him feel heavy, then by all means he should choose white wine, suitably matured, yet delicate and of ripe flavour. But let it be watered down a little, yet be sparkling and. . . . . drunk in moderation.

The adoption of wine as a celebratory drink is, in fact, almost universal, for example at elections, engagements, marriages, christenings, at anniversaries or Christmas and end-of-year parties, and even after funerals. St Paul seems to have had a predilection for it. . . when he said: 'Drink no longer water, but use a little wine for thy stomach's sake and thine often infirmities.' *St Paul's Epistle to Timothy*, Ch.5, V.23

The literary references are legion, of course. If one wanted to be lyrical, one could join the poets who throughout history have sung hymns of praise to wine, from the Greek Alceus (his was the wine with added resin flavour which is continued in present-day 'Retsina') to Horace who praises 'Falernum', to the heavy drinking of Rabelais's 'Gargantua', to our own Pulci's 'Morgante'; (or even to Persia with Omar Khayyam): all toasting the pleasure of wine in song, forgetting the troubles and the routine of everyday life, almost as though one felt God-like.

For opera buffs, one could choose from the wine-drinking scene in the first act of Verdi's *Otello*, the 'Brindisi' in his *La Traviata*, Mascagni's *Cavalleria Rusticana* (a drinking song there which is a prelude to tragedy), or even Berlioz's fascinating wine song in the *Damnation of Faust*; there are others, of course.

And let us not forget that we toast events in wine. 'Cheers', 'good health', 'campai', 'salud', 'chinchin', 'salute', 'prosit' and a great many more. The Romans always toasted five times, namely to 'good health', 'pleasure', 'sleep', 'love' and 'riches'. How right they were! Realistically, however, I believe that Galileo was right when he remarked simply that: 'wine is none other than sunshine mixed with the sap of the vine'.

The history of wine, however, is really that of man since remnants of winemaking have been found even in prehistoric dwellings; indeed, some writers suggest that fossils of vines can be dated back sixty million years. There are references to it in the hieroglyphics carved on the stones of ancient Egypt, in the cuneiform writing of Babylonia and in Cretan wine containers of the Minoan civilization.

The Jews of course knew it; it is mentioned in the Old Testament, as well as in the New. There is reference to it in the Bible (see Psalms 104, 15 where it is recorded that wine cheers the heart of man; Noah is said to have planted a vineyard); and in the New Testament, one cannot forget the marriage ceremony at Canaan and the miraculous transformation of water into wine.

According to legend, Dionysus, the son of Jupiter and Semele, better known to the Romans as Bacchus, discovered the plant in India. He is said to have helped it to grow by planting it in the bone of a bird and from there to have taken it to Greece, whence it found its way to Rome. In Homer's time, wine was an ordinary commodity among the Greeks; in Greek mythology, Dionysus is said to have been the first to teach Oenopion, the son of Ariadne, how to make wine.

In the fourth century BC, the Greek Democritos spent some time trying to discover the origin of the grape vine and after him the Carthaginian precursor of the Roman experts, Mago, who was called 'the father of agricultural sciences', tried to do the same. The Romans, Columella and Pliny, added to our knowledge of wine. Pliny described ninety-one varieties of vine, identifying fifty different types of wine and classifying nearly two hundred.

That the vine came from the East is now undisputed, despite Greek mythology sometimes attributing its creation on Mount Nysa, in Libya, to the god Dionysus. Even if one looks at the word 'wine', it seems that in many languages this is none other than a rendering of the Sanskrit 'vena', meaning an offering of wine. One finds the word in the Italian, Polish, Spanish 'vino', the French 'vin', the Greek 'oinos', the Catalan 'vin', the German 'wein', the Celtic 'gwimen' and the Ethopian 'waien'. The Armenians say 'ghini' and the Georgians add a 'g' to the Russian 'vino' to get 'gvino'. (On the other hand, the Hungarians call it 'bor', which certainly is not derived from Sanskrit, it being a word of Turkish origin identifying a greyish colour.)

Special wine-producing species of *vitis vinifera* were cultivated in the Near East in at least 4000 BC, if not earlier, and were known to the Egyptian (evidence has been found in the Pyramids), Minoan, Greek and Etruscan civilizations. However, it is essentially to the Greeks and to the Romans that we owe the development of the first recorded wine industries.

Whilst there is no doubt that the many tribes inhabiting the Italian peninsula two thousand years before Christ enjoyed some form of vine cultivation and wine production, it took the arrival of the Greeks in the south and the Etruscans in the central and northern districts to put wine production onto any sort of formalized basis. Moreover, although the two civilizations were separate, the Etruscans were nevertheless influenced by Greek customs and systems, including the adoption of certain of their winemaking techniques. And they were also arguably Italy's first wine exporters as Etruscan wines sold and transported in amphorae to Gaul are well recorded. Fairly recent discoveries (1956) have confirmed this 'export trade'. Ruins have been unearthed indeed in the proximity of Civitavecchia, at Pyrgi, of the port that served the Etruscan Necropolis (nowadays) of the town at Cerveteri.

The Greeks named their Italian mainland provinces Oenotria (Enotria – 'land of wine' from the Greek 'oinos') generally taken to mean the land of trained vines: the name *greco* is still used in Italy to refer to low pruned bush vines and *etrusco* for vines trained up into trees: suitable credit, surely, for Italy's first winemakers. The Etruscans extended their activities far into the north of Italy as evidenced by an archaeological find in the Trentino area, now to be seen in the Museum of the Buonconsiglio Castle in Trento, of a very ancient, sacred vase which contains an inscription in Etruscan of its dedication to their young God of Wine, Lavisio. (Incidentally, the Roman historian Livy records that the reason the Gauls first invaded Italy in the fourth century AD was because they wanted to get hold of the Etruscans' wine and methods of wine production. To do so, they travelled as far down as modern Tuscany.)

Then came the Romans, who sensibly profited from the best of these earlier vine and wine techniques and improved on them. There is a substantial body of written works on Roman agriculture in general and vine husbandry in particular, including advice on climate, planting, pruning, vine varieties and even the economics of wine production. Moreover, many Roman medical texts refer to wine as playing an important part in medical treatments, and there is as much information there regarding colour, flavour, quality and effect as in any modern tasting notes. Naturally, what can only be described as a miniature wine industry developed, so certain districts and wines became recognized for their inherent quality. The beginning of wine quality grading systems was already in its infancy with Falernian (Falerno) and Caecuban (Cecubo) as the Barolo and Chianti of Pliny's day; valued wines followed later by Praetutium from the Adriatic coast, Lunense from the Ligurian coast, Rhaeticum from the central Alps and Mamertinum from Sicily.

We owe pasteurization to a Frenchman, of course, but the Romans themselves had developed their own method for storing wines when they diverted the steam from their hot baths and kitchen ovens into a specially designed room in which the amphorae containing wine were positioned, the heat and the steam hastening chemical reactions which caused young wine to mature very fast.

So important was wine to the Romans that they built at the source of the River Tiber a 'Forum Vinarium', the first international centre for wine's exchange and exportation. The wines were stored in amphorae for this purpose. Indeed, as we know, the Romans were very keen on their wines. If they were meant for ageing, the amphorae were sealed. In Petronius's 'Satyricon' (or 'Satyrica', if you like) at Trimalchio's extravagant dinner (Book XXXIV) glass amphorae were produced, bearing, no doubt hilariously, the label '100-year-old Falernum of Opimius Consul'. (Falernum is also mentioned by Marcus Aurelius in his 'Meditations'.)

The Romans were justly proud of their viticulture. In his 'Natural History' (Book XIV) Pliny the Elder remarks that one of the starting points is the vine, 'as regards which Italy has such an unimpeachable supremacy as to give the impression that, with this alone, it has exceeded the wealth of any other country'. (In fact, he classified a total of 195 wines, eighty of which he considered to be of major quality.) Their pride was justified, for they started applying technology to vine growing. One example will suffice: the Etruscans had allowed the vine to grow unimpeded, climbing over walls and tree trunks; the Romans introduced pruning, first described by Pliny. (Although it should be noted that the practice of allowing the vine to grow climbing over walls and tree trunks is still to be found in many parts of some southern Italian regions, (e.g. in Campania, in the Massico, at Aversa, Nola and so on.) Nothing unusual here, given the Greek influence; on Crete, in the days of Minos, vines were trained up elm trees.

It is interesting to observe at this stage that the Romans were at times ambivalent in their approach to wine consumption since in their highly efficient and organized social structure the evils of alcohol abuse were a matter of concern. For example, wine was not officially allowed to those who had not reached their thirtieth year and, in any event, was absolutely forbidden to women: indeed, in Roman law, wine drinking by the wife was one of the grounds for divorce.

Furthermore, the Romans usually drank their wines diluted with water which, to some extent, ensured that the alcoholic impact was less and contributed to the creation of a mentality that drunkenness was not a good idea. The Romans, in this context, exhibited some contempt for the inhabitants of Gaul, the Gaulois, who drank their wine neat and, partly as a result, were inclined to drunkenness.

Pliny recorded Cato's belief that relatives kissed women when they met them, not out of love but merely to ascertain whether they had been drinking wine. Wine consumption was fairly widespread and the so-called celebrations of the mysteries of Bacchus, or the rites of Dionysus, often resulted in uncontrollable orgies. Indeed, in the year 186 BC the Consul Spurius Posthumius embarked on a very tough crusade to ban the consumption of wine. Interestingly, the Romans always drank their wines chilled. The practice of serving wines, especially the reds, at room temperature only came to the fore in the nineteenth century.

For centuries, both the Greeks and the Romans stored their wine in 'amphorae' or in a 'dolium'. (Indeed, the earliest amphora yet found with a cork stopper belonged to the Etruscans and dates back to at least 500 BC.) Both were made with baked clay and, as a result, were exceptionally fragile and not suited to transport over long distances, despite attempts to find a shape that could travel better. It was only when the Romans expanded into north-eastern Italy, in the area of the Dolomites, that they discovered what the Gauls were doing, namely storing wine in wooden containers. Again, Pliny the Elder has our thanks for recording this fact. In his 'Natural History' (Book XIV) he states: 'There are many methods for keeping wine. In Alpine regions it is stored in wooden containers reinforced with metal ribbing; and especially in hard winters it is preserved from frost by lighting fires. . .' As a result of this discovery, two things happened: 'amphorae', which the Etruscans were already using some 2500 years BC, were consigned to the museum of history and wooden barrels evolved, making transport of wine much easier than it had been.

Many of the strictures and constraints suggested to winemakers at that time cannot be faulted even today. The need for cleanliness was constantly stressed, and the wisdom of carefully positioning the preparation yard and the press itself in the coolest possible environment was emphasized, but possibly the finest text is the following: 'The best wine is one that can be aged without preservatives; nothing must be mixed with it which might mask its natural taste. For the most excellent wine is one which has given pleasure by its own natural qualities.' Nowadays, the most up-to-date international winemaking philosophy is stated as 'Grow the best grapes you can and mess about with them as little as possible', which neatly paraphrases our Roman author of two thousand years ago.

Unfortunately, after the fall of Rome, all these techniques were lost. If any wine was produced it was strictly domestic or, at best, local – and often more for medical than for pleasurable purposes – whilst monasteries and other places of religious devotion, having need of wine for sacramental purposes, also maintained a winemaking presence. Not until the late Middle Ages was wine again evident, and even then records and reports are rare as 'Italy' simply did not exist as we know it today and the host of principalities, papal states, city republics, duchies and the like that occupied modern Italy seemed too concerned with other matters to bother about wine. Wine was simply a convenient beverage with welcoming properties, and there was already strong evidence that the constant Italian defect of utilizing invariably good and often exceptional growing conditions for quantity rather than quality had started to become a disconcerting habit.

Until more recent times, wine was not drunk on its own. One could say that it has been mixed throughout history with practically everything under the sun. The Romans used to mix it with honey, herbs and spices. (For example, their 'vinum absinthatum' was made with an infusion of absinth blossoms. It is said that Cicero enjoyed making this wine for himself on his country estate.) Both they and the Greeks used it to sterilize water; the Greeks put resin in it to make 'retsina'. It is a matter of record that some of the old spiced wines were fairly well known (for example, that brewed by Hippocrates more than four hundred years BC). The Portuguese have added brandy to make port; wine has indeed acquired different tastes at different times in different parts of the world. The Spaniards used to store it in containers made from pigskin and the resultant drink was quite far removed from what the modern person would consider is the genuine taste of wine. When the Italian seafaring republics (Venice, Genoa, Pisa and, to a lesser extent, Amalfi) brought back from the East a great variety of spices (cardamom, cloves, ginger, nutmeg, etc.) they used them both as a preservative and for their tonic effect in the wines being produced at the time. This use of spiced wines continued for many centuries, although with the passage of time there may have been a tendency to develop in particular directions. More recently, wine is mixed with herbs to make vermouth.

Even the way in which grapes were used to make wines has differed. Some grapes were initially turned into very sweet wine and only later on, in the nineteenth and twentieth centuries, were adapted to make dry ones.

There are also many superstitions attached to wine. In Mediterranean countries, for example, and especially in Italy, to spill wine or champagne is said to bring good luck, especially if the bottle gets broken in the process (an occurrence to some extent reminiscent of the practice, at weddings in Greece and other countries, of smashing crockery to wish happiness and good fortune to the spouses). There are literary precedents for this. In the first book of the *Aeneid*, the Latin poet Virgil records how when Aeneas was entertained at dinner by the Queen of Carthage, she poured wine on the table in order to wish them both good luck (Book 1) as well as between the horns of a milk-white heifer (Book 4). She was, of course, in love with him but that is by the way. It did not work, because he left her not too long after that and she committed suicide by falling on her sword.

But the practice, at least a variant of it, still prevails in Italy, manifested sometimes also by dabbing champagne behind one's ears like perfume or dipping a finger in champagne and touching the lips of new-born babies (a similar practice occurs in Cataluña). Harmless superstition, no doubt, in the case of a drop on the baby's lip; a tragic waste otherwise. . . !

One thing, however, has remained more or less unaltered in the last few thousand years, namely that we have a northern limit of cultivation of the vine in Europe at latitude 48°. At the southern end, overall the limit of cultivation follows latitude 35°N, with a small exception in the case of the Cape Verde Islands at 16°N, because of the favourable combination there of air and sea temperatures. This fact is a mark of the flexibility of the vine which has adapted itself to different latitudes and even to varying water levels. The reader might like to know that there is a vineyard in Sicily adjacent to Lake Gurrida where, when the waters of the lake reach their peak, the local Grenache vines end up below water to a depth of more than two metres, so much so that sometimes they disappear completely!

Following the voyages of Columbus, Europe exported grape culture and winemaking techniques all over the world practically and, more particularly, to Argentina, Mexico, South America, South Africa, Australia, New Zealand and California and, of course, other parts of the USA.

The Americans, however, did not show much gratitude for this because, in the second half of the nineteenth century, they, in turn, exported to Europe from the eastern US three infestations which devastated European vineyards, costing wine growers much effort and money to put right, namely the vine louse known as *phylloxera vastatrix* (1894), the fungus of powdery mildew (*oidium* 1852), as well as of downy mildew (*peronospera* 1880) or *plasmopara viticola*, damaging but less destructive than the vine louse. Fortunately, we were able to graft *vitis vinifera* scions (detached shoots including buds) onto the American species native to the eastern USA, thus allowing the new *Riparia* hybrids to salvage the European wine industry and develop what are now recorded as 5,000 varieties of *vitis vinifera* alone.

Apart from the variety of grape used, it is a fact that it is the sun and soil (what the French call the *terroir*) which determine the type and quality of the wine. The true significance of the soil is rather difficult to assess but, that apart, it may be said that the process of making wine is reasonably straightforward, although the chemical reactions occurring in the fermentation process are quite complicated.

Everyone knows that wine is the exclusive product of the fermentation of fresh grapes or fresh grape juice. It contains water, ethyl and methyl alcohol, tartaric, citric, lactic, succinic and acetic acids, glycerine, sugar, mineral salts and other substances (pectin, mucillage, etc.) the skins of the grapes contain colourants (anthocyanins), flavours and tannins. There are, in addition, imperceptible quantities of organic and mineral acids, salts, lipid essences and esters, proteins, vitamins (more specifically, appreciable quantities of vitamin A, fair amounts of vitamin B2 and of vitamin C, traces of vitamin P and B1), polyphenols (in varying percentages from 250 to 5000 milligrams per litre) and flavonoids, all elements which, with tannin, have a significant effect on the bouquet of the wine, and possibly on one's health, especially if we consider the more recent enquiries into the anti-oxidant effect of quercetin and resveratrol, two substances which have now been analysed in great detail, the latter being hailed as a 'miracle' molecule in health terms, especially since it is said to provide cardio-vascular protection.

Grapes are harvested and crushed either completely to extract red wine or pressed more gently to derive either whites or rosés. The juice is allowed to ferment by the introduction of yeasts and then clarified. There are varying methods of clarifying wines, using fining agents (nowadays mainly bentonite), filtration, centrifugation, refrigeration and, less commonly, heating.

Most successful of all, are egg whites. Freshly beaten egg whites are traditionally the most effective way of clarifying wine, although a number of winemakers maintain that they are very messy. There is a technique to this which is dependent upon how much tannin one wishes to extract from the wine; though I observe that excessive fining of this type tends to deprive the wine of much of its flavour. Fining and filtration technology is changing fast: there are now becoming available stainless steel cylinders with filtration capacity reduced to 0.45 micron (one millionth of a metre). So much for the record.

The enzymes or yeasts that are added to the wine transform the sugars into alcohol and carbon dioxide. This is known as alcoholic fermentation, which, the reader may be surprised to learn, of itself produces some sulphur dioxide (although not in sufficient quantities to stabilize the wine; this aspect is dealt with later). It may, increasingly nowadays, be followed by what is known as a malolactic fermentation, the purpose and effect of which is to transform the malic acid (a strong acid) existing in the must into lactic acid, which has a softer taste, contributing at the same time to balance the acidity of the wine.

At the time the grapes are picked, fermentation is made easy by the relationship existing between acid and sugar concentration. If the grapes are very ripe they contain many sugars: this will result in a wine with full body and a reasonably high alcoholic content. Grapes of this nature will only mature where the sun is hot and the season is long.

The wine requires to be stabilized, so that it will not spoil and will travel better. A number of methods are adopted and, until recently, especially in the New World, pasteurization was believed to be the most efficient. Its drawback was that the wine ceased to be a living thing because all its micro-organisms were destroyed. Nowadays, pasteurization is less common and it would be beyond the scope of this guide to delve too deeply into this rather technical aspect of the matter.

Some wines are strengthened in flavour and in alcoholic content by distilling grapes that have shrivelled or dried up. There are two ways of achieving this. The first is to gather the grapes for winemaking rather late ('vendange tardive'), when the bunches have begun to wilt and occasionally in Italy, but more often in France, are covered by *botrytis cinerea*, a particular kind of rot which, because of the wonderful results that it produces, has now become known as 'noble rot' ('pourriture noble'). It has the effect of taking the water out of the grape and concentrating the sugars in it without causing any damage. This is what one may term the natural way of using grapes which are no longer fresh.

The other way more often used in Italy is either to stretch out on matting on soil, well exposed to the sun, the required quantity of grapes or to hang the bunches in dry and ventilated environments which are called 'fruttai'. The net result of this kind of drying out of the grapes is not only that the sugar content increases, thus allowing the resultant alcoholic content to rise, but also a grape which possesses more aromatic qualities and is richer in ingredients or extracts. This latter process is known in Italy as 'appassimento' and is used extensively in the Veneto region, but also elsewhere, of course. One of Italy's best known wines, Amarone (q.v.) relies substantially on this method. (A variation on 'appassimento' is the 'ripasso' procedure (v. Glossary).) The strength of a wine may also be increased by the addition of alcohol (v. Port and Marsala).

Still current, and probably inevitable until a new technology is evolved, is the practice of adding sulphur to the wine. Given the importance of the practice it is treated separately and fully in Chapter 11.

CHAPTER 2

GETTING PERSONAL

B efore considering Italian wines in detail, it occurred to me that I should make a few personal observations which may help the reader to understand my point of view and my approach to wine generally.

I would like to start by acknowledging the obvious fact that the power of advertising very often brings to the fore varieties of wine that were previously not so well known. This does not only happen in Italy, of course. Take Chardonnay. Until about twenty-five or thirty years ago, it was not that popular in Europe. Quantities of it were grown in France and north-east Italy, but, as a generalization, it was not a wine in which the Italians at least had much interest. (I discount for present purposes the fact that the Chardonnay grape is the main component in champagne.)

Indeed, I recall watching on BBC1 a few years ago a very well-known producer from Piemonte (a specialist when it comes to high-class wines such as Barolo, Barbaresco, Dolcetto) being interviewed. When it was put to him that his children, who were taking over the firm as he was retiring, had started producing Chardonnay, he shrugged his shoulders and said, 'That's not a wine.' Idiosyncratic, perhaps, but indicative of a mentality which, until recent years, has prevailed throughout many wine-producing regions of Italy.

The producers from the New World then decided that, especially in its oaked version, it would be a great popular success. (In California, in the late 1970s, the area dedicated to Chardonnay rose from 6,250 hectares to over 44,000 hectares in the year 2000.) They were right and everybody now drinks it: it is found everywhere. It has 'invaded' Italy, where vines existing since time immemorial are being up-rooted to appease not too discerning consumers swayed by the power of advertising. Chardonnay is merely a fashion wine. In my view, oaked Chardonnay compounds the unpleasantness of the trend and it can hardly come as a surprise to those who are interested in wine that the abbreviation ABC (to stand for 'Anything but Chardonnay') is now acquiring some currency! I am of course aware of the fact that there is a long-established natural affinity between oak and Chardonnay, as witness the Burgundy whites; it does not worry me – any more than the fact that some producers of 'Chablis' are maturing it in small barrels. (See Chapter 8 for my thoughts on oaking.)

The increase in popularity of Chardonnay occurs where least expected. For example, quite recently a number of producers of 'Cava' have added to the long-established, traditional grape varieties ('parellada', 'macabeo' and 'xarel-lo') Chardonnay in varying quantities. What next?

Fashion and market requirements are affecting a number of Italian wines which are undergoing changes – some good, some bad. An example of brilliant experimentation are the 'super Tuscans' to which further reference will be made. But before doing so I would like to make a few general comments that reflect my own taste, experiences and beliefs. The reader, as recommended throughout, will form his or her own judgement; all I ask of him or her is to approach the matter with an open mind.

1.   Are reds better than whites? And what about rosés? Current thinking rather more than tradition has it that red wine is much better than white, and only reds make 'great' wines. Furthermore, modern recommendations consistently promote the fact that reds contain a number of flavonoids which are good for the heart: more particularly, it was discovered in the 1990s that a polyphenol known as resveratrol is to be found in the skins of red grapes. Therefore, so runs the moral, drink red wine if you want to protect yourself against heart disease.

Maybe it is true that reds drunk in moderation are better for you than whites; but it is certainly not accurate in a gastronomic context. There are certain foods with which a red wine would be totally inappropriate; there are some whites which are infinitely to be preferred to a red on a hot summer's day. Furthermore, there are some people who cannot drink red wines either because it gives them a headache or because they have serious health problems drinking reds. The question of whether, and if so why, women appear to prefer whites to reds, as is often said, is considered separately in Chapter 9.

2. The neglect of rosé wines is inexplicable, since there are a number of excellent ones. Here, I must confess that I am rather drawn to rosé wines because, ultimately, they are reasonably flexible. They are not so heavy as reds, but they are more flavourful than whites; they are as fresh as whites but many of them, especially those from southern Italy, can be fairly full-bodied. In short, they can be drunk throughout the meal without having to worry unduly about finding the right combination with food. Having said that, I should add that it is not as though Italy produces many rosé wines of a high calibre and it must be admitted that in this particular field the Italian wine industry could do better; nevertheless, there are some good rosé wines in Italy, as I shall point out.

The greatest producer of rosé wines is France followed by Italy. Third comes Spain. The primacy of France is hardly surprising because, as Hugh Johnson records, its origin can be traced back to the fifteenth century in the Bordeaux area when they started producing 'claret', i.e. a 'one night-stand wine', if I may use that term, since it was obtained leaving the squeezed juice of the grape on its skin for no longer than twenty-four hours simply to allow fermentation to commence which would then be continued in the barrel.

Interestingly, I am not aware that any special studies have been made to ascertain whether rosé wines may have a contribution to make in the context of cardiac health. I should not wish the reader to form the impression that there are no good rosé wines in Italy. It is true that until the early 1940s rosé wines were not even bottled in Italy. Maybe this was due to the belief, which is commonly held in other parts of the world as well, that rosé must by definition be an inferior wine since it is a mixture of red and white wines. (For the record, it is illegal both in France and in Italy to obtain rosé wines by mixing red with white; an exception is made in the champagne area where almost all the rosé wines are obtained 'par melange'.) This is not true: it is merely the result of a different method of vinification, but that is a separate story. It was the well known firm of Leone de Castris of Salice Salentino that first bottled rosé wines commercially in Italy in 1943, consolidating a production begun in 1925.

As a final observation under this heading, I have little hesitation in stating that rosé wines are beginning to make a come-back and will increasingly receive the attention and appreciation they deserve.

3.   And what about sparkling red wines? This is a field where Italy

can boast of quite a variety of reds which, at first glance, one would not associate with bubbles; and yet, they emerge as very successful. The classic Italian dry reds, which can be found in a sparkling version, are Barbera, Brachetto, Freisa, Bonarda, Grignolino, Recioto, Nebbiolo, obviously the Lambrusco and, perhaps surprisingly, the Aglianico del Vulture. One is ignoring, of course, the great number of aromatic wines, such as Aleatico, Malvasia and Moscato. There is also produced in Veneto a lightly sparkling *sweet* red, Recioto Spumante, which is a variety of Valpolicella; it is a most unusual but highly enjoyable drink, especially chilled. Nor should we forget the original Vernaccia di Serrapetrona in the Marche, a red sparkling version of the more commonly found white Vernaccia grape (and there are many others).

4. One should not ignore the contempt which is often felt by some wine writers for sweet wines. It is not for me to consider whether a Chateau d'Yquem is to be preferred to a Muscat de Rivesaltes, when eating chocolate pudding; we are considering here only Italian wines. Certainly, you would not drink an austere Barolo when you could more profitably imbibe a Chambave from the Val d'Aosta, a Marsala Vergine from Sicily, an Aleatico of Portoferraio (a remarkably powerful and flavoured red from the island of Elba) or, indeed, an Anghelu Ruju from Sardinia, or even a Recioto from Soave (again, there are many others). The truth is that in this, as in other aspects, one must maintain a sense of proportion.

5. To some extent I find it inexplicable that, even in Italy, still wine should not be drunk more often as an aperitif. This neglect has happened recently when the consumption of wine in Italy has dropped. In Venice, for example, it had been customary for centuries to go and have an 'ombra' (literally, a shadow, sometimes referred to as an 'ombretta') which really meant to go and drink a glass of white wine first thing in the morning in order to cheer oneself up for the rest of the day. (A brief note for the linguist. 'Ombra' in Italian means 'shadow'. The noun, often changed into 'ombretta' (a small shadow), is said to be derived from the fact that one would sit outside bars in St Marks Square sipping a glass of white wine in the shade of St Marks bell tower round about midday.) This does not happen quite so often nowadays, even in Italy; whilst the popularity of cocktails is reducing, the trend seems to be towards either 'Prosecco' (q.v.) or no alcohol at all.

In the countryside, in the wine-producing areas of Piemonte, workers and peasants always carried about a small barrel, not quite pocket size, containing their favourite red wine, a sort of hip flask. Again, this 'tradition' seems to be disappearing, although it should be recorded that others are coming to the fore. For example, whilst the old Italian 'osteria' or shop of the 'vinaio' is less evident these days, the 'enoteca' seems to be on the increase in the major Italian cities. The 'enoteca' is what I would term, perhaps somewhat condescendingly, a more civilized version of the British 'wine bar'. Until some twenty years ago, 'enoteche' were practically unknown in Italy, save for the truly major enterprises which were more like a wine museum than a place where people congregated to drink and talk. Now, however, there are over a hundred, some – especially in the large towns – quite important establishments where top wines can be sampled and where comparatively young people seem to congregate after work, 'happy hours' style.

6.   And yet, I record with pleasure that there are parts of Italy where still white wine is commonly served as an aperitif, or as a thirst-quencher. There are places in Florence where this occurs and where the offer of a fine dry white wine is accompanied by olives, nuts or other 'nibbles'. Those who have been to San Gimignano know full well how enjoyable it is to walk up or down the high street, popping into one or the other of the various 'caves' where the local 'Vernaccia' (a white wine) is served accompanied by olives or ham or whatever.

Indeed, there are some places where even a red can be sampled as an aperitif, as anyone who has walked through the high street of Soave will confirm.

7.   One thing, however, is certain, namely that there can be no doubt as to the increasing popularity of wine. With it, have come what I would term some unfortunate sales gimmicks.

For example, it is now quite common, at least in France, Italy and Spain, to find wine dispensed in bars and cafes 'on draught'; red, rosé and white, suitably chilled. In the same countries, especially in motorway service area restaurants, wine of all types is now offered for sale in plastic bottles (screw top, of course). But as if that did not suffice, it is now possible to buy in Italy wine dispensed from a carton (suitably advertised, of course, on television and elsewhere) in the same way as milk or fruit juice.

I prefer to say nothing about its quality: I tend to believe that there is a connection between the container and the contents so that as a rule when it comes to wine the more expensive stylistically and qualitatively the container, the better, at least in theory, the contents. Fortunately, the Italian authorities have intervened, possibly concerned by the fact that the traditional way of marketing wines in bottles is being overtaken by technological advances. It has been decreed that packages containing wine must show both the date of 'bottling' (packaging, of course) *and* that of expiry. The latter must not exceed nine months from the former.

8.   One final thought concerns the taste of wine. This has changed from the days of the Romans who used to prefer spiced wines to modern times. The Greeks, of course, loved their Retsina but this is clearly for most Westerners a summer wine and not something one would enjoy in the middle of winter.

But tastes do change, usually (and I was about to say, inevitably) influenced by economic considerations. It would have been anathema to an Italian vintner, until say the 1970s, to rely solely on oaking to produce good wines. Nowadays, it is commonplace.

This neatly brings me to the taste of wine.

Here I feel that most Anglo-American writers have gone over the top. Wine is such a fundamental drink, to some extent like beer and water, that inevitably it has inspired countless writers to attempt to define its taste. Leaving aside water, which theoretically at least ought to be tasteless, one can generally identify the taste of wine (and beer). Equally, one can identify their smell. All one has to do, in fact, in order to recognize immediately the smell of wine, is to enter an empty pub or one of the ever-decreasing number of places in Spain, France, Italy or Greece, where wine is dispensed out of barrels rather than bottles.

What happens, however, is that we all want to go further. Having identified wine – and the culture of wine is spreading fast in the Anglo-American and Scandinavian worlds and elsewhere – we feel that we must, each of us, make a contribution to wine vocabulary. In the process, unfortunately, we forget something very simple, namely that wine is grape, and grapes, no matter of what variety, have only a small range of flavours. The distillation of the grape and more particularly the maturing of the wine in oak may add a touch of subtlety to those essential flavours, but it does not alter them fundamentally. However, one need only watch some of the popular TV wine-tasters to realize the absurd lengths in terms of descriptive gobbledygook they go to in order 'to be different' for its own sake. If they only confined themselves to explaining how a Burgundy tastes of, say, strawberries, and a Bordeaux, say, of raspberries, that would not be too bad. But enthuse they must, linguistically. I am exaggerating, of course; but the point being made is that we are becoming too sophisticated in terms of taste, smell, colour, density, clarity, etc. Some are self evident, of course, but taste and smell are more difficult to analyse for the amateur.

Nevertheless, all wine writers, myself included, have to make their own contribution. Accordingly, one finds that incredibly extravagant adjectives are applied to qualify the taste and the smell of a wine: I feel that the brain has taken over from the gut. In my view, there are only about a dozen or so natural tastes and smells that can be identified in unadulterated wine of any kind throughout the world. Anything other than that is a rationalization on the part of the taster or drinker.

Furthermore, it is a false rationalization for at least one reason, namely, that the taste and flavour of any wine, which is pure (I discount artificially treated and chemically adulterated wines) change according to a number of factors and especially the time of the year, the weather and, above all, the altitude. For example, a wine drunk at sea level on a summer's day on the coast running from Naples to Salerno has a completely different flavour if tasted at 6,000 ft in the Alps. Not only does the flavour change, the alcoholic content is affected, and the wine's effect on the body is also altered. It is metabolized much more quickly at higher altitudes and, for that reason alone, if no other, it has a totally different effect on the person who is drinking it, also in terms of taste and smell.

A further point worth bearing in mind is that, as I see it, wine should be drunk with food because if tasted on its own, it loses its character. I shall no doubt be unpopular with professional wine-tasters when I say that one of the dangers of those exercises where no substantial amount of food is available, is that the taste you derive from the wine is not necessarily the same as that which will be appreciated by the palate when it is drunk at a meal.

At this point, I should like to add a note of warning. Supermarkets have been instrumental in educating the local public to drink wines from many more parts of the world than simply from France. Italy has gained a great deal from the general supermarkets' interest in its wines and, to that extent, I do not complain too much. However, when exercising their marketing power, especially with the lesser producers, and insisting on showing on the back of the bottle a description which is meant to assist the client in choosing the wine, they have indulged in a form of wishful thinking inspired mainly by the need to make the wine more appealing. For example, about a year ago, I bought from a major supermarket chain twelve bottles of a white (no names) French wine from the Pays d'Oc area. Not a bad wine. On the front it was identified as a wine with 'tropical notes' and on the back label the description was expanded into the wine's 'tropical flavours and tasting of apricot'. No doubt suggestive and more exciting than the wine itself was; and in any event quite wrong. I have tried over many months at regular intervals to detect any trace of apricot (impossible to identify a tropical flavour) but could only reach the conclusion that what I was tasting was not apricot, but gooseberry. Nothing wrong in that, in itself; many wines, including Italian whites, are allowed to have and indeed do have a gooseberry flavour. But the description is advisedly, I believe, imprecise since an apricot-flavoured wine is more likely to be chosen than a gooseberry-tasting one.

Which brings me to another point that I touched on earlier, namely that I feel very strongly that in much of the contemporary writing about wines the language used tends to be so flowery and imaginative it ends up being confusing, and therefore meaningless. I propose analysing this phenomenon, briefly.

But before doing so, I should remind the reader that there is nothing new. The Romans knew about this. They were connoisseurs of wines and had their own wine-tasters; some of the descriptions they applied to wine have, in fact, come down to us so we know of a number of different terms used by them. Choosing at random: 'austerum' (austere); 'durum' (hard); 'crassu' (quite flavourful); 'lene' (soothing); 'molle' (soft); 'severum' (severe); 'sordidum' (unclear) and 'vile' (even in their day the Romans made poor wines!).

In the nineteenth century, a Frenchman by the name of Norbert Got, wrote a book entitled *La Degustation des Vins*, which contains a chapter where he provides over two hundred descriptions, some most unusual, that can be applied to wine, like 'fiery', 'heady', 'amber-coloured', 'of fair colour', 'velvety', 'spicy', 'smooth', 'tangy' and even 'amorous'. (In a sense, he was anticipating modern technological developments since it is now established that laboratory equipment is capable of identifying at least two hundred different scents that a wine produces. These are the result of varied associations of chemicals, such as fatty acids, terpenes, ethers, esters and aldehydes. It is these, ultimately, that will determine whether the flavour of the wine can be recognized as fruit or flowers or something different.)

Unfortunately, the average human sense of smell and taste is, in my view, quite insufficient to relate back to such a huge number of flavours: hence my suggested reduction to basic scents/flavours which may, at first sight, appear as an over-simplification, but which ensures that the layman at least is not fussed about refined definitions or descriptions.

In the English language, we have not been left behind.

Choosing at random, here are some of the adjectives or expressions used to describe wines as tasting of roses, violets, jasmine, lime and acacia, grass, green peppers, thyme, resin, tea, mint, truffles and hay and, believe it or not, even green or black olives.

Of course, according to most wine writers, the taste of wine can also be equated to that of fruit, whether it be citrus fruit of any kind, or apricots and peaches, pears, melons, apples, cherries, redcurrants, blackcurrants, quinces, gooseberries, strawberries, raspberries, blueberries, mulberries, blackberries, black cherries as distinct from red cherries, lychees, pineapple, passion fruit, mango and rhubarb. Other wines will be flavourful of earth, chalk and even of volcano (Has anybody *tasted* a volcano?), of slates, stone, gravel, wax and petrol.

Nor is the animal kingdom ignored because wines can actually be said to taste of farmyard, venison, damp fur, wet wool, leather, musk and even cat's pee. (Clearly, it must be a pretty horrible wine to drink; and in any event, one may have smelled it, but can any of these 'experts' say that they have actually tasted 'cat's pee'?) Different varieties of wine may taste or smell of cloves, butterscotch, liquorice, vanilla and aniseed or be full of the aroma of hazelnuts, walnuts, almonds, prunes, raisins and dark chocolate.

The oaky wines will, understandably enough because it is often used to line the barrels, also taste of tar, or even of toast, but that is not enough; caramel and butter come into it and honey and maybe even tobacco (. . . . . !).

Some writers feel that they can best describe the wine by saying that it tastes of kerosene (I would not choose to drink wines tasting of petrol!), although some major Rhine wines appear to have this 'taint'. Nor should we forget wines that taste of nettles and grass, asparagus, green peas, leaves, guava or lanolin and, why not, even marzipan, lavender, red wine gums, coconut, eucalyptus, tomato, peppers, liquorice, dill, leaf mould, mushrooms, smoke, overcooked meat, burnt rubber and overripe game?

I have also seen wine described as tasting of fruitcake and dried figs, as distinct of course from fresh figs, as having a green, leafy smell or that of pipe smoke and even of 'sweet/sour tomato and soy sauce'. (I have borrowed the majority of the above descriptions from Michael Schuster, to whom I am grateful, taken from his excellent *Essential Wine Tasting*, Mitchell Beazley, London, 2000).

The reader may feel that we have already gone too far: not at all. Recently (November 2005), I was perusing some wine-tasting notes which started off by classifying the smells that a wine threw up. It was said that these could be described as flowery, fruity, herbaceous, of dried fruit and of jams, spicy, toasted, of aromatic herbs and of animals, as well as (dear me!) ethereal. The animal smells, apart from including all those mentioned, comprised also the smell of 'sweat'. Words fail me.

All these descriptions have been applied to wines, especially the red variety for which stronger words are usually employed, than for white ones. Are these identifications of flavour and smell meaningful to the average drinker? I suspect not. I would encourage the reader to beware. Beware in particular of wine writers, myself included! A few are excellent and many are good: but the majority are only to be trusted if their advice is taken with more than a pinch of salt.

By all means, believe what they say when they recommend one wine rather than the other as being value for money; by all means, too, accept almost blindly that they are right when they tell you which vine and in which percentages, went into the wine. And of course, if they tell you that it is red or white, or even rosé, again they are to be believed! But when it comes to taste, do not trust anybody: just trust yourself.

That is not to say that you will be as good as they are, although you might be, with experience. But you are the supreme judge of what you like and there is no point whatever in drinking something simply because a particular journalist has recommended it, since his/her taste buds may not be the same as yours. Arguably, they may be better; but you are paying for the product and it is your taste buds that should prevail.

The reader should not misunderstand; it is not my intention to criticize wine-tasters and experts; but it is one thing to taste wine at a show, a trade fair, in the cellars of the producers, or in those of established importers. There, one is in effect expected to take notes, to say things, to comment on the wine, describe it, eulogize it, if such be the case. It is inevitable that in such a context one will get carried away, endeavouring to use terminology which others present may well understand better than the average consumer of wines, simply because they themselves may be inclined to use words of the same ilk.

But what about the 'ordinary' person who is trying to organize a dinner for his/her friends or colleagues at work, who then finds that he/she has to choose a wine in keeping with a particular menu that has been chosen for the occasion? At this point of decision-making, all the above descriptions of flavours and smells become totally irrelevant. What the person making the selection wants to know is that he/she can buy a particular type of wine which *maybe* tastes of strawberries or apples, and can be happily combined with the food that is on offer. Nothing else really counts, except perhaps the price!

Furthermore, a point I feel strongly about is that a number of Italian wines which are highly tannic suffer if sampled without food. It is only the oil and other fat in food that helps with that particular type of tannic wine, also because the tannin itself marries quite well with meats and sauces.

Leaving these considerations aside, wine can be described much more simply and that is why, quite often, I have used in Part II's 'Wines and their Characteristics' the terms 'sapid' (to mean something that tastes interesting) 'vinous' (to indicate that the wine tastes as wine should) where the flavour could not be accurately identified save by the use of excessive imagination! In my view the following are the fundamental flavour/smells of any wine, of any colour:

Fruit flavours – apple, blackberries, blackcurrants, cherries, gooseberries, plums, raspberries and strawberries.
Flower flavours – acacia, jasmine, roses, violets.
Various flavours – almonds (nuts generally), caramel, vanilla, grass

and chocolate; and oak, of course.

And that is it for flavours and smells, other than to mention the vanilla-like effect of oaking!

CHAPTER 3

STORING, SERVING AND SAVING WINE

T his subject is the delight of the boffin, the territory of the wine snob and the realm of the out-dated 'connoisseur'. In the UK market, where 95% of all the wines bought are drunk within forty-eight hours of purchase, considerations such as decanting cradles, serving baskets, wine thermometers and so on – an area called 'wine artifacts' in the United States – are almost academic.

First, a few general observations.

STORAGE

Noteworthy are the changes that have taken place since the old days when wines were kept in cellars. Although nowadays there are some electrically operated wine storage units, which can cater for both reds and whites, it is true to say that the average householder probably keeps his/her bottles either under the kitchen sink, or the stairs, or in the garage or shed: in terms of storage temperature, not a good idea.

The reason is simple. What mainly affects wine is not its actual temperature, but temperature fluctuations. Accordingly, wine should be stored where the temperature is reasonably constant. Variable temperatures, due to expansion and contraction of the volume of wine in the bottle, act as a pump. They draw in and expel a microscopic amount of air around the cork with each 'breath'. This has the effect of accelerating the ageing process, although it is worth noting that the same development will not occur with the silicone corks or the metal caps that are now increasingly being used. The observations that follow, however, are mainly related to the use of cork stoppers.

A cool, even temperature is best. However, a warm, stable temperature is better than a constantly varying one. Ideally, all wine (red, rosé, white, sparkling) should be stored within the temperature range 10°-14°, no more. But it is not only temperature that affects wine, since another five factors are also important, namely, humidity, ventilation, light, noise and vibration.

Undoubtedly humidity is important: too little and the cork will dry out, allowing air to penetrate into the bottle: the wine will quickly deteriorate; too much and the labels will come off the bottles! A hygrometer is indispensable to ensure an even degree of humidity in the ideal range 60-70%. One may well ask how that can be achieved, which brings us to consideration of the third important factor, namely ventilation, preferably from outside. Our forebears used to recommend that cellars should face north, with a small window that would supply natural ventilation. Unpleasant smells must be avoided at all costs; furthermore, good ventilation will prevent any form of fungus growth, which will damage both the wine and its labels.

Wines should always be stored away from noise and vibration which interface with the biochemical development of a wine intended for long-term storage.

Last, but not least, of the spoiling factors is light, especially sunlight which causes oxidation. Wine prefers darkness if it is to develop its characteristics. Put differently, and begging forgiveness for what some might consider a sexist remark, food and wine are like a good woman: they need a great deal of tender loving care and should be kept out of harm's way!

SERVING

Striving for simplicity, I observe that in any event the temperature at which wines are drunk (as distinct from that at which they should be stored) is, on the whole, very much a matter of personal preference. Such preference in turn depends on one's wine education, if I may use that term, the place where the wine is drunk, the season and possibly also the company.

Wine writers can scream until they are blue in the face that a good red wine should not be chilled: but in many parts of the world, such wines are, in fact, chilled on a hot summer's day; and especially so in Italy.

There is, of course, nothing new about this. Writing in 1673 (*Observations Topographical, Moral and Physiological Made in a Journey,*

London, at p. 267) an English visitor to Italy, the botanist John Ray, observed that 'all the Neapolitans. . . and generally the Italians drink their wine and water snowed'. By that, he meant, chilled wine and chilled water.

It is indeed very common in southern Italy, for instance, at the height of summer, to serve even such a full-bodied wine as a Falerno slightly chilled; nor is there anything unusual about this, since the Roman tradition of drinking wines cooled, if not chilled, continues to be practised. This practice is not exclusively Italian: indeed, I have seen a red Sancerre being served chilled in good French restaurants, even when the weather is not too hot, and unquestionably the less full-bodied, almost rosé red wines – especially from flavourful grapes such as Pinot nero – may well profit from a light chilling.

The general rule is that if you chill any wine too much, you reduce its taste whereas if you warm a red wine excessively, the alcohol becomes too obvious.

Personal preferences apart, the following generalizations may be helpful:

1. All sparkling wines, champagne included, should – I was about to say 'must' – be drunk chilled. There is no exception to this rule, and by chilled, I mean at a temperature between 6° and 9°C (43°-48°F). Obviously a vintage Krug may be able to tolerate 1° or even 2° more than an indifferent Prosecco; but this is a minor variation on the principal theme.

2. White wines with an alcoholic content not exceeding 13°, should also always be served chilled. One can have a debate as to the exact temperature, that is to say whether we should serve a light, dry, white wine at a slightly colder temperature than a full bodied, dry white. The former should be cooled at 7°-9°C (45°-48°F) and the latter at 10°-14°C (50°-57°F). I make an exception for strong 'Mediterranean' whites, e.g. the 'Vernaccia di Oristano' which can, in fact, be drunk at room temperature: (as to which, see later) but that is explicable on the basis that their minimum alcoholic content, like that of many other whites from, say, the Greek islands, is 15°.

3. Rosé wines, too, should always be served chilled but, in my view, at a slightly higher temperature than whites.

4. Sweet wines, whether red or white, should usually be served quite chilled, the whites probably at a lower temperature than

the reds; as a general rule, the sweeter the wine, the lower the temperature at which it should be served.

5. Problems arise when we are dealing with red wines. The reason is that, as a rule – albeit with some exceptions – red wines have much more flavour and tannin. If we were to serve them cool or chilled or cold, we would be reducing the amount of flavour that is released and we would thus be less able to taste the tannic qualities of the wine. Because of this, it is a general recommendation that, broadly speaking, full-bodied reds, especially if aged or with much tannin, benefit from being served 'at room temperature'. This is a wonderful expression that is bandied about, but it is a fact that the temperature of a room varies depending on the occupier of the home. The expression 'room temperature' is meaningless as such, there-fore, unless it is specified at which temperature the wine should be served. In my view, for this kind of wine the serving temperature should not be lower than 17°C and should be closer to 20°C (63° and 69°F).

Less full-bodied wines or, as they are often termed, medium-red wines, can be served at a slightly lower temperature, say 16°-18°C (61°-65°F) subject, of course, to what has been said above about drinking some types of reds at the height of summer, on a beach in either the Mediterranean or a tropical island.

6. Red sparkling wines should normally be served chilled, the precise temperature here being a matter of personal taste.

So much for generalizations. More specifically, we should be aware of the following:

It is unlikely that when one picks a bottle of wine from one's stock or buys it from a supermarket or a shop, it will be at the right temperature, although the number of wine cabinets which provide the right temperatures both for reds and whites is increasing, despite their high price.

Therefore, if we have a white wine which is not cold enough, we can cool it by either putting it in the freezer or in the fridge, depending on how much time we have at our disposal. It will take no more than half an hour to cool any white wine in a freezer and more than three hours in an ordinary fridge. (But please do not leave it in the freezer for too long: after, say 3½ hours, you risk finding frozen wine and frosted pieces of glass!)

Of course, in an ideal world, we should not do it that way: we should try and cool the wine gradually.

The best is a wine bucket, but not all of us will go to the trouble of using one. In any event, to chill a bottle by immersing it into a wine bucket, will certainly take no less than ten minutes, but to bring it down to the desired temperature will probably take twenty or maybe even thirty minutes, much depending of course on the target temperature as well as on the ambient temperature, the quantity of the ice put into the bucket, etc.

When dining in restaurants, beware the ice bucket. If the wine is served too warm, then it will certainly need a bucket, but as wine is consumed from the bottle, the ice and water have an increasingly rapid effect on the quality of what remains in the bottle. Animated conversation is dangerous because one does not notice that, having got down to the last two glasses of the high quality white that had been chosen, the guests are condemned to drinking ice lollies until the bottle is empty. I suggest that when that stage is reached the bottle is taken out of the wine bucket and left to stand on the table.

There are available now the so-called 'rapid ice' sleeves, both for wine and for champagne bottles. These are certainly effective but one must reckon on about ten to fifteen minutes for a white and probably slightly more for a champagne, the glass of the bottle being thicker. There are also 'gadgets' on the market that are both wine coolers and warmers!

A point worth bearing in mind, is that when served at table, wine will rise in temperature by at least 2° in about ten minutes.

What should not be done is to put ice cubes inside the glass. We have all done it occasionally, at the seaside maybe: but not to be repeated elsewhere! The fact is that every wine has a water content ranging between 85 and 90%: adding ice cubes to it not only dilutes the alcoholic content but also changes the flavour of the wine because the water which is inside it is something more 'alive' and with a different flavour than that which comes out of a tap.

The reverse process applies to reds which have to reach the famous or infamous room temperature. Much depends on the original bottle temperature, but if one wanted to do it the 'natural' way, one might have to keep it for at least twenty-four hours in a room having a temperature of say 18°C. The higher the temperature of the room, the shorter the period of time required, but what will do harm is a sudden rise in temperature if, for instance, the bottle is placed too close to a source of heat or, as I have sometimes done myself, on top of a radiator when one is in a hurry.

A better way would be to immerse it in tepid or even warm water, although that will damage the label.

Obviously, the simplest way is to warm the wine by holding the glass in one's cupped hands; that may be otherwise inconvenient and possibly require extra willpower! Some maintain that the microwave oven is ideal. I cannot go along with that, probably because I do not own one! However, do not be too disturbed by the screams of horror from so-called experts: this can be an efficient way to raise the temperature of the whole mass of wine in the bottle at the same time. Having made this point, I am not sure what the consequences are on the wine itself, although I appreciate how efficient the system can be for raising temperature. But concern must remain about the effect of the microwaves on the flavonoids in the wine. Maybe the bottle itself is adequate protection, but until more research is done, doubts will remain, especially since a recent (November 2003) study concluded that when broccoli are cooked in the microwave they lose 97% of the flavonoids. Worrying, perhaps, for wine lovers.

If the wine contains no sediment, then the bottle can be laid on its side on a folded kitchen towel for twenty seconds at a low setting; if on the other hand the bottle needs decanting first, then it should be decanted and the decanter itself put in the microwave for the same length of time. The only point of concern is that one needs to take care to ensure that no metal foil enters the microwave. Even though you think the 'foil' contains no metal, it is safer to remove it.

Of course, one may either 'frost' the glasses in the case of a white, or warm them up in the case of a red.

Also, under this heading the reader will, no doubt, be aware that there are wine thermometers available. I believe that the simplest gadget, however, is the band (metal or plastic) which one slides around a bottle. The temperature display is fairly immediate and, overall, quite accurate.

A final point to be borne in mind both at home and especially in the restaurant is that if one has a good red that needs to be served without having had time to uncork the bottle, say at least two hours prior to it being either served or decanted, a very effective way of allowing the wine to breathe is to pour it into a jug, preferably of the kind with a very wide neck and give the jug more than a gentle swirl.

This may be anathema to purists, but, I can assure you, it is very effective.

DECANTING

Decanting is a fantastic idea: but how many of us, and how often, have the privilege of drinking the kind of wine, namely vintage wine or a full-bodied wine with much sediment, which will benefit from decanting? It seems to me, at the cost of being slated by the professionals, that the only benefit of decanting a good bottle of red wine is to allow it to breathe, rather than to get rid of the sediment.

Decanting should certainly be done for some of the better types of wine. I suggest that it would almost be compulsory in the case of vintage full-bodied reds.

It must always be remembered that the technique of decanting red wine is not simply used to take the wine off its lees: it is much more important to 'open up' the wine.

I also suggest that we should forget about the nonsense of 'drawing the cork' a certain number of hours before the red wine is consumed since a very long period of time would be required before one could see any effect: the only wine in contact with oxygen would be the tiny disk in the neck of the bottle. If one is decanting to let a red wine breathe, as one should, then what is required is that the wine itself should be exposed to as much oxygen as possible. Therefore what one should do is to pour it into a decanter, not gently using the lager-pouring technique of running it down the side of the vessel or the same subtlety as one must adopt when pouring champagne, but rather by easing the wine out of the bottle directly into the decanter, ensuring that as much bubbling as possible takes place and, preferably, from as high a position as possible. In the case of particularly 'close' wines, such as a vintage Barolo, this operation may have to be carried out more than once.

Not all connoisseurs of wine, however, favour this procedure since many of them maintain that to 'carafe' the wine in this manner destroys its intimate structure, whatever that expression may mean. Opinions must differ on this issue.

So what would an experienced sommelier do?

He will:

a)   select the wine and bring it up from the cellar in the morning, decide if it will need decanting and if so, carefully, without shaking the bottle, place it upright on a sideboard in the dining room, a few hours before serving, draw the cork, tilt over a candle flame and decant it off the lees, or, more likely select the wine and bring it from the cellar in the morning

b)   a few hours before serving draw the cork or, ever more likely, before dinner bring the bottle up from the cellar and place it on the back of the kitchen stove, then subsequently draw the cork and serve the wine

Well, that is the theory. It would be much easier to wait for the wine to be chosen, pull the cork, decant it if necessary and put the decanter into the microwave for twenty seconds. I am told that some of the best palates in the United Kingdom have drunk the very finest class growth clarets served in this way and have then proceeded to pay compliments to their host for the . . . . .'perfect condition of the wine'. And why not?

Of one thing, however, I am absolutely certain: a good glass may not make much difference to a white wine, but will dramatically affect the flavour and impact of both a champagne and a good red.

For the former, a flute is to be preferred; and for the latter, a goblet-type glass. (There are many good manufacturers of wine glasses: I prefer the Riedel range, probably the best in the world. The company was founded in 1756).) And if you wish to be a perfectionist, or are not too certain of the absolute cleanliness and lack of odour of the glass you intend to use, then adopt the old Italian custom of pouring some wine (not too much!) into it, swirl it round the glass a few times and then throw that small quantity away. A baptism for the glass, a useful precaution for the experienced suspicious drinker.

SAVING WINE

When there is any wine left in the bottle, and one wishes to keep it for later, it should be remembered that the greater the quantity of residual sugar in the wine and the higher the alcoholic level, the longer the storage life expectancy. Thin 10.5-11° wines, unless they contain very high quantities of sulphur, will not last very long.

As a general rule, light-bodied, dry white wines will normally stay in good condition for twenty-four hours, especially if evacuated with a VacuVin or sealed with a wine preserver aerosol; sometimes they will last without noticeable deterioration for as long as forty-eight hours. I do not recommend either of these systems simply because I believe that once a good bottle of wine is opened, it deserves being drunk at once. But I mention the matter for the sake of completeness.

Heavier, more fruited white wines, which usually have higher alcoholic levels, will last for up to four or five days. Dessert wines, particularly if fortified, will actually last for months.

Reds, however, can be more problematic. Whereas white wines change from good to evil very quickly – they fall, so to say, 'off the edge' – reds usually take a slower road towards undrinkability. The reader may like to know that at almost all the top international wine competitions where aerosol wine-savers are regularly in use, there is an expectation that any red of substance and quality should last at least a week in prime condition, and longer in many cases.

This is an area where New World-style wine producers have a distinct edge as their quest for fruit-tasting wines leads them to let grapes ripen fully. The two consequences are high sugar and, inevitably as a result, higher alcoholic levels than traditional European wines. Thus, a level of 13.5 or 14° is quite normal and 15° by no means uncommon in a situation where it must be admitted (and I put it this way, because I am not too fond of New World wines generally) both fruitiness and alcoholic content are in perfect balance. At that stage, the 'storability' of these wines is greatly enhanced.

CHAPTER 4

INTRODUCING ITALIAN WINES

A BRIEF NOTE ON ITALY

The Italian peninsula is long and narrow, running from north-west to south-east, for a length of about 1,200 km. Its land boundary is about 1,800 km; the remainder is coastline, extending to about 4,500 km (7,500 km if one includes the Italian islands). Its surface area is approximately 301,000 square kilometres, 65,538 square kilometres of which are classified as woodland.

Italy hangs in the Mediterranean Sea, almost like a reversed appendix from the intestine: its usual description is a 'boot'. Its northern part is clearly attached to central Europe. Its southernmost tip of Sicily is almost contiguous to Africa (indeed, it was once joined to the African continent); summers are hot, but winters are cold.

Its northern regions of Lombardia and Piemonte are fertilized by the River Po (at 652 km, one of the longest in Europe) which intersects an almost rectangular plain well cultivated and irrigated, with good centres of activities and excellent communications.

Although Italy is largely a mountainous country (plains cover only 23% of its total land mass), it has a wide range of soils and varying climatic conditions which make for an extraordinary variety of wines. There are many hill slopes (e.g. the Monferrato and the Cuneese in Piemonte, the undulating countryside of Toscana and Umbria) and the variations in altitude, from the Alps to the Apennines that run, as a spine, for a total length of 1,350 km (starting south in Calabria and ending in the north-west with Liguria), through the whole of Italy, combine with the fertility of the soil to produce assortments of flavours that are not to be found, in my opinion, in any other country of the world. There is gravel, clay, limestone, and what is produced on the slopes of Vesuvius and Etna after the regular coverings of volcanic ash: little wonder that there is so much to choose from. Less obvious is the fact that the whole of the territory that produces wines in the central province of Lazio (Frascati and many others) is also of volcanic origin and exceptionally rich in potash. But the variety of choice has one enormous drawback: it is confusing for the layman and has resulted in every village or small town having its own wine to boast of, without a concurrent development of refinement in winemaking techniques. All this is changing, as I shall endeavour to show.

Tradition in winemaking in Italy has ensured that wines have been made following rules laid down centuries ago. Furthermore, wine has always been looked upon as a complement to food and not, as in the Anglo-American and Scandinavian world – at least until recently – as something out of the ordinary.

Wine has never been lacking, even in the poorest households, at mealtimes; nobody ever bothered to consider which wine (red, white or rosé) should be coupled with particular foods. It sufficed that some wine was there, regardless of the temperature at which it might correctly be served. Indeed, there is a Piedmontese saying that it is better to drink warm wine than cool water!

Keen though the Italians are on drinking wine, they are not the greatest imbibers in the world. The record is held officially by Luxembourg where in 2003 the 'per capita' consumption of wine was 66.1 litres.. However, I do not entirely believe these statistics, because I know from direct personal experience that many people travel to Luxembourg from other parts of Europe in order to purchase wine of all kinds, which is considerably cheaper there than elsewhere. Discounting Luxembourg, therefore, the leading position in yearly personal consumption of wine goes to France, with 48.5 litres. Italy comes close behind with 47.5 litres, followed by Portugal (42), Switzerland (40.9), Hungary (37.4), Argentina (34.6), Greece (33.8), Uruguay (33.3), Denmark (32.6), Spain (30.6), Austria (29.8), Finland (26.3), and Germany (23.6). The South Africans consume much less, 8.26 litres per person and, perhaps surprisingly, are beaten by the United Kingdom with 20.1 litres per person. (Appendix 5 shows the full table.) Interestingly, it is recorded (*The Times*, 9 February 2005) that Britons drank more than a billion litres of wine in 2004, sales increasing by more than 30% during the period 1999 (£5.8 billion) to 2004 (£7.6 billion).

It was only in the eighteenth century, by which time France had long established its wine supremacy, that the activities of the Grand Duchy of Tuscany, with a zonal definition for Chianti and the establishment of a wine academy, show signs of recognising and developing the local potential. These stirrings were followed in the nineteenth century by the importation of French concepts into Chianti by Baron Bettino Ricasoli and into Barolo by Louis Oudart, the start of sparkling wine production in Asti by Carlo Gancia who imported French Champagne methods, and the production of fortified wines in Marsala pioneered by an Englishman, John Woodhouse.

By the end of the nineteenth century, the Risorgimento having unified (if you are Italian) or created (if you are a political realist) the nation, a sense of vinous unity also developed. Nationally, those who could afford to, began to care about wine quality and overseas fledgling export markets – usually created by expatriate Italians seeking a taste of home – began to beckon. Sadly, just as Italy started to be recognized for quality, the twin scourges of phylloxera and oidium struck, and in the confused aftermath not only were many valuable (by repute at least) indigenous varieties lost, but replantings often favoured imported varieties and, almost invariably, heavy cropping versions over intrinsically high quality vines.

The Italian legacy today is confused. The most widely planted white grape (Trebbiano) is only found in other countries mostly for distillation purposes, and the most widely planted red variety (Sangiovese) is essentially a blending grape needing the support of other varieties, rather than as a stand-alone type. Alongside these difficulties are those resulting from politics and the politics of agriculture, especially in the last ten years or so when a number of major Italian vineyards have been sold to foreign, mainly American, buyers whose principal concerns, apart from profit of course, are uniformity in the wines produced. The result is that tradition, original flavours and varieties are sacrificed on the altar of such concerns and of new vinification techniques.

The late 1970s and the whole of the subsequent decade saw a major shift in Italian winemaking: one could say that the professionals took over from the amateurs. This was reflected not merely in the up-dating and/or change of equipment, of storage vessels (for instance, concrete containers were replaced by stainless steel) but also by determined efforts not only to regulate the composition, quality, labelling, etc. of the wines but also by the attempts, (sometimes, as in the case of the super Tuscans, extremely successfully, though not always so) to create new types of wine, usually of a higher alcoholic content and smoother, to take into account the tastes of the ever-increasing wine-drinking public.

Things are changing, and changing fast. Certainly, as far as the man in the street in the UK and the US is concerned, Italian wines nowadays are becoming better known and much more appreciated – not unlike Italian cuisine.

ITALIAN WINES CONSIDERED

A point that must be made at the outset is that a number of misconceptions abound concerning Italian wines. Time and time again over the years I have heard many wine drinkers say that they know little about them because they have never tried them. In all likelihood, they have sampled them but in a different garb: for decades, there have been trainloads of strong, flowerful, red wine travelling from the cellar of Italy, as it is known, namely Apulia in the south-east (as well as from Sicily), to France and other non-Mediterranean countries. This wine of 15/18° alcohol that goes from Puglia to the north is known as 'miere' (from the Latin 'merum' – and in English 'mere' – meaning 'pure' wine). Importantly, it travels well to its northern destinations where, in a sense, it undergoes castration by being 'cut' with weaker, almost inferior wines, with which it is blended into local products to give them the extra flavour and higher alcoholic content which the local grapes cannot provide. Lest the reader should be in any doubt about this particular statement, I refer to Hugh Johnson's *The World Atlas of Wine*, 3rd edition, 1997, p. 177, where it is recorded that France and West Germany took (in bulk) more than half the quantity, i.e., in excess of 18 million hectolitres.

This figure is reported for what I would term historical reasons. Since the third edition of Hugh Johnson's work was published, a number of changes have taken place in the marketing of Italian wines. These changes can be summarized by stating that there has been an overall reduction in the export of Italian wines in bulk and an increase in that of bottled wines.

Evidence for the above statement is clearly provided if I mention that the total volume of Italian wine exported in 2006 was 7,839 million hectolitres.

The percentages for the countries that are the main importers of Italian wines (bottled) are as follows:

USA	30%
Germany	28%
UK	12%
Switzerland	7%
Canada	5%
Japan	5%
Austria	3%
France	3%
Sweden	3%
The Netherlands	2%
Denmark	2%

In the years since 1998, there have been three main changes in the pattern of exports: Germany that was the major importer of Italian wines has given place to the USA (where for the past three years Italy has been exporting more than France) and quantities imported into the UK have, in fact, increased. The only country which, during the same period, appears to have shown the greatest reduction is, in fact, France, although minor adjustments have occurred with respect to Austria, Japan, Denmark, the Netherlands and Sweden.

Other customers for strong Italian red wine are Switzerland and the USSR. Italian wines can be found in such far-flung places as Japan, which is importing ever greater quantities of it and China which, it is hoped, will become a major market. I should also mention the potential of the Indian sub-continent: in January 2007, the show-case exhibition of Italian wines, VinItaly, was held in Mumbai. Similarly, since the turn of the century, exports have increased substantially to the new members of the European Union, namely the Czech Republic, Poland, Slovakia, Hungary, Malta, Lithuania, Estonia, Latvia, Slovenia and Cyprus, with Latvia and Hungary vying for first place. Interestingly, in 2006, the value of Italian wine exports represented nearly 20% of the country's total exported products.

Strange though this may sound to many, there is nothing novel in the idea of wine going from Italy to France. Archaeological evidence has recently been discovered of a wreck in the Tyrrhenian Sea, where a ship foundered some 2,500 years ago carrying hundreds of amphorae of Etruscan wine from either Lazio or Toscana en route to Marseilles or Lattes in France (as revealed in a Channel 4 television programme entitled 'Lost Worlds', shown in December 2002). Incidentally, I recommend a visit to the Archaeological Museum in Lattes!

Nor is there anything unusual about this either. Archaeological discoveries have unearthed a wine 'pipeline' made of clay which helped to load the wine being shipped out of the port at Sibari, a town on the Ionian Sea in Calabria. The transport of wine in large quantities by sea has been confirmed by the underwater discoveries that have been taking place over the past two decades all along the southern Italian coastline where hundreds of terracotta jars dating back to the first century AD have been found.

Until comparatively recent times, the British general public was quite ignorant about wine matters. Of course, the man in the street knew that you drank champagne on special occasions, had heard of claret, may have known of the broad difference between Bordeaux and Bourgogne, and in all likelihood had some inkling that once a year there was a 'race' to bring over to England a comparatively innocuous, if not sharp, and definitely uninteresting French wine by the name of Beaujolais 'nouveau'. The reader should not think for one moment that I am being chauvinistic in making this remark. A Frenchman, Francois Mauss, President of the Grand Jury of European Winetasters, is on record as having stated in the summer of 2002 that Beaujolais 'is a crap wine' ('C'est un vin de merde'). See *The Times*, 11 January 2003. I do think this comment is somewhat unfair, however, because, occasionally, one does find a rather pleasant Beaujolais nouveau! Nor is this to be taken as a criticism of the French who have always been very successful in blending their wines and highly competent in advertising them (as witness the Beaujolais 'race', the sales of the Hospice de Beaune, 'Les Tastevins', 'Les Confrèries du Vin').

Indeed, it would be fair to say that until, say, the mid-seventies, any English wine culture which might have existed related almost exclusively to France (leaving aside port, Madeira, Marsala and sherry wines). In developing, blending, publicising and marketing their wines, the French, as far as the UK, the USA and possibly other countries are concerned, have been undisputed masters for some two hundred years.

There is no denying that during this period the French

winemaking industry has had the upper hand. This is under-standable because not only has it been supported by first-class products, but it had a perfect theoretical basis if one considers that the Frenchman Lavoisier, a great chemist, established in the eighteenth century the equation of alcoholic fermentation and one century later another Frenchman, Louis Pasteur, bequeathed to humanity not only the hot sterilization apparatus that he had developed but also his studies on modern winemaking. On the other hand, and perhaps chauvinistically, I should record that it was way back in 1787 that the Florentine Adamo Fabbroni published the first 'technical' book on wines entitled *Dell'Arte di Fare il vino* where he demonstrated that wine fermentation could take place even in an airless atmosphere.

At the same time, the man in the street then began to realize that there were some good wines emanating from Spain which were cheaper than the French. Rioja became a household name, although some might argue that it is not even the best Spanish wine-producing area and Cava began to be appreciated, primarily because it could be bought for under £5 when the equivalent bottle of mediocre French champagne cost around £15, if not more.

But Italian wines took a long time to break down the almost impenetrable barrier of French marketing expertise. They have now succeeded in doing so, of course, but the effort was prolonged and substantial. It is worthwhile pointing out at this stage that one of the reasons – apart from bad organization – why until, say the mid-1980s, Italian wines were less well known than they deserved to be, is simply because they were made to be drunk locally.

Being generally unpasteurized and containing, long before the European Directives came into force, reasonably modest amounts of sulphur, they did not really travel well. In effect, they suffered because of their comparative purity.

In the UK, in particular, until say the 1970s, the only Italian wines having any kind of reputation for the man in the street were Chianti (red) and Frascati, Orvieto and Verdicchio (whites). One could add that those varieties are no more representative of Italian wines than a light ale is of English beers, though typical of them as far as the British were concerned.

Maybe it was the popularity of the flask that made Chianti the Italian wine by definition. Representations in films or in advertise-ments showed the family sitting at a meal, at a large table, with grandfather and grandmother at the head of the table, and the flask of Chianti being passed round. The reader should not misunderstand: Chianti is a fine wine, but there are many other Italian reds that are just as good, if not better. The advertisers then caught hold of the fancy, amphora-shaped bottle of the Italian dry white wine named Verdicchio and that became popular too. Again, without wishing to be unkind, there are many better Italian whites.

Later, British supermarkets decided that Lambrusco would prove a popular wine; cheap at source, sparkling, sweetish, eminently saleable. There are, of course, some excellent Lambruscos to be drunk in the area of production, but it is fair to say that what is exported is not the best wine.

This comparative ignorance of Italian wines on the part of the Anglo-American public is compounded by an absolute lack of knowledge of Italian grape varieties. The man in the street who takes an interest in wine may have heard of Cabernet Sauvignon, but I suggest he could not name a single Italian indigenous grape variety. And yet, some of these varieties are important. To give but one example, Barbera is a very ancient, dominant and versatile red wine grape, which in Italy is grown almost exclusively in the north-west, but which has been successfully exported to other countries such as Argentina, California, Australia (especially the state of Victoria), Brazil, Uruguay, Mexico and Peru. It is an extremely prolific, though at times uneven, grape, which non-Italian winemakers are trying to exploit to advantage. It also has an ancient lineage, for although one cannot say for sure, it is conceivable that when the Greek geographer Strabo was talking about the vineyards surrounding the town of Asti some two thousand years ago, he had Barbera in mind. It is first officially mentioned in a document of the thirteenth century (1249, in the Church of Sant'Erasmo at Casale in the Monferrato), although it was really classified only at the end of the nineteenth century and came to the fore during the first thirty years of the twentieth century, when the vines were replanted on American root stocks following the phylloxera epidemic.

Barbera was exported to California over a hundred years ago but did not become popular there until the 1990s. (A leading UK supermarket is now selling a Barbera produced in California!) The 'oenological' connection between Italy and the United States is, in some respects, quite marked. In the early 1990s, there was a movement initiated by the Californians to import into their region some of Italy's most successful grapes. Interestingly, the initiative was taken by top Californian vintners and some of the Italian varieties (Barbera, Sangiovese) are proving quite successful. (I pause to observe in this connection that three of the principal Californian wine producers – Mondavi, Ernst & Julio Gallo and Rossi – are of Italian origin, emanating respectively from the Marche, Fossano and Dogliani in Piemonte.)

Bonarda is also a very successful grape (more commonly known in Italy at least as 'uva rara') and is becoming increasingly popular in the Argentine where it is blended often with Malbec.

Nebbiolo is a generous, strong grape that goes to produce some of the best red wines of Italy (Barbaresco, Barolo, Gattinara, Nebbiolo) and which is now being used in the New World. (There is available in the UK a screw-cap Nebbiolo made in Australia!)

Sangiovese goes into a number of reds (also as 'Sangioveto') (the best known being Chianti), as well as being popular in other parts of the world. A mark of the increasing popularity of the Sangiovese is its availability as an IGT wine. (See Chapter 5.) Often of a fairly nondescript character, the 187cl bottles are, in fact, offered by one of the major UK airlines on some of their flights. And it is not that bad a variety.

Trebbiano, that goes to make much white wine and one of the most widely grown grapes in the whole world, probably on a par with the Spanish variety Airen, is increasingly being planted in Australia and was exported many years ago to Argentina thanks to the Italian immigrants there.

A number of Italian grape varieties have been 'naturalized'. The Primitivo of Apulia (claimed by some to have Dalmatian origins) has become the 'Zinfandel'! of California. (Some wines made with the Primitivo (q.v.) grapes are called in the alternative Zinfandel with the IGT qualification); 'Sangiovese' is now grown also in South Africa to be blended with other grapes. 'Refosco', a grape native to Friuli, is now grown in California.)

When the Hungarian vineyards were ravaged by the phylloxera in the second half of the last century, they were revived by the importation of European/American hybrids as well as by a number of vines of Italian stock. For example, one of the Hungarian varieties is called 'Bakator'. This name is the corruption of the Italian 'Bacca d'Oro' and is clear proof of the origin of the particular grape variety.

The area of Hungary which is known as the Hungarian Sea, namely that surrounding Lake Balaton, is associated with a number of good local wines. But the grape variety which is most widespread is the Italian Riesling, which can be found all around the hills of Badacsony, Balantonfured and Csopak, simply because it is the type of Riesling which is very prolific and, above all, has a high sugar content. A variety, I add, which, although not common in Germany, is well known in Austria and Switzerland and parts of Eastern Europe.

Italian Riesling certainly seems to suit the basalt type of soil that is to be found around Lake Balaton. I appreciate that some experts maintain that it is not an indigenous Italian variety but it is derived from either Austria, or Germany relying on names such as Welschriesling and/or Olasz Riesling.

It is, of course, well beyond the scope of this guide to consider a number of matters that are of importance when dealing with varieties of vines, especially the way in which they are trained and pruned. There are so many permutations (the single this, the double that, the trellis here, the canopy ('pergola') there, the bush type plant, the 'small tree' (alberello), the bow, the espalier and so on), much of them related to traditional approaches, which are being constantly re-appraised. Ultimately, however, it is the weather that determines how a vine will be trained, in order either to shelter it from, or expose it to, the elements and sunlight. To give one small 'Italian' example: on the island of Pantelleria, the southernmost part of Italy where grape is grown, quite close to the African continent, vine is cultivated in a particular way, low in the sand, with a view to protecting it both from the wind and from the salt of the surrounding sea.

Italian vines can speak for themselves, but the French have been much better at advertising their great oenological ability. In Italy, we have been more concerned to produce quantity rather than quality wines: however, the picture is changing at a very fast pace. As already noted, the most recent statistics confirm a reduction in the quantities produced in Italy with a concomitant increase in those from France: the different emphasis being reflected in the variations in price structure of Italian and French table wines in the UK, the former increasing and the latter reducing. (In this connection it is interesting to record that the number of 'sommeliers' in Italy has risen steadily over the past fifteen years: there are now in excess of

40,000, 31,000 alone representing the membership of AIS – the 'Associazione Italiana Sommelier'.)

But as I have already stated, the problem is that Italian wines have always been considered by their producers as something analogous to food: a necessity much more than a luxury. They have been created, and only occasionally blended, in line with local requirements and were never intended to travel half way round the world. The modern sophisticated methods of pasteurization were not needed and the wine remained something living, a world of micro-organisms, minerals and flavonoids. It is only over the last two decades that consideration had to be given by the Italians to producing the kind of wines that would suit the palate of northern and other peoples generally, tasting more of the oak into which they were matured than of the grape from which they originated, essentially a means to liberate the spirit of those people whom a strong sun seldom comforts, a prelude to that abandonment, if not drunkenness, which, on the whole, was not until recent days a national Italian trait.

As with everything else, there is a fashion in wine. This is particularly true about Italian wine.

There are some DOC or DOCG (as described later) wines (e.g. Taurasi and Primitivo, whether di Manduria or of the more common type sold generally in 'wine bars' throughout Basilicata and Calabria) which pour into the glass almost in the same manner as 'Ribena'. They are full of thickness, colour, body, as wine writers call it, and flavour. They are real wines, they are 'strong wines' and suffer no comparison.

There is a sensual excitement in watching them being poured, which is not to be found with any other wine. They are, if women readers will forgive me, 'men's wines'. Certainly, they are not so famous or expensive as a Chateau Lafite, or as respected as a Chateau-Neuf-du-Pape or a Crozes-Hermitage: but they are real wines, colourful, reliable, strong (their alcoholic content varying from 12.5° to 15° or more). They are solid, yet fragrant. Try out any of the following short selection of dry reds:

Aglianico	Gattinara
Amarone	Primitivo
Barbaresco	Sagrantino di Montefalco
Barbera	Salento

Brunello   Solopaca
Dolcetto   Taurasi
Falerno

If you have a sweet tooth, then I recommend any one of the following: any virgin (dry) vintage Marsala, Moscato di Pantelleria, Moscato di Trani, Moscato di Noto, Picolit, Vernaccia di Serrapetrona, and any Vin Santo Toscano.

If you prefer dry wines, then try a vintage Brunello di Montalcino, a good Vino Nobile di Montepulciano, Nero d'Avola, Primitivo di Manduria or Salice Salentino. And Barolo, of course!

When you read about these particular Italian wines, you may find that the wine-taster or writer approves of what is being tasted, but with a certain amount of hesitation and indeed condescension; as if anything that were supposed to be valuable in the world of wine could only come from France. Regrettably, this is a fairly widespread attitude, at least in the UK and the USA. It calls for criticism, redress, rectification, education, enlightenment and, at the end of the day, enjoyment. I have yet to meet any English-speaking person who, when offered wines of the kind described (and the names mentioned above are a small sample of the number of other flavourful, solid and reliable Italian wines) has not burst into praise of one kind or another. It would be too simple to assume that it is the high alcoholic content of these wines that has precipitated such praise: the contrary is true. The imbiber has suddenly found – in all likelihood, much to his or her surprise – that there was an extra quality to these wines, which he had not yet come across drinking those of other countries, whatever they might have been. That quality is a combination of alcohol and taste, but ultimately, of excitement: something, if I may say so with much pride, typically Italian.

The recent greater concentration in Italy on quality rather than quantity is also highlighted by two factors which are important. In the first place, wine has now become much more of a news item: the number of articles in newspapers and magazines and, more particularly, the amount of television space dedicated to wine are increasing all the time. Furthermore, there are over 10,000 new entries every year in Italy of boys and girls in the age group between eighteen and twenty-five who take the sommelier course, a clear reflection of the interest in wines.

More significantly, perhaps, is the fact that there has been an increase in the number of Italian women taking the Italian equivalent of the Master of Wine course and many more of them are coming to the fore in the oenological world, as experts on wines but, above all, as owners or directors of powerful wine enterprises. To choose a few at random and in alphabetical order: Anna Maria Abbona manages one of the best known Piedmontese wine estates at Barolo in the province of Cuneo, specializing in Dolcetto wine; Albiera, Allegra and Alessia Antinori are well known representatives of their family, famous for its Chianti; Vinzia di Gaetano Firriato, together with her husband Salvatore, won the title of 'Italian Cellar of the Year' and, in 2004, with her Nero d'Avola, that of wine of the year for her firm, Firriato of Parero (Sicily); Diana Frescobaldi is associated with what is probably one of the most famous names in the world for Chianti, namely that of the Marchesi de'Frescobaldi; Elisabetta Geppetti and her husband Stefano have come to the fore with the Morellino di Scansano; Serenella Moroder has, with her husband Alessandro, been instrumental in the transformation of the Conero reds into very successful 'modern' wines; José Rallo, a member of the well-known Rallo family at Donnafugata (Marsala) is known as much for her firm's enterprising use of the Nero d'Avola grapes as for a barrique matured Chardonnay; Teresa Severini Lungarotti is, with Chiara Lungarotti, in charge of the family enterprise (practically an all female operation) at Torgiano (in the province of Perugia), famous for its red wines (Rubesco, Torgiano and Vigna Monticchio); Maria Silvaggi and Dora Celentano are associated with a resurgence in the Massico (Aglianico, Taburno); Nadia Zenato manages the well-known Zenato Enterprise at Peschiera del Garda in the province of Verona (well noted for its Cabernet, Lugana and especially Amarone).

There are many others whose names come to mind, such as Francesca Colombini, a well-known producer of Brunello di Montalcino and Giovanna Folonari from Tuscany, especially what I would term the up-and-coming generation of women vintners, some quite young and yet knowledgeable.

Indeed, it emerged on the 8 June 2006 that of the 100,000 or so firms that produce wine in Italy, some 25,000 are headed by women; perhaps not so surprising an item of news given the fact that in December 2006 it was confirmed that of all the agricultural enterprises throughout Italy 43% are controlled by a woman.

Not all is rosy, of course, in the Italian wine garden. The multiplicity of grape varieties are at best almost invariably destined for a DOC blend when the world is asking for strong character, single-variety wines, and at worst condemned to be sold by weight and sugar content to a co-operative to be transformed into high-strength, high-colour bulk-blending wines as transfusion material for anaemic wines in France, Germany and even, on occasions, Spain.

These are, to many Italians, unpalatable truths. But it is impossible even to begin to consider where Italy stands in today's international wine market without understanding the background to the reasons for production difficulties or sales disadvantages, or the unwillingness, at least until recent times, to cease relying so much on Garganega and Sangiovese and to exploit instead the wealth of autochthonous vines. There is much that is good, there is even more that is immeasurably better than just ten years ago, there is some wine production that can only be called superb, and an iceberg's tip of the simply 'ethereal'. It is much the same in other countries, but Italy's iceberg is just a whole lot bigger than anyone else's and that means there's an enormous base of anonymity supporting a very small summit of excellence.

But that is my main purpose in writing this book – to lead you towards those wines literally 'at the top'. Those that are quintessentially Italian, that simply could not be produced anywhere else in the world, that shout 'I'm Italian and proud of it'. I hope that you will look and learn and, even more importantly, ENJOY!

ITALIAN WINE BOTTLES

For the most part (three out of four of the major types), Italian bottles are of French origin.

1.   *The Bordeaux type* ('Bordolese'). This is the straight, I was about to say standard size, wine bottle nowadays containing 0.750L (0.375 for the halves); it is more frequently used for red wines and can be either white or amber-coloured; the former more commonly used for rosé, young red and white wines; the latter for the more mature reds. They can also be used for whites in what one can only term an off-white glass colour.

2.   *The Borgognona-type* bottle. This is of Côte d'Or origin, a conic, almost fattish shape. It is used in fact throughout the world in

0750L and 0375L sizes.

3. *The Rhenish-type* ('renana'). This comes from Germany, as its name indicates and was exceptionally favoured in the eighteenth century in the European capitals. It is flat-bottomed and is usually of a light green colour, occasionally white. It is found mainly in north-east Italy for champagne-type wine with variations on the actual size and shape. It is used for most of Italy's sparkling wines.

The above represent the principal shapes but just as Italy displays great variety in its wines, it also shows some imagination in the types of bottles used. For example, in Piemonte, over the past twenty years or so there has been a revival of older-type bottles such as the 'albeisa' and the 'astesana'. The amphora-shaped bottle of the Verdicchio from the Marche is still the same as it was for a very long time. A container similar to the Tuscan flask but more of an oval shape is used quite frequently for the Orvieto whites.

The Moscato Rosa (Rosen Muscateller of north-east Italy) very often comes in long, narrow, brown or green bottles, of varying capacity, as does the Barolo Chinato (I am ignoring miniatures and fancy bottles which emerge from time to time, which are not quantitatively significant).

CHAPTER 5

UNDERSTANDING THE ITALIAN SEARCH FOR EXCELLENCE: A HISTORY OF IGT, DOC AND DOCG WINES

After the Second World War, a few long-established and respectable wine producers, mainly in Piedmont and Tuscany, together with a myriad of smaller enterprises – mostly family businesses – were all competing with one another in providing an extraordinary variety of wines of quality ranging from what might be described as the sublime to the ridiculous.

Successive governments slowly came to realize that, instead of earning foreign currency by exporting trainloads of strong, flavourful red wine of high alcoholic content from Apulia and Sicily to other European countries, but especially to France, for blending, they should concentrate on developing a national wine industry instead.

The formation of producer co-operatives was encouraged and gradually people began to see the benefits of controls on the production of wine, which until then had not been the case. More especially, it became apparent that the government should intervene to give legislative support and endorsement to regulations and practices which had grown up in a somewhat haphazard fashion over the previous hundred years or so and to ensure that quality, rather than quantity, should become the principal aim.

It is true that the nineteenth century had been, for the Italian wine industry, an era of substantial change and reform; but choosing at random, wines like Barolo and Chianti, which are now known and respected the world over, were then of most uneven quality. The former tended to be almost sweetish and not suitable for ageing; the latter lacked statutory control, although thanks to Baron Ricasoli it was one of the first wine areas of Italy to organize itself into a 'Consorzio' in 1902, later with a distinguishing mark on its flasks and bottles (the black cockerel).

In 1963, however, the first Italian law controlling production nationally was passed (Presidential Decree No. 903) which codified the concept of a *denominazione di origine* (the Italian equivalent of the highly profitable concept of *appellation controlée*, which the French had introduced in 1936). This proved so successful that on the 10 February 1992, what is now known simply as law 164 (promoted by the then Minister of Agriculture, Goria), revised and strengthened the concept of denomination of origin. The regulatory system thus set up was reinforced by two later 'Statutory Instruments', namely on 21 May 2001 and 10 April 2002, which endorsed but also tightened previous practice extending it to vine growers, wine-makers and bottling plants by introducing further controls both on the must and on the wines. These effectively followed upon European Commission Regulations 822/87 and 823/87 which clarified concepts and wording.

Regulation 822/87 defines wine as follows: 'It is the product which is obtained exclusively from the total or partial alcoholic fermentation of fresh grapes, whether pressed or not, or of grape musts.' Regulation 823/87 provides further requirements such as wine's own production zone, type of grape, etc. It also laid down the wording to be used in describing wine, as set out hereunder. As a result, we now have in Italy what one can term a pyramid of quality and classification of Italian wines.

At the base of the pyramid, comprising some 40% of national production, there are what the French would call the *vins de table*, table wines, in Italian *Vini da Tavola*, abbreviated to VdT or VDT. These are standard production wines, which can be blended or unblended and the sole control over which is that they should be of good quality and contain no chemicals, other than prescribed quantities of 'sulphur' (and tartrates).

Above that, representing 30% of national production, we have the *vini a indicazione geografica tipica* (meaning 'wines having a typical geographic indication') (more commonly known as IGT wines) introduced in 1992 by law 164, referred to above.

These are not necessarily superior to table wines, but usually perform better for the simple reason that they have to be identified by specific areas of production (namely, the region from which they originate, e.g. Sardegna), thus ensuring some kind of uniformity. They will usually show on the label the grape variety (e.g. Sangiovese) and also the year of the vintage. It must be admitted that many IGT wines are emerging that cannot easily be distinguished from ordinary 'unqualified' table wines. A certain amount of care is required when choosing IGT wines. At the same time, however, it should be noted that there are some excellent IGT wines which, but for the regulations, would certainly qualify for a DOC. For reasons of space, a very small number of them are considered here although there are others (for example, Dogajolo, Carpineto) which are of standing both in quality and in price terms.

The regulations also prescribe that IGT wines must correspond to certain parameters: amongst these are the maximum grape yield per hectare and the minimum natural alcohol content at distillation and the projected alcohol content at consumption. Statistically, it is claimed that at least 85% of IGT wines actually derive from the geographical zones whose name they bear.

The third tier is represented by DOC wines, namely the wines of *denominazione di origine controllata*. These are wines whose label must make clear that they are produced in a particularly well-defined area, that have features especially associated with that area and whose composition and taste are essentially, and in detail, controlled by specifications laid down by law. They represent 25% of national wine production.

The wine that qualifies for a DOC label is specific to a particular territory and is the result of traditional winemaking techniques. A wine cannot normally obtain DOC status nowadays if it is created, so to say, out of the blue as a result of novel blending or vinification processes: all DOC wines must have had a long history and tradition and are associated with a particular territory or region. However, there are successful wines – to which reference will be made below – that have been made over the past twenty to thirty years as a result of blending various types of grapes, some of which are not even indigenous to the particular area. In other words, a wine may be made in Tuscany with grapes that have recently been planted there but originated from other parts of the country, or from abroad. These, as the law stands at the moment, do not normally qualify as DOC, even though they may be high quality, expensive wines.

The scope of DOC protection extends nearly 2,000 kms from the north-western regions of Italy (Aosta and Piemonte) as far down as practically to Africa if one considers that on a volcanic island situated not too far from Africa, Pantelleria, there is a DOC Moscato wine.

The law of DOC wines covers the type of wine (e.g. has it been matured for a particular period, does it come from a late vintage), the grape variety that can be used in its production (if of a single variety) and if a blend of different grapes, the percentages of that blend. But more particularly, the law lays down the quantity of grape that can be produced in each hectare (for example, 90 quintals per hectare), the ratio of wine to the grape (for example, 60%), as well as the type of maturing used for the wine (in metal barrels, steel vats, or oak casks, or in bottle) and the actual ageing period.

This does not mean, of course, that all DOC wines are perfect: but a DOC wine is more likely to be good than bad. One should look carefully at its bottle description (as to which, see later).

A number of DOC wines are now being blended. For example, one can now find a Pinot Grigio blended with Garganega, a Primitivo blended with Merlot. The results are varied but one thing is certain: the DOC label cannot be applied to such blends which are then sold either as IGT products – the more common situation – or as table wines.

At the very top, representing 5% of national production, we have wines which can claim that they are not only DOC, with their denomination of origin being *controllata*, that is to say controlled by law, but *controllata e garantita*. What this means, in theory, is that the state itself to some extent guarantees the wine by way of the regulatory framework and inspections to which it is subject. The description of these top quality wines, abbreviated to DOCG, applies only to wines of particularly interesting quality, that have enjoyed DOC status for at least five years and that have overcome tests (to them) based on their chemical and organoleptic composition. The first test occurs, as for DOC wines, when they are produced, and the second when they are bottled.

The procedure that allows wines to qualify for particular denominations of origin, especially for DOCGs, is very tight, for not only must it be proved that the wine is 'particularly worthwhile', but a precise specification must be laid down. This covers the areas where the wine is produced, the quantity per hectare, acidity, minimum alcoholic content, vinification techniques, bottle type, capacity and labelling. A consultation period follows as well as a public hearing and time is allowed for objections.

I mention all of this to show the strictness of the criteria applied before the state acknowledges and guarantees the particular wine.

DOC and DOCG wines are further defined by European law as being of VQPRD, that is to say 'wines of quality produced in specified regions' (*vini di qualitá prodotti in una regione delimitata*).

Another authorized identification is the abbreviation VLQPRD, which stands for *vino liquoroso di qualitá prodotto in una regione delimitata*. This label is utilized for liqueur-type wines (sweet, dessert drinks) of most types such as Marsala, Aleatico and so on.

There is a further description that can be applied only to wines of DOC and DOCG classification, namely VSQPRD which stands for *vino superiore di qualitá prodotto in una regione delimitata*.

The final description is VFQPRD which is *vini frizzanti di qualitá prodotti in regione determinata*.

From the technical point of view, the abbreviations VFQPRD and VSQPRD must be shown on DOC and DOCG wines. Where, however, one has sparkling (spumante or frizzante) wines which are merely table or IGT wines, this description cannot be applied (see EC Regulation 1439/1999 Annex 7).

For those who are interested in figures, there exist at present in Italy 352 DOC and DOCG wines (319 DOC and 33 DOCG), as well as 120 IGT wines. A full list is in Appendix 2.

In recent years, substantial criticisms have been voiced regarding the DOC system – by Italian wine writers, of course, but in the main by foreigners, especially English and American writers. Amongst these criticisms is the fact that the system imposes constraints which are based on a traditional view of winemaking that, it is said, is no longer in keeping with modern tastes, which have become much softer and blander; that, as a result of these constraints, there is a considerable lack of imagination on the part of Italian wine producers who are effectively prevented from experimenting; that some of the traditional systems of winemaking are now obsolete; that the DOC label often extends over very wide, and possibly undefined, areas where, especially because of the number of territories covered, it embraces wines of extremely varied quality; that the insistence on using only particular types of grapes or mixtures of grapes, in categorically stated percentages, is ultimately boring in terms of taste; that the existence of highly detailed production codes, whilst ensuring the identity of the wines, is detrimental to quality and that the Italian situation should be compared with the French, since in France there is no production code laying down the percentages of different grapes and the manner and time of maturation of the wine; that the codes themselves do not provide any inducement to improve quality; that there is no standard (can one exist?) by which qualitative controls of the wines are in fact carried out at least in the sense that the panels appointed by local chambers of commerce to supervise the enforcement of Law 164 appear to be more concerned about uniformity than quality; that by identifying well defined geographical areas and confining DOC and DOCG denominations to those particular areas, changes have been made in the various territories which may have resulted in lesser quality vineyards being included in a higher quality denomination. (This has happened quite often with Nebbiolo vines which, as a result of the re-definition of the respective areas, have, even where of inferior quality, ended up by being included in a Barolo DOCG where perhaps, more appropriately, they should have remained either in the Nebbiolo or in the Langhe definition.)

That the system may be self-defeating if a clear-cut limit is not imposed on the number of *new* DOCs. That, accordingly, Law 164/ 92 should be reviewed to take into consideration more what the public wants than what tradition dictates.

There is, of course, an element of truth in all these criticisms, although one cannot help observing that there is nothing to stop any winemaker in Italy from experimenting provided he does so outside the framework of the DOC system.

Many, in fact, have done so. To achieve different results, they took the view that it was time we forgot about the centuries-old local traditions of winemaking, some of them (like only pressing the grapes at particular times of the month) being based (according to them) on old wives' tales. Consequently, it was decided to import wine experts from those very places (Australia, New Zealand and California) where, in fact, winemaking on a successful scale occurred mainly because of the knowledge and influence of French and Italian immigrants. The humour in this situation will not escape the reader.

Did we Italians have much to learn from these imported

oenologists? Maybe; certainly we learnt to import 'foreign' grapes or grapes which were not widespread in Italy (take, for example, Cabernet Sauvignon in Toscana and elsewhere), and perhaps greater sophistication in blending and vinification processes. One should not forget, however, that vines moved from one country or area to the other do not always perform either so well or as expected. Indeed, the non-successful transplantability of the vine was highlighted by Pliny the Elder in his 'Natural History' (Book XIV), where he makes the point that 'there are some varieties of vine that have such love for the land on which they grow that they leave in it all their reputation and cannot be transplanted elsewhere'.

No doubt, some excellent wines are now made in Italy as a result of these 'foreign' influences and a few of them, the so-called 'super Tuscans' (e.g. Solaia, Ornellaia, Sassicaia and Tignanello) are now better known on some markets than the traditional Barolo, Barbaresco and Brunello. But there is a danger in this situation since the new vinification processes that we have imported from abroad are being used indiscriminately rather than selectively. The result is that there are now produced in Italy wines (whether DOCG, DOC or whatever) which are becoming indistinguishable from those of other countries and especially from New World wines. This is a dangerous trend, for it is conceivable that competing in terms of style with, say, an Australian Shiraz may not prove quite so advantageous for an Italian wine as its vintner may think.

What is worrying, however, is that although we may end up achieving extreme uniformity, we appear to be discounting the inherent values of the enormous variety of our indigenous vines which up till now have allowed us to produce 'different' (at least in terms of taste) wines which, whilst perhaps incapable of competing in terms of quantity, could actually prove superior in terms of quality to many New World and South American products. Surely we would be better off trying to be different so that our selling points would, in fact, be the varied features of our wines over a wide spectrum that, in the final analysis, wine drinkers throughout the world would appreciate and want to treasure.

We are undoubtedly doing this quite successfully with our food. It seems a pity that we are not always able to maintain the same consistency of approach when it comes to our wine production.

What these criticisms discount completely is the fact that the DOC has ensured the historical continuity and flavour of certain wines, inevitably associated with a particular locality; furthermore, it has provided a disciplined framework within which the winemakers had to operate if they wished to take advantage of the DOC labelling. It has enforced a rise in quality of the DOC wines, as well as of the IGT indirectly, and by prescribing the registration of bottling plants (the bottling register number *must* be shown on the label and on the cork, represented by a number and the identification letter of the province; for instance, for a Brunello di Montalcino, say 711 (province of Siena) it has guaranteed that the system of control and supervision allows for better classification of Italian wines generally. To give but one example, just in the province of Cuneo (in Piemonte, the principal wine-producing area of Italy), there are 250-odd registered bottling plants for Barolo wine alone!

But there is a further point which is ignored when one criticizes the DOC system. Here is a simple example.

One of my favourite wines is Barbera (q.v.). This is a red wine from Piemonte, made exclusively with the Barbera grape, a most prolific vine, seldom matured in oak (there have been of late many attempts to do so, some quite successful). The wine tastes good. It is a vibrant, darkish, thick red of high alcoholic content (13-13.5°) usually drunk young although it can be matured for up to ten years quite successfully, sometimes 'slightly effervescent' (or 'vivace', as the locals call it). It is a robust wine that suits people of a certain temperament. You cannot confuse it with a Burgundy or a Bordeaux. It has a friendly quality of its own, it warms the cockles of your heart, if the reader will forgive the expression. In a nutshell, it is Italian. Why should anyone want to blend the Barbera grape with anything else, thus achieving a non-Italian flavour which may be French or Spanish? As it stands, Barbera cannot be confused with any other wine. (There are some blends of Barbera and Nebbiolo available under the Langhe label which are excellent.)

And this is where the criticisms of the DOC system ultimately fail. You may want to drink an Italian wine of a particular kind, made in a particular manner. You may have been drinking it for the past fifty years or more. You may feel that there is no need for change in that particular taste.

Having said all this for the sake of the record, it must be acknowledged that there are too many (330) DOC qualifications and the Italian Association of Oenologists must be right when, on 10 July 2005, they made the point that there should be no additions to the DOC listing unless the wine has already qualified as an IGT for more than five years. More controversially, they suggested that there are some DOC wines which are hardly known to the public. Accordingly, steps should be taken to 'deprive' those particular wines of a classification which, whilst historically explicable, is no longer justifiable in commercial terms. One can see difficulties in this kind of argument, but it cannot be denied that the situation calls for review.

As far as the more progressive Italian wines are concerned, and one thinks in the main of the so-called 'super Tuscans', they have come about not only as a result of new attempts at vinification, which are wholly praiseworthy, but also because of very substantial investments in advertising, publicity and public relations which are not usually available to smaller producers, and I wonder whether, ultimately, they are good value for money, as far as the average wine drinker is concerned. Historically, the 'super Tuscans' can be traced to the late 1960s. Sassicaia was first produced commercially in 1968 from Cabernet Sauvignon vines (allegedly from the Chateau Lafite vineyards) imported from France and replanted in Bolgheri, an area until then not well known for its wines.

For the record, Sassicaia is the first (and so far the only) 'super Tuscan' wine that has received DOC recognition and is properly described as Bolgheri Sassicaia, Bolgheri being the locality in the province of Livorno where one of Italy's most famous wines is produced at the San Guido vineyard.

In 1971, the long established house of Antinori released onto the market the wine which they called Tignanello that had been produced the year before: it was an immediate success. All these super Tuscans are excellent but, regrettably, also very expensive wines, especially since they are produced in rather limited quantities. At the end of the day, one is entitled to ask whether any of them is to be preferred, in terms of value for money, to a Taurasi or a Salento, which can be purchased at a fraction of the price.

As usual, the reader is invited to form a view. If he or she can afford to buy these 'new' Italian wines, then appropriate comparisons can be made. But they are not cheap! At the time of writing, for example, there was a 1995 Sassicaia retailing in London at £102 per 0.750 lt. bottle and it is worth noting that it is most unlikely that one will find a bottle of this wine, of any vintage (save in Italy), retailing at less than £75. At a Christie's wine sale in Milan on 30 November 2001, a bottle of 1985 Sassicaia was sold for just under £1,250. In any event, most of them (e.g. the latest and possibly best so far Sassicaia of 1998) are very difficult to come by.

The European Union has issued specific regulations concerning labelling (No. 2392 in 1989 and 3201 in 1990) and the Italian State has actually carried the matter further. The whole subject-matter has now been codified in European Regulation 1493/99 which incorporates and/or amends previous regulations such as 3292/89, 3201/90 (see also Regulation 884/2001).

An example of the labelling of Italian wines is provided overleaf:

A TYPICAL LABEL

(Front)

Name of Producer

1996 (1)

AMARONE DELLA VALPOLICELLA

Denominazione di origine controllata (2)

CLASSICO (3)

Imbottigliato da ....
a .... (4)

---

75 CL (5)   14° (6)

---

(1)   this must represent at least the minimum ageing prescribed
(2)   this could be a DOCG or an IGT description
(3)   produced in a particular region
(4)   bottled by.........., at.........
(5)   could be 50 CL or 37.5 CL or even 1 Lt or 1.5 Lt depending on bottle
           size
(6)   must always be no less than prescribed
(7)   literally, do not dispose of glass within the environment. This warning
           must appear on ALL wine labels by law and is a reminder to the general
           public of an environmental obligation to be tidy and to recycle.

A TYPICAL LABEL

(Rear)

Name of Producer

1996 (1)

AMARONE DELLA VALPOLICELLA

Denominazione di origine controllata (2)

CLASSICO (3)

Non Disperdere il Vetro nell'ambiente(7)
Continen Solfiti (8)

Imbottigliato da ....

a ....

OR

Messo in bottiglia da ....

a .... (4)

A description will then usually follow, in Italian, or in English, or in both, indicating the grapes used (though not necessarily in which percentages), the suitability of the wine with different dishes and whatever else (history of wine, gold medals won, etc.) the producer feels the buyer should be aware of. A combination of useful information and advertising elements.

(1)	this must represent *at least* the minimum ageing prescribed
(2)	this could be a DOCG or an IGT description
(3)	produced in an original territory
(4)	bottled by.......... at....................
(5)	could be 50 CL or 37.5 CL or even 1 Lt or 1.5 Lt depending on bottle size
(6)	must always be no less than prescribed
(7)	literally do not dispose of glass within the environment. This is a wording which by law must appear on ALL wine labels and is a reminder to the general public of an environmental obligation to be tidy and to recycle.
(8)	contains sulphites.

The front label is compulsory. All bottles of wine produced in Italy must have one showing the information as listed.

The back label is optional: the producer may wish to add notes about his wine, which could prove helpful to the purchaser. This is more a marketing exercise than a requirement. Some producers show two labels, others only one. (If a second label is not provided, the front one must bear the notice about glass in the environment.) In truth, one could say rather cynically that the better the quality and the reputation of the wine, the less likely it is that a second label will appear on the bottle, although it should be noted that many bottles of average quality wine show no second label, the producer thus hoping that the buyer will consider it a more valuable product! The lesser known wine may require explanation, especially for the non-professional drinker, and the second label does provide a useful introduction to the wine, firstly because as a rule it gives the grape variety from which it is derived or, if more than one, the blend, though seldom the percentage; but more particularly because the producer will set out his own view of the foods with which his wine may be associated.

As a rule, these associations should be treated with respect; as knowledge of the particular wine progresses, however, the drinker will reach conclusions which sometimes are at variance with what is shown on the bottle.

In addition to the label/s, however, the neck of the DOCG bottle must have round it, or vertically along it, a little label, supplied by the State, of green (for white wines) or pink (for red wines) colour with green, brown and/or black printing which must contain the following indications:

a) the quantity, 0.750 litres, usually, or whatever the true contents might be

b) the serial number, say AAA 01363982

c) the description of the wines, e.g. Vermentino di Gallura. This may be just Vermentino di Gallura or Vermentino di Gallura Superiore.

d) the stamp of the state, which is the badge of the Italian Republic, with the letters DOCG and the wording *denominazione di origine controllata e garantita*.

e) optionally, in small print, which is hardly legible unless one has either perfect eyesight or a magnifying glass, a reference to the 'Ministero delle Politiche Agricole e Forestali', that is to say to the Italian equivalent of our own Department for the

Environment, Forestry and Rural Affairs (DEFRA).

The cork itself is also a distinguishing feature, since it will identify the bottling plant and it will also bear the 'national' badge with the wording: 'INE – Italia – marchio nazionale' – as well as the name (and trade mark, or badge, if applicable) of the producer and the vintage year. This provision, together with the controls imposed by DOC and DOCG legislation, is essential in enhancing and thus guaranteeing the traceability of the wine.

Below is a glossary of other terms that one might find on an Italian wine label:

Abboccato – slightly sweet

Amabile – medium/semi sweet

Annata – the year of the vintage

Appassimento – this is a process used extensively in the Veneto region. Grapes are stretched out on matting on soil well exposed to the sun, or hung in dry and ventilated environments which are called 'fruttai'. The drying of the grapes results in an increase in sugar content (making for greater alcohol) and a wine which is more aromatic and richer in flavours.

Asciutto – very dry

Azienda (Agraria/Agricola Vitivinicola) – estate

Barricato – fermented in oak, in barrique, to use the French word

Barrique – a French term to describe a small barrel

Bianco – white

Botte – cask or barrel

Bottiglia – bottle

Brut – dry, same as in French

Cantina – cellar or winery

Cantina Sociale – co-operative winery

Caratello/I – a small barrel, the precursor of the barrique.

Casa Vinicola – wine enterprise

Cascina – estate (literally farmhouse)

Chiaretto – rosé

Classico – describes a DOC wine that comes from an historically settled and well-defined wine area, as distinct from territory added more recently.

Consorzio – consortium of producers

Contiene Solfiti – contains sulphites

Cooperativa – co-operative, an alternative to 'Cantina Sociale'.

Corpo – body

Cru – the Italians have borrowed the French word to identify a particular plot of land or the wine from it.

Denominazione – the wine name equivalent to the French 'appellation'

DOC Denominazione di Origine Controllata – as described in the text

DOCG Denominazione di Origine Controllata e Garantita – as described in the text

Dolce – sweet

Enoteca – wine library

Etichetta – label

Fattoria – farm or estate

Fermentazione naturale – natural fermentation

Fresco – fresh

Frizzante – sparkling or semi-sparkling, fizzy

Frizzantino – lightly fizzy

Fruttato – fruity

Governo (or, more correctly, 'Governo all'uso Toscano') – this is a procedure adopted for most Chianti wines. What happens is that a wine that is ready for storing or bottling is made to circulate over partially dried grapes: this results in what one could term a secondary fermentation, which it is said gives more body, but above all, more flavour to the wine so treated. The practice is somewhat similar to 'Appassimento' and 'Ripasso'.

Gradazione Alcoolica – % of alcohol (by volume)

Grigio, as in Pinot – grey

IGT Indicazione Geografica Tipica – as described in the text.

Imbottigliato all'origine – estate bottled

Imbottigliato dal Viticoltore – as above

Imbottigliato/a/da – bottled at/by

Legno – wood

Liquoroso – a wine of high alcoholic content, usually sweet, generally above 14°, sometimes fortified. Strong bodied wine (either naturally or fortified with distilled alcohol). Usually sweet.

Masseria – farm or estate

Messo in bottiglia da. . . . . a. . . . . – estate bottled

Metodo Charmat – more correctly, Metodo Charmat/Martinotti,

but normally abbreviated as shown; a re-fermentation method (in stainless steel vats) to be distinguished from the 'metodo classico' (champenoise).

Metodo Classico – will appear on most bottles of Italian sparkling wine to indicate that it was made in a similar way to Champagne. Bottle fermentation method.

Metodo tradizionale – ditto

Millesimato – vintage

Nero – red

Non Disperdere il Vetro nel'Ambiente – literally, do not dispose of glass within the environment. This is a wording which by law must appear on ALL wine labels and is a reminder to the general public of an environmental obligation to be tidy and to recycle.

Novello – the equivalent to the French 'nouveau', namely a newly fermented wine sold within a very short period from its production.

Passito – a wine resulting from the appassimento process (q.v. in text)

Pastoso – semi dry

Podere – small farm or estate

Produttore – producer

Profumato – scented

Ripasso – a process used mainly in the Veneto region for Valpolicella and Amarone wines, whereby a fully fermented wine goes over the lees

Riserva – this has no overall legal meaning. It can be merely some sort of puff. Theoretically, it ought to identify a better quality wine and there is no doubt that wines which bear the 'Riserva' label are more expensive than those that do not. Quality apart, it usually shows that the wine has been aged for a longer period than the ordinary version of that particular variety. It is worth noting, however, that certain statutory or customary local specifications for wine may actually prescribe a special meaning for the word 'Riserva'. That is to say, they may actually dictate that you could only apply the word 'Riserva' to a particular type of wine complying with special characteristics.

Rosato – rosé

Rosso – red

Secco – dry

Semi-secco – medium sweet

Spumante – sparkling

Stravecchio – literally very old, applied almost exclusively to the longest aged sweet wines like Marsala and, less frequently, to spirits

Superiore – a wine with more alcohol than the minimum prescribed by the regulations, matured for longer

Tenuta – farm or estate

Tranquillo – not that common, meaning in essence not sparkling

Uva – grapes

Uvaggio – the grape mix (blend) in any particular wine

Vecchio – old, applied occasionally to certain long aged DOC wines

Vendemmia – vintage harvest

Vendemmia tardiva – used for some wines, e.g. Nebbiolo – late harvest

Vigna * – vineyard (similar to the french 'cru')

Vignaiolo – grape grower

Vigneto – ditto

Vino da Tavola – table wine, used to describe very loosely all wines which do not have a IGT, DOC or DOCG classification

Vino Novello – new wine which, by regulation, must be bottled within the same year in which the grapes are harvested. Usually, though not necessarily, applied to red wines

Vite – vine

Viticoltore – grape grower or winemaker or both

Vitigno – vine or grape variety

Vitivinicola (usually preceded by the noun 'azienda') – a wine producing commercial enterprise

Vivace – literally lively, applied more usually to bubbly wines, especially in northern Italy

* strictly controlled and defined by law, with clear-cut boundaries and the imposition of separate vinification for the grapes derived from it.

As observed above, the cork itself will bear, as is the practice in Spain, though not always in France, the number of the bottling plant (in Italy, 'R.I.' + no.; in Spain 'R.E.' + no.). Indeed, the Spaniards are much more specific because after the indication 'R.E.', followed by a number, they also show the initials or the identification of the region e.g. 'R.E.233.-MU', that is say bottling plant no. 233 in Murcia.

The Italians are not so strict. The cork does not necessarily bear the imprint of the bottling plant for lesser quality wines.

In passing, let me say that there is circulating an IGT wine from Sicily (a blend of Sangiovese and Merlot); interesting to observe that neither of these grape varieties is indigenous to Sicily; Sangiovese comes from Tuscany, and Merlot from north-east Italy where the 'plastic' cork bears no identification whatsoever and the bottling plant is only identified on the label. Not too critical, the reader might think; but one would like to see some consistency in this context, since the indication of the bottling plant can be significant.

ITALY'S WINES CLASSIFIED BY REGION			
	DOCG	DOC	IGT
Piemonte	9	47	-
Toscana	6	34	5
Veneto	3	24	9
Lombardia	3	14	12
Campania	3	17	9
Umbria	2	11	0
Sardinia	1*	19	15
Emilia Romagna	1	20	0
Friuli-Venezia-Giulia	2	9	3
Valle d'Aosta	1	0	0
Marche	1	13	0
Abruzzi	1	3	9
Lazio	0	26	5
Puglia	0	25	6
Sicilia	0	20	7
Calabria	0	13	13
Liguria	0	8	0
Trentino Alto Adige	0	7	2
Molise	0	3	2
Basilicata	0	2	0

* it is in fact the Vermentino di Gallura, the first Italian *white* to be granted DOCG status
(As at December 2006)

CHAPTER 6

EXPLORING ITALY'S WINE REGIONS

(NOTE: The regions are referred to starting in the north-west and moving clockwise southwards)

Piemonte is Italy's principal region for quality wines. Not surprisingly, it is not at the head of the table for quantity; this is taken by Sicilia, Puglia, Veneto and Emilia Romagna. Numerically, however, its quality wines stand supreme. In total, it has 9 DOCG wines and 47 DOC wines. No other region of Italy can boast of such numbers, although Toscana comes a close second with 6 DOCG, 33 DOC and 5 IGT wines. At the other end of the scale, the area with the lowest number of DOCG and DOC wines is the Valle d'Aosta, which has only 1 DOC. A full list can be found in Appendix 2.

The production of red wine in Italy stands at 48.3% of the total, the remainder being white and rosé.

The principal thirteen wine-producing regions of Italy (without distinguishing between red and white or rosé) are set out in order below. (The quantities produced in the remaining seven regions are not significant.)

Region	million hectolitres [As at 31-12-01]	million hectolitres [As at 31-12-06]
● Sicilia	8.0	6.550
● Puglia	7.2	7.520
● Veneto	6.8	7.090
● Emilia Romagna	4.7	6.620
● Piemonte	3.4	3.360
● Abruzzi	3.3	3.120
● Lazio	2.9	2.490

• Toscana	2.2	2.920
• Campania	2.0	2.010
• Marche	1.8	1.090
• Sardegna	1.1	0.830
• Friuli-Venezia-Giulia	1.0	1.040
• Trentino-Alto-Adige	1.0	1.1610

The first two are the regions of Italy which are also the most important exporters of strong, high alcoholic (13-16%) basic red wines for blending.

They also happen to be the principal regions of Italy (there are others, of course, such as Campania and Sardegna) where northern Italian and foreign viticulturists have made a number of investments based on the meteorological advantages and general wine-producing potential.

These have manifested themselves in the acquisition of existing wine-producing enterprises, as well as plantings of 'northern' vines basically new to the area but with great potential. It is not unusual to find Chardonnay, Merlot, Sauvignon and Syrah growing side by side with local vines. At present, none of these 'new' wines qualify for DOC or DOCG classification; many of them, however, can take advantage of the IGT denomination but where that is not possible, they are bottled under 'fancy' names and sold as 'vini da tavola' (VdT). Some of the investments thus made are fairly substantial and are not confined to large wine producers from Piemonte or Veneto; more than one well-known Tuscan firm has invested in Sicilia and Puglia.

REGIONS OF ITALY

Valle d'Aosta (An autonomous region of Italy since 1947)

In viticultural terms, Valle d'Aosta could be said to be unique. It is located at the north-westernmost corner of Italy, close to the Dolomites peaks. Historically, this is not a rich part of Italy, where the farmers who grow the vine display what can only be termed heroic qualities because of the low temperatures.

And yet, the production of wine here was already well known in Roman times because Varro, in his seminal work *De re rustica*, speaks favourably about the wines of this area.

There is only a small area of 650 hectares under vines, and the annual production is 31,000 hectolitres which, by Italian standards, is insignificant.

This is due to the fact that only one part of the region grows vines, namely the valley of the local tributary of the Po River, the Dora Baltea. Here, soil levels rise from a hilly 1,200 ft to a maximum of 3,600 ft. And yet, at this altitude, wine is still produced. Not a red with strong body, obviously, but the local white whose alcoholic content starts at 9°. The fact that it is so low is indicative that here grow some of the highest and coldest vines in the world. Indeed, at Morgex, within sight of Mont Blanc, the vintage takes place round about mid-December, when there is snow on the ground and temperatures fall below freezing. A local oddity is the wine made from grapes thus gathered known as 'chaudelune': a sweet wine, of which only a few thousand bottles are made. (A similar sort of 'ice wine' is also made in one or two villages of the 'Langhe' in Piemonte.)

Inevitably, the choice of produce is limited: not too many exciting reds, almost rosés, and the remainder Chardonnay, Muller Thurgau and the Pinots, all white, plus an outstanding sweet wine, the Chambave.

Piemonte (Piedmont)

Piemonte means at the foot of the mountain, which is a very apt description of the whole area since it is surrounded by mountains on the north, the west and its southern sides (respectively the Alps, the Alpes-Maritimes and the Ligurian Apennine) which protect the area in more ways than one. Viticulture is carried out mainly on undulating hills, a beautiful sight, both in autumn and in spring. A number of vines are typical of the area: Barbera, Bonarda, Dolcetto and Nebbiolo for the reds and Arneis and Moscato for the whites. There are others, of course, and most notable of all has been the recent increase in plantings of the fashionable Chardonnay .

Quality is the hallmark of Piedmontese wines: 9 DOCGs and 47 DOCs (no IGTs), with an area under vines of 58,000 hectares and a production which, on average, exceeds three million hectolitres. It is interesting to note that at least 80% of wine production in this part of Italy is of such high quality as to merit DOCG and DOC status, the split between white and red grapes being respectively 30% and 70%.

Recently, there has been a trend to imitate what was done in Toscana when the so-called 'super Tuscans' were created. Whether any super wines will emerge from the new experiments that are being carried out in Piemonte with non-local vines (e.g. Merlot and Syrah, in particular), it is too soon to tell. Meanwhile, we can enjoy the fact that this is the region of the three 'Bs' (Barbaresco, Barbera and Barolo) as well as of the wine with the delightful name, the Grignolino, a charming light red to be drunk young.

Statistically, Piemonte leads Italy in the production of sparkling wines and only north-east Italian regions (Trentino Alto Adige, Friuli Venezia Giulia) can compete; in terms of quantity Emilia Romagna with its Lambrusco comes a poor third.

In 1997, a new DOC came into existence called 'Piemonte' which is an umbrella denomination to cover sparkling wines, Barbera, Bonarda, Brachetto, Cortese, Chardonnay, both varieties of Moscato and all the Pinots. What this means is that the above-mentioned wines can be produced in any part of the Piemonte region provided the vineyard is recorded in the DOC classification register.

In 2005, Piemonte produced 6% of the overall national production of wines in Italy, 20% of such production representing its export rate.

Lombardia (Lombardy)

There have been wines in Lombardy since the time of the Romans. The poet Virgil, who came from Mantua, refers to the hills around Lake Garda where the vine grew, together with the olive and the corn. Nowadays, it can boast of growing, in addition to local vines such as Bonarda and Croatina, the ubiquitous Nebbiolo, and the Pinot Noir. It has 3 DOCG wines: 2 reds, the Sfursat and the Valtellina Superiore and probably the best Italian sparkling wine, the Franciacorta made with Chardonnay, white Pinot, as well as with black Pinot. There are two excellent types of this sparkling wine, namely the Satén, white, and the Rosé.

In addition to that, it can boast of 13 DOC and 12 IGT wines, grown over about 27,000 hectares and producing about 1.1 million hectolitres of wine.

In 2005, Lombardia produced 2% of the overall national production of wines in Italy, 5% of such production representing its export rate.

The cultivation of vines in the Valtellina region is noteworthy.

They grow on terraces excavated in rather rocky ground on soil which requires a great deal of attention, rising sometimes to 800 metres above sea level.

Trentino Alto Adige

This region is high up in the Dolomites and it was known to the Romans as Rhetia. The locals can be grateful to the Etruscans who, between 1500 and 1000 BC, introduced vines to the area, which the Romans later developed successfully. In fact, the Romans held Rhetian wines in high esteem. Augustus is said to have enjoyed them and Pliny reminds us that 'Rhaeticus' came from an area north of Verona where it was kept in wooden barrels bound with wicker hoops. Near one of its principal towns, Bolzano (Bauzanum to the Romans, or Bozen in Austrian) remains have been found of large barrels, dating from pre-Roman times, where signs of hoops were evident.

Its principal grape variety is the Schiava (which had, and still has to some extent, a significant role by giving a particular character to wines) but a number of varieties of French origin such as Pinot and Cabernet as well as other foreign vines, such as Riesling, were grafted on to the Schiava, and are now predominant in some parts.

Trentino produces good, reliable whites (Pinot Grigio, Prosecco di Valdobbiadene). The overall production is substantial and quite enjoyable. Not outstanding, at least in the sense that there are no DOCGs, but there are 7 DOCs and 2 IGTs. It is interesting to observe that in this region DOC wines account for just under 70% of total production (Veneto and Piemonte claim this record as well!) which is far from negligible: and indeed, is one of the highest percentages of DOCs throughout Italy.

Total production amounts to 1.16 million hectolitres over 12,800 hectares of vines. The reader should note that this area, whilst technically part of Italy, is almost half Austrian. Trento may be called thus in Italian and Trent in German; Bolzano is also Bozen and Alto Adige is Südtirol (south Tyrol).

Traffic apart, it is a particularly pleasant experience to drive from Verona to Trento surrounded wherever one looks by vineyards. In the whole of this area, the vines grow as trellises and the hillside vineyards are indeed a beautiful sight, a very typical part of a unique Alpine landscape. One can, for example, suddenly come across a rustic whitewashed and red-capped cottage hidden behind trellis arbours. The trellises have the double advantage of protecting the grapes from extremes of heat but also from frost.

Many of the grape varieties are German/Austrian (Müller Thurgau, Gewürztraminer and Sylvaner, which are often found growing above 500 metres of altitude) and what is important to know is that the wines from this area, although they have to comply with the same requirements as other wines in Italy as to labelling, etc., may in fact still so comply although they are labelled in German. The wines themselves may use both names (e.g. Lago di Caldaro becomes Kalterersee and so on.)

Here the two provinces of Trento and Bolzano have joined forces to establish a very efficient winemaking industry in the valleys that climb the slopes of the Alps. Although both provinces concentrate on popular whites (Pinot Grigio and Chardonnay, and others of course), the reds of the area are by no means to be despised. The DOC wines are known as Trentino followed by the name of the type of wine so, for example Trentino Chardonnay, Trentino Merlot. For ease of reference, however, in the list of wines that follows the DOC Trentino has been placed after the type of wine so one gets Chardonnay Trentino DOC. Similarly, for the Alto Adige or dell'Alto Adige (Sudtirolo-Südtirol) wine.

Wine quality in this area is high. An interesting region, it is also well known for the fact that it yields 50% of the whole Italian apple production. Trentino Alto Adige produced in 2005 2% of the overall national production of wines in Italy, 12% of such production representing its export rate.

Veneto

This region of north-east Italy (somewhat surprisingly, perhaps, the flattest in Italy despite its mountains) produces great quantities of wine (7.090 million hectolitres each year) over a cultivated area of 75,000 hectares. It is covered by some 200,000 wine-producing firms, more especially in the province of Verona, which alone accounts for some 54,000 hectares and about 2 million hectolitres of production.

As far as quantity is concerned, it is comparable to Puglia and Sicilia, but the quality of Venetian wines is very high; its percentage of DOC wines competing with the adjacent Trentino-Alto-Adige and with Piemonte (and Toscana, of course) as being the highest in Italy. It can boast of 3 DOCGs, 25 DOCs and 11 IGTs. Most people know its Valpolicella, but there is a lot more. There is that extremely pleasant wine produced on the banks of Lake Garda, Bardolino, brilliantly ruby in colour and beautifully scented but the kind of wine that can only be drunk when no more than three or four years old. The amber-coloured Soave (many cheap exports, but some of the best Soave is drunk in Italy) is said by some, though not by me, to be the complete white wine.

An event worth recording is that in 1953 the 1950 vintage Valpolicella was bottled by Bolla under the name of Amarone, a wine destined to become famous as arguably amongst Italy's best.

Over recent years, in addition to local grapes (Merlot, Corvina, Rondinella, Cabernet and Garganega – there are others, of course) Chardonnay has begun to be planted in Veneto, following the current fashion. Veneto has been an important region for over 2,000 years where the Romans developed winemaking techniques which are still current today. For example, they made a wine called Acinaticum by drying grapes on racks or mats for, say, three months, to derive from them extra sugar and flavour (a process nowadays known as *appassimento*, used for Amarone). Interestingly, perhaps, it is also the region of Italy where more white wine is produced than red. For example, in 2005 Veneto produced 4 million hectolitres of whites with slightly less than 3 million hectolitres of reds. In 2005, Veneto produced 14% of the overall national production of wines in Italy, 28% of such production representing its export rate.

Friuli Venezia Giulia

This area is adjacent to Trentino Alto Adige and is amongst the smallest of the Italian regions. The vines in the rough northern ground in its upper region require a great deal of attention and hard work. It can boast of 2 DOCG's; one, a most uncommon and practically unknown wine, at least abroad, called Ramandolo produced in rather small quantities; the second obtained recently (November 2005) for the old-established, but still rather scarce, sweet wine called Picolit, now to be known as Colli Orientali Del Friuli Picolit, 8 DOC's, 3 IGTs and many other excellent wines, from Tocai to Cabernet and Riesling. The local Chardonnay is also outstanding, although probably the most interesting wine of the area is the sparkling Moscato Rosa, a rosé sparkling wine. A well known part of this region is the Collio.

The Collio is to be found in the extreme north-east of Italy, close to the Slovenian border. It is a very small wine-producing area of only about 1,600 hectares; in a sense located strategically, because it is only twenty miles from the sea and about the same distance from the mountains and on south-facing slopes. This situation provides shelter from Alpine winds and is sufficiently close to the sea for temperatures to be not too low. The production in the Collio area is small, about 0.75% of Italy's total.

It is usually said that this region is only famous for its white wines. That is not strictly speaking true because some of its Cabernet wines can be very good. Be that as it may. It produces 1.04 million hectolitres over an area of 19,000 hectares, but what is worth noting is that of these, at least 600,000 hectolitres cover DOC wines. In 2005, Friuli Venezia Giulia produced 2% of the overall national production of wines in Italy, 2% of such production representing its national export rate.

Liguria

This is a small wine-producing area (only 5,000 hectares delivering around 250,000 hectolitres each year), the region being of elliptical shape running from the French border all the way down the curve of the Gulf of La Spezia. The comparatively small production is amongst the lowest in Italy, firstly because the size of the individual ownerships of vineyards is small and secondly because, perhaps surprisingly, it is the most heavily wooded region in Italy.

There are some pleasant wines there, but none outstanding. No DOCGs, 8 DOCs and 3 IGTs. The whites predominate and the only DOC red (Rossese di Dolceacqua) though famous, is in my view not that exciting. But I may be wrong. The best are the whites that you associate with fish, coming from both the eastern and the western side of the Riviera, namely Pigato, Vermentino and Cinque Terre (dry and sweet) (Sciacchetrá) (in the province of La Spezia).

Historically, it should be noted that wines from this part of Italy were much better known in the past than they are now. The area production is around 5,000 hectares and the quantity around 250,000 hectolitres. In the past decade or so attempts have been to improve, if not rehabilitate, some of the wines in this area, e.g. the Ormeasco. In 2005, Liguria produced 0.02% of the overall national production of wines in Italy, 1% of such production representing its export rate.

Emilia Romagna

This is a major wine-producing area. It can boast 1 DOCG (Albana), 21 DOCs and 13 IGTs.

Foreigners probably know it best because of its Lambrusco wine. Regrettably, the Lambrusco you drink abroad is, in most cases, of fairly inferior quality. If you want a good Lambrusco you will have to go and drink it locally, since there is very little worthwhile Lambrusco in other countries, although much is imported; but there is an abundance of good Lambrusco available in Italy. From Modena and Reggio Emilia, the Lambrusco of Sorbara, the Lambrusco Salamino, the Grasparossa di Castelvetro, the sophisticated Salamino di Santa Croce, the red or rosé Lambrusco and the naturally sparkling Novello (nouveau). There are approximately 63,000 hectares planted with vines, producing more than 6.62 million hectolitres per annum.

Emilia Romagna is also the region of Italy which claims to produce its best food. Even leaving aside Parma Ham and Parmigiano of all types, it is an acknowledged fact that the locals are famous for and much appreciative of their cuisine. It may therefore not be entirely a coincidence that this is also the region of Italy where the greatest amount of wine is consumed and where no less than 65% of the population are wine drinkers.

The region is historically interesting because, as both Varro in his *De re Rustica* and Cato in his *De Agricoltura* record, the Romans found there the non-cultivated vine or *vitis vinifera silvestris* – from which present-day vines are derived through cultivation; they called it 'Labrusca' from which the current name Lambrusco is derived.

In 2005, Emilia Romagna produced 12% of the overall national production of wines in Italy, 5% of such production representing its export rate.

Toscana (Tuscany)

This is inevitably the most popular region of Italy, because Chianti grows there. It has been defined as the heart of Italian wine, first because of its history (its wines go back at least five centuries) and substantial production, and second because the vine is to be found throughout the region. More than 60% of the total area is hilly. It produces 6 DOCGs, 37 DOCs and 6 IGTs, an impressive performance, second only to that of Piemonte.

The most important wine-producing areas are concentrated

between Siena and Florence and wines that come from there are known throughout the world, Chianti of course in its several varieties, Brunello di Montalcino and the Nobile of Montepulciano, amongst the reds and the Vernaccia di San Gimignano, amongst the whites. (The first Italian white to earn the DOC label.)

Backbone to the characteristic flavour of Tuscan wines is the Sangiovese grape, the only Italian grape which, it is claimed by some, can compete with Cabernet Sauvignon. But there are wines of all kinds, including two excellent sweet ones, the Vin Santo and the Aleatico di Portoferraio. Of its annual production no less than 45% is dedicated to DOCG and DOC wines.

Tuscan vines cover an area of 63,500 hectares, with a yearly production of 2.920 million hectolitres. More recently, as has already been mentioned, Tuscany has produced the so-called 'super Tuscans', wines newly made by blending different grapes and following oenological criteria which, to some extent, are novel for Italy. The backing they have received by firms with considerable financial muscle has allowed them to come to the fore. I have already commented on them and shall say no more under this heading. In 2005, Toscana produced 5% of the overall national production of wines in Italy, 16% of such production representing its export rate.

Marche

Wine production here commenced in the Iron Age. Remnants of *vitis vinifera* have been found in the area, which is hilly but capable of producing some very nice wine. It produces 2 DOCGs, 15 DOCs and 1 IGT. The most popular white is the Verdicchio and the most successful red the Montepulciano. The production is hardly negligible: 1.090 million hectolitres from 24,500 hectares.

In 2005, Marche produced 2% of the overall national production of wines in Italy, 1% of such production representing its export rate.

Umbria

This is the green enclave of Italy, the region being landlocked, entirely surrounded by Toscana, Marche and Lazio. It has 2 DOCGs, 11 DOCs and 6 IGTs, which is a small percentage (about 25%) of the total production from 16,500 hectares, which yield about 1 million hectolitres per annum.

Probably better known to the English public because of its white Orvieto (there is also a red variety which is hardly exported) but producing a DOCG red which can compare with the best in Italy, namely Montefalco Sagrantino, or, more correctly, Sagrantino di Montefalco. In 2005, Umbria produced 2% of the overall national production of wines in Italy, 1% of such production representing its export rate.

The last decade or so has seen an increase in plantings of non-indigenous grapes such as Merlot and Syrah.

Molise
This region is mentioned for the sake of completeness since few of its wines are exported and it was the last of the Italian regions to obtain for its wines the DOC label, it being provided for its Biferno as recently as 1983.

And yet, it is said that there are some 35,000, mainly family-type, enterprises which represent some 65% of the total agricultural output of the region. It only has 3 DOC wines – representing a mere 5% of total production – and 3 IGTs; and although there are new plantings of Montepulciano, Sangiovese, Aglianico, Trebbiano and others, it has yet to make an impact on the Italian wine scene. The area under vines is small: 9,000 hectares yielding about 500,000 hectolitres.

Lazio (Latium)
This is the area, with Rome as its capital, where Frascati originates. But there are many other wines of quality, mainly whites (as well as at least one excellent red, the Cesanese del Piglio.) There are 26 DOCs and 5 IGTs.

The region, one of the largest in Italy, is quite active in wine development and is known for having recently introduced 'foreign' vines such as Cabernet Franc, Cabernet Sauvignon, Merlot and Syrah. In Roman times its wines were appreciated perhaps much more than today. In one of his 'Odes' (Ode XI) the Latin poet Horace wonders whether he might drink with his mistress a barrel full of Albano wine matured for nine years. . . . .

Lazio wines are produced in the hills around Rome (the 'Castles') – Castelli Romani – where in addition to Frascati one finds Albano, Castel Gandolfo, Genzano, Marino, Nemi, Rocca di Papa, as well as the red wines from Marino and Velletri.

The production is substantial; 2.490 million hectolitres, of which about 20% goes to yield 24 DOC wines. The area under vines is 48,000 hectares. In 2005, Lazio produced 5% of the overall national production of wines, with exports accounting for 1% of total production.

Campania

In ancient times, this was the preferred area for the supply of wines to the capital, Rome. They imported from there the classic Roman wines, *Falernum* and *Caecubam*. The former is still available in Italy in some quantity, but the latter is disappearing. Nevertheless, with a production of 2.01 million hectolitres of wine over 41,000 hectares, Campania is a very prolific region and can boast 3 DOCGs, 18 DOCs and 9 IGTs.

One of the DOCGs is extremely worthwhile. It is amongst Italy's best reds, Taurasi, of great body and high alcoholic content. But Campania also has another less well-known fine red, Solopaca, as well as the Falerno del Massico. Its whites, however, are amongst the best that Italy produces, namely Greco di Tufo and Fiano di Avellino, which in my opinion can stand comparison with any white wine available in the world today.

In 2005, Campania produced 4% of Italy's overall national wine production with exports accounting for 1%. Not especially high, some might think, but we must at least give it credit for being the only region of Italy which, at least so far, has not been persuaded to plant non-indigenous vines. It is correct to say that at least 95% of the vines grown in Campania are from the locality.

Abruzzo

This is a mountainous region on the eastern coast of Italy facing the former 'Yugoslavia'. Some of its peaks can be quite high, reaching 9,000ft. It has 2 DOCGs (one obtained in May 2003, the other in October 2004), 3 DOCs and 10 IGTs. A lot of wine is not even bottled, but supplied to outlets for distribution in restaurants and bars, etc. Overall, there are 33,000 hectares under vines, giving each year 3.12 million hectolitres. In 2005, Abruzzo produced 7% of the national production of wines, of which 2% went for export.

Basilicata (formerly Lucania)

This is a land of Greek traditions – poor and mountainous – with a small production (approximately 600,000 hectolitres) over 11,000 hectares. In its northern reaches, known as the Vulture, it produces one of the best reds of Italy which is one of the two DOCs for the area (the other being the *colline teramane*) namely the Aglianico del

Vulture. This is a wine that ought to be matured for at least five years, of intense colour, veering to orange when aged. Only one wine, but how different. It is a pity that it represents a mere 3.5% of total production. The region can also claim 12 IGTs. It is said that there are some 40,000 enterprises in this region dedicated to wine production. In 2005, Basilicata produced 1% of the overall national production of wines in Italy, with none going for export.

Puglia (Apulia)

As my table shows, this is a very substantial wine-producing area. More than 7.52 million hectolitres and almost 107,000 hectares of land are dedicated to the vine, making Puglia the cellar of Italy. In times past it used to be called 'the cellar of Europe'. By the way, it is also the region of Italy producing the greatest quantity of olive oil – expanses of olive trees stretching over miles in the countryside making a most unusual and pleasant aspect.

It has no DOCGs, but 25 DOCs (as well as 6 IGTs) accounting for only 4% of the total production of the area; the remainder is bulk wine for local or foreign consumption: known as 'miere' it travels north in trainloads. But there are some gems, like the sweet Moscato di Trani, the powerful Primitivo di Manduria and the well-known Salice Salentino, an outstanding full bodied red.

Local table wines are equally worthwhile, especially some DOC whites (Locorotondo, Castel del Monte). One is bound to wonder how the northern, but especially the foreign, winemakers would cope without the 15°/17° dark, strong wine supplied by Puglia.

The region's rosé wines are outstanding and, in my view, probably the best in Italy. It is here that the first Italian rosé ever to be bottled was produced in 1943. It should also be noted that over the past decade attempts have been made to diversify by occasionally planting 'northern' grape varieties but more particularly to build on the existing types of vine, especially the 'Uva di Troia'.

In 2005, Puglia produced 17% of the overall national production of wines in Italy, with 2% going for export.

Calabria

Like Apulia, Calabria – the toe of Italy – is surrounded by sea. In fact, it is the Italian region with the longest coastline. Not a great production (approximately 830,000 hectolitres over 24,000 hectares). Only 5% of it goes to support the 13 DOCs and the 13 IGTs.

Again, it is a region of the Greeks, who introduced to it the art of cultivating the vine. A number of local varieties are, in fact, of Greek origin. The Greeks were so impressed with this area, that they called it 'Oenotria', namely 'the land of wine'. Its best known wine is the Ciró, but there are many others such as the elegant, if not majestic, Verbicaro (DOC) about to disappear since so little is produced that it does not even get onto the national market, Savuto (DOC) known since the sixteenth century, the Greco di Bianco (DOC), which the locals say is even better than the whites from Campania and the Donnici (DOC). In 2005, Calabria produced 1% of the overall national production of wines, none of which went for export.

Recent studies have established that the wines of Calabria, especially because of their high alcoholic content, were well suited to travel. Evidence has emerged that, from the port of Tropea, they were not only sent to other ports along the Italian coastline but got as far as Barcelona and Valencia in Spain, Bruges in Belgium and, it is said, they even reached London.

Sardegna (Sardinia)

The region was invaded successively by the Phoenicians, the Carthagenians, the Romans and the Spaniards; each of these peoples left their mark in the local wines which deserve to be more widely appreciated than they are. The island produces about 1 million hectolitres each year, but it can boast that 20% of total production is in respect of DOC and DOCG wines. It can also claim the first white DOCG wine, namely the Vermentino di Gallura, an outstanding product from the north-east of the region. Apart from that single DOCG, there are 19 DOCs and 15 IGTs.

Alone amongst Italian wine-producing regions, it offers Vernaccia di Oristano (q.v.), which one could term the Italian 'sherry'. It has a minimum alcoholic content of 15° and is matured, in its better versions, for a minimum of three years, or in, so to say, the top of the range, the Riserva, for a minimum of four years.

There is also what is known as a Vernaccia Liqueur in two versions: sweet with an alcoholic content at 16.5° and dry with an alcoholic content of 18°. The liqueur version of the Vernaccia could only be drunk as an after-dinner potion, but the remainder of the Vernaccia (not the sweet one, of course) is eminently suitable because of its dryness as an aperitif and, some maintain, can be drunk throughout the meal. After the dark years of the Middle

Ages, the first mention of local wine production in Sardinia is to be found in a work of 1395 entitled *Carta de Logu*. This is the work of the first recorded woman judge in Europe, Eleonora of Arborea, who published the code for the region of Sardegna originally drafted by her father Mariano, who was also a judge.

In 2005, Sardegna produced 2% of the overall national production of wines, little of which went for export.

Sicilia (Sicily)

Here, too, the Greeks introduced the vine. Archaeological finds show that wine was being made in Sicilia at least two thousand years before the birth of Christ. Sicilia is a great producer of wine: over about 6.55 million hectolitres derived from over 140,000 hectares, the highest in Italy, most of which is distilled. But there are excellent whites and a red which is becoming quite popular, namely the Nero d'Avola. (An Eloro DOC.)

It can boast 1 DOCG, 21 DOCs and 7 IGTs and both reds and whites are produced successfully. And, as most people know, Marsala comes from there.

In 2005, Sicilia produced 15% of the total national production of wine, 3% of which went for export.

CHAPTER 7

THE ART OF EATING AND DRINKING

Many people find the art of matching wines and food somewhat arcane, which is a pity. The trouble is that one looks for absolutes, for specific pairings like 'roast beef with Barolo' or 'grilled plaice with Vermentino'. A point to be borne in mind is that many British people come to discover wines, as it were, after having sampled the local offerings whilst on holiday abroad. This can have rather unusual effects. To give a poor example, perhaps, Retsina drunk in Greece or in the Greek Islands can be quite pleasant to some; but those very same people who enjoyed it with many foods by the seaside would probably find that it does not mix well with English dishes and is certainly unsuitable in the middle of a British winter. This alone causes difficulties when trying to combine wine sampled abroad with food cooked at home. Life is not simple, and for reasons which we shall come to, in matters of food it is getting more complex all the time. Looking at it positively, however, here are some of the problems and, hopefully, a few solutions.

We must all delight in the fact that Britain has developed into one of the best, though most expensive, places to eat away from home, at least in Europe in the medium-to-high price ranges. Apart from France, Italy and Spain at the lower end of the price scale, in Britain we can claim as much variety and invention as anywhere else, thanks mainly to the adoption of foreign dishes: and this poses the first problem. There is no doubt that courses are becoming more complex since chefs draw on wider and wider inspirations, such as the ethnic or Pacific Rim cuisines; (we even have nowadays the neologism 'Mediterrasian' cuisine!, which is to be added to what has been termed 'Britalian' cooking!); furthermore, an ever greater range of herbs and spices has become a universally acceptable feature of modern gastronomy. As a result, the flavours that one seeks to find a match for, the dishes that one needs to balance with the drink, proliferate; complex flavours, whilst they may make for a better, more interesting dish, do not do the person choosing the wine any favours at all.

Another problem is that it is not always easy to decide whether wine should be chosen to complement the food or to create a contrast to it. As an example of complementing wine with food, one would offer the same wine as is used in the sauce: accordingly, 'pollo alla cacciatora' from Emilia Romagna should be matched by the same Sangiovese di Romagna that was probably used in preparing the sauce. That is not too bad. But when it comes to contrasting wine with food, how about trying to combine two extremes such as Vin Santo and Gorgonzola?

One should not discount too easily the suggestion made by some writers on food and wine that one should always choose a wine (red or white seems immaterial) from the same region where the particular dish originates. The suggestion is made that there is a symbiosis between types of food and wine since they both originate from plants grown on the same type of soil. There is much truth in such an observation; in reality, however, the planning required to achieve such a result is perhaps more than the average host or restaurateur would either care to put up with or find the time for.

Nor should one forget that when combining wine with food, colour is a determining factor. For example, red, bloody meat mixes well with a red wine, lighter meats go down satisfactorily with a rosé, whereas with fish or white meat there is a tendency to prefer white wine.

Quite clearly, complementing flavours is much the easier exercise and one can say as a generalization that, in its most simplistic form, it means choosing a wine of the country or area from which the dish originates. This is, of course, a generalization which may not always work: nevertheless, it is a good rule of thumb and a lot of people maintain that simple Italian reds usually work surprisingly well with a pizza (there are others who maintain that you should only drink water over carbohydrates; but that is a different part of the argument). Furthermore, the greater the quality and age of wine, the more difficult it is to combine it with food. It is claimed that the more famous chefs prefer a less important wine so that the flavour combinations are easier.

There is then the more important question: 'what about the sauce?' Nowadays the use of sauces has become more and more common and whilst it is very easy to match meat or fish cooked simply (for example, poached salmon with Riesling, seared tuna with a young Merlot, duck with Pinot Noir, chicken with Chardonnay or Pinot Bianco, and so on), the moment one adds a sauce the scene changes.

Poached salmon with hollandaise sauce would destroy most Rieslings and certainly needs a more substantial wine (perhaps a Chardonnay from Trentino Alto Adige, or a Vernaccia di San Gimignano); seared tuna with a zippy Thai sauce requires a wine with more residual sweetness, such as a medium Muscat (there are many varieties to choose from amongst Italian Moscato wines); the citrus in duck á l'orange necessitates a move to a pungent white, such as a Pinot Grigio or a (Traminer) Gewürztraminer: both are to be found in abundance in north-east Italy.

On the other hand, chicken with a balsamic vinegar sauce signals a move away from white wine towards light reds; eminently suitable would be those from Val d'Aosta, a light Valpolicella or a Grignolino. A fact never to be forgotten when combining wine with food is that where sauces are used, sauce is king: therefore, the key to a successful outcome is matching the sauce rather than the main ingredient of the dish.

The next consideration is the mix of dishes. The old rule of white with starters and red with main courses looks silly. Consider, for example, what would happen if one started with devilled kidneys, followed by a baked fish as the main course. I suggest that, here, salvation is to be found – in restaurants at least – in wine by the glass. A restaurant offering a variety of eight or ten wines by the glass, especially when dessert wines are also offered, enables a more subtle and suitable choice to be made. Where this does not happen, choosing a suitable wine becomes a dreadful and, almost invariably for some, an unsuccessful compromise. This may explain why so much Anjou Rosé and Mateus Rosé used to be sold in the UK (and in the USA): both caterers and customers had insufficient confidence or knowledge to make a choice and plumped for the worst of all possible compromises.

Another question which can be vexing is what wine to choose with cheese. The cheese course used to be seen as a way of soaking up red wine left over from the main course, but with increasing refinements of taste it is now more common to take cheese after dessert (a practice which is not really Italian): as a result, more people now see sweet wines as a far more likely marriage with cheese and even our English supermarket chains have been running evening get-togethers encouraging people in that direction. Clearly, the range of cheese now available in the UK makes absolute combinations an impossibility, but one rule of thumb I would proffer, namely that the saltier the cheese, the sweeter the wine. Nor should we forget that matching cheese with alcohol opens the way for beers and grappas as possible alternatives.

Finally, we come to the no-go area. Artichokes, lemon juice, eggs, vinegar and, for some people, even tomatoes are said to be ingredients that will ruin any wine. But a creative cook can find ways around the problem: use wine in a vinaigrette instead of vinegar; eggs with runny yolks are the real problem so let us avoid that and ensure the yolk is well cooked (hard boiled eggs with a Gavi di Gavi, perhaps), and if one is determined to have wine with artichokes, I would suggest a strong, dry, flavourful red wine, such as the Sardinian Cannonau.

Furthermore, the lemon embargo only applies to serious concentrations of citric acid so let us extend the lemon juice with sweetish wine such as a light Moscatel; and a dash of lemon can actually enable a buttery dish to accept a wine complement more easily.

It must be admitted that today one of the greatest salvations for the amateur is the proliferation of inexpensive books offering hundreds of recommendations for dishes and wines. Therein, however, lies a danger: it is sometimes best to avoid slavishly following suggestions that are made in this context but rather simply use them to provide either direction or inspiration. I must continue to insist that individual preference should always rule. If someone enjoys Barbaresco with kippers, for example, or sweet Moscato with steak, so be it.

The relaxation of a well-loved pairing, however 'officially' inappropriate, is often worth all the agony and soul-searching in finding something which is appropriate and correct. But given the present approach and the fact that both food and wine are meant to be enjoyed, one should not turn the choice of wine into an agonizing process. Looking at it dispassionately and bluntly, if you drop a complete clanger and the wine does not match the dish at all, drink water with the food and leave the wine for when the course is finished.

Finally, let us remind ourselves that there are some rare occasions when a wine is such perfection that it almost seems a shame to spoil it by eating at the same time. Hence the recent birth of the expression 'meditation wines': no food allowed, but perhaps only a cigar or a good book; maybe some music. If you have a sweet tooth, then I recommend any one of the following: Moscato di Pantelleria, Moscato di Trani, Moscato di Noto, Picolit, Vernaccia di Serrapetrona and any Vin Santo Toscano.

If you prefer dry wines, then a vintage Brunello di Montalcino, a good Vino Nobile di Montepulciano, Nero d'Avola, Primitivo di Manduria, Salice Salentino, or virgin vintage Marsala.

□

Our taste buds recognize a number of sensations and flavours. Without joining the debate engendered by a determination to quantify the resultant findings, suffice it to say that there are four fundamental tastes which most normal people are capable of recognizing when eating food. They are acidity, bitterness, saltiness and sweetness. Try it out on yourself and you will find that most of your tasting experiences can be classified under these four headings. The result is that the same four tastes come into play when drinking wine, save that in the case of wine one may experience more than one of these fundamental tastes at the same time.

For example, you could have an essentially sweet wine which is, at the same time, acidic in flavour; or you might find the wine a little too bitter for your tastes. One might think that perhaps saltiness cannot be tasted in a wine, but that would be wrong. There are some Italian wines from grapes grown on volcanic soil (wines from Campania, for example) where the tangy taste does remind one slightly of salt in the same way as a Manzanilla (of the genuine Sanlucar de Barrameda type) clearly does.

As with food, one often finds that one or more of the fundamental flavours are of noticeably higher intensity in a wine. When that happens, the wine is unsatisfactory because it is unbalanced, either as too smooth and lacking in character or as too sharp and consequently unpleasant.

These fairly elementary notions must be borne in mind when we try and match food to wine and they are becoming much more significant in an era like ours marked by increasingly hedonistic tendencies. Gone are the days where the peasant was not bothered about what wine was to be drunk at meals and where a thorough appreciation of the significance of combining wine with food belonged purely to the rich and powerful, the nobility of good living, if not of spirit. Nowadays the man in the street is much more knowledgeable about certain aspects of wine/food-matching than his forebears. (I hasten to correct myself: so is the woman in the street, now that she is taking a much greater interest in the choice of wines.)

I shall be offering certain broad rules later on, but for the present it suffices to say that the four fundamental tastes referred to which can, in food of course, be influenced by other factors. These are mentioned as they spring to mind and certainly not in order of importance. They are:

1. **The use of 'herbs'**, especially, as far as Italian cuisine is concerned: bay leaves, basil, capers, fennel, garlic, oregano, parsley, rosemary and sage. Leaving aside peppery influences of any kind (white, black, red pepper, cayenne and paprika) it must be remembered that, as a rule, herbs (basil is an obvious exception) give off stronger flavours when cooked. To match food prepared with herbs with a gently tasting pale bodyless white wine is to court disaster.

2. **Bitterness**. It is not often that one says that a food is bitter and yet, Italian food can be just that. It is not merely a matter of the herbs to which reference has already been made, but also the addition, for example, of liver, whether alone or in combination, the fact that a strong red wine may have been used in the sauce or the cooking, and so on.

3. **Fat**. There is plenty of it in Italian cooking, butter in the north, olive oil in the centre and the south. If too much oil is used, the tongue appears to be coated by a greasy film which, whilst not in itself unpleasant (and indeed, almost a fundamental occurrence when eating strongly flavoured Italian foods) does make the choice of wine exceptionally difficult.

4. **Consistency**. The more solid, compact and 'tough' the food, the longer the chewing process which, in turn, produces greater quantities of saliva that can affect the sensitivity of one's tastebuds.

It is probably true to say, as one of the generalizations which I am trying very hard to avoid, that the greater the consistency of the food, the more likely it is that one needs a strong wine with high alcoholic content; preferably, but not necessarily, a red.

A runny dish (for example, a clear soup) needs a totally different approach from 'lasagne' or roast pork.

5. **Sweetness.** This is probably one of the easiest taste perceptions which we all have grown accustomed to from a very early age. To what extent one uses sugar, honey or other sweetening substances in main courses is dependent upon local gastronomy. In general, one may say that in such courses sweetness does not create too many problems as far as wine compatibility is concerned. On the other hand, when dealing with puddings and desserts generally, there seems to be no way out: a dry wine is not usually appropriate (unless it be a sparkling one of quality or a fine Marsala Vergine) and a sweet wine (white or red seems immaterial) is almost compulsory.

In this, as in everything else concerned with the matching of food with wine, two factors are fundamental: one's preferences and a certain amount of common sense.

6. **One final general observation.** Whatever the combination, one should ensure at all times what I shall term a natural balance between wine and food. Neither must be allowed to predominate. This explains why great chefs do not get on too well with (great) sommeliers because it is practically impossible to successfully combine outstanding food with outstanding wine, since each component in the equation will have a tendency to take over. Indeed, there can be no question that the greater the quality and the age of a wine, the more difficult it is to combine it with food, so much so that famous chefs have a tendency to prefer the choice of a lesser type of wine so that flavour combinations can be made easier. Furthermore, the flavours of a dish should not be so powerful as to overcome the tastes of the wine.

By parity of reasoning, the body, the consistency of a wine, should match the structure of the food. A delicately flavoured dish will be ruined by a strong-bodied wine; equally, an imposing rich main course will not benefit from associating with a light Frascati.

Crudely put, a dish with a lot of fat and sauce needs to be paired with a wine whose alcoholic content and tannins can be equal to the fight. In a strange sense, one could say that a fat dish might almost benefit from a wine with some fizz in it.

In conclusion, I have tried to strike a balance between personal preferences and dogma. Whenever I had to swing towards one consideration rather than the other, I have been guided by my Italian background. I have done so, first, because I could not help myself and second, because I am extremely conscious, and proud, of Italian gastronomic influence generally on the cuisines of most countries in the world.

Here are my own preferences as to which *Italian* wines can usefully combine with food, and how. I shall append to the list my own recommendations of what Italian wines to use with a number of items of food as well as, in some cases, on the cuisine of other countries.

HORS D'OEUVRES

If these are based on meat or vegetables, then I favour dry (not sweet) rosé wines. I suggest Rosato del Salento, Chiaretto del Garda, Castel del Monte Rosato or even Bardolino, and, finally, Cerasuolo degli Abruzzi. There may be other combinations, of course. To mention but one, the pleasant Chiaretto of Ischia, and obviously, the well-known Orvieto and Frascati and the lesser known Lugana and Cortese, white or dry rosé wines, although a dry Lambrusco would also be quite suitable.

The variety of hors d'oevres (antipasti) available in Italy is so great that it would take too long to be specific. There are so many regional variations on the antipasto theme (some Italian writers have said that there are over a hundred in Piemonte alone) that to list them all, and to find suitable accompanying wines, would take many pages.

I shall confine myself to observing that the traditional, refined Italian antipasto consists of an assortment of thinly sliced prosciutto (raw and cooked ham), salami and 'mortadella' (and there are just as many varieties of salami, as there are Italian regions) with some filleted anchovies, maybe quartered hard-boiled eggs, marinated mushrooms, green and black olives. The choice here becomes very difficult because one would have to know what follows during the remainder of the meal but, broadly speaking, I would opt either for one of the stronger rosés from Puglia (Castel del Monte Rosato or a Five Roses of De Castris) or a sparkling Freisa.

Pickles are not often available in Italy as a separate hors d'oeuvres but, insofar as they are, it would be preferable to drink no wine with them but only water; the combination of wine with vinegar being always fatal. The same may be said for any food that has been pickled.

If the hors d'oeuvres are based on sea food or oysters then the choice is very wide indeed. From Soave, Lugana and Pigato to Fiano di Avellino, Vermentino di Gallura and Vernaccia di Oristano.

SOUPS

The thin chicken broth-type soup lends itself to either one of the dry white wines already mentioned or a not-too-strong rosé. But there are many other heavier types of soups in Italy – 'pasta e fagioli' (pasta with beans), 'pasta e ceci' (pasta with chick peas), 'pasta e piselli' (pasta with peas) which make the choice somewhat more difficult. Again, as a generalization, with this kind of soup, short of drinking no wine at all as some have recommended in the past, I would suggest one of the stronger rosés from Puglia.

PASTA & RISOTTO

When it comes to these dishes, the Anglo-American public is quite indiscriminate. Let us have a nice glass of red wine with a nice plate of pasta. Wrong.

In the first place, one has to determine what sort of red wine one would drink, but it is not the pasta that tells you which wine to choose, rather the sauce that accompanies it. If the sauce is based on lobster, prawns and any other kind of seafood, then dry white wines are infinitely to be preferred to any red. In this connection I recommend a dry Frascati, a Verdicchio or a Falanghina. If the sauce is meat-based (e.g. 'bolognese') then one would obviously opt for a red, but not a robust one and I would recommend generally a Chianti. The only exception to this would be the rare occurrences where the meat sauce is based on game (a practice mainly to be found in northern Italy) when it is permitted to have one of the strong classic red wines – Barolo, Barbera, Barbaresco, and so on.

All the above can also be said about rice dishes. We Italians have a saying that 'rice is born in water and dies in wine'. But we are less sophisticated about explaining which type of wine. Rice can be made with as many sauces as pasta: accordingly, my recommendations must be the same for rice as they are for pasta, as concerns wine combinations. I make one exception, namely, 'risotto ai tartufi' (rice with truffles), where I would recommend drinking a sparkling Freisa, or preferably, if one can afford it, a Franciacorta Saten.

A point to be made conveniently perhaps, at this stage, is the thought that our sensitivity to wine gradually reduces the more we eat and this is one of the reasons why the general recommendation is made of having stronger wines as you progress over the meal.

FISH DISHES

Here I would recommend the same wines as with fish hors d'oeuvres. One could go further and include the Vernaccia di San Gimignano and Greco di Tufo, but there are so many other white wines, as will be shown in the lists that follow, which could prove so suitable that, as we say in Italian, one has only the embarrassment of making a choice.

A differentiation should be made between sea fish and fish from rivers and lakes. Both are abundant in Italy, of course, but if you are in the mountains having trout, then the wines that I have just mentioned would not only be inappropriate but occasionally also difficult to find. Much more suitable would be the wines from Trentino Alto Adige and Friuli Venezia Giulia which are mentioned in the text.

At the same time, there are local variations. In Piemonte, for instance, we have from time immemorial been preparing trout with Barbera; not everybody's cup of tea, but an example of how significant flexibility can be when mixing food with wine. I myself under the heading Lambrusco have recommended that particular wine with trout. As an alternative, and staying in Piemonte, a Favorita could well be quite enjoyable.

There is fish which is reasonably fat. I am thinking of the eel (of different varieties). Here, a white wine may not necessarily be that appropriate: I would recommend a not-too-strong red, possibly a

Sangiovese (but there are others). A number of gourmets suggest that Riesling makes a clever combination with smoked salmon. I do not disagree.

ROAST MEAT

A distinction should be drawn between white meat (chicken, turkey, rabbit, for example), red meat generally and the kind of dish which is common to north-west Italy, but is also to be found elsewhere of course, namely boiled meat ('bollito'). Personally, with any kind of 'bollito' whether 'misto' or singly, I would recommend either a sparkling Barbera, a sparkling Freisa, or a Grignolino. But there are other permutations based on light white wines, which combine very well with 'white' meats.

For example, I have often enjoyed a Greco di Tufo with roast chicken or roast, (not stewed, for which a red is more appropriate) rabbit.

A Vernaccia di San Gimignano is eminently suited to cold, white meats of any kind, as is an Orvieto. A classic Italian cold meat dish is the 'vitello tonnato' which consists of thinly sliced veal with varying sauces (anchovies, eggs, capers and so on). For this, I would prefer a Gavi di Gavi or a rosé Lagrein.

Game dishes deserve separate attention. Here there is no doubt that the stronger the flavour of the wine and its body, the more successful the result, hence, I recommend Gattinara, Recioto Amarone, Brunello di Montalcino, Vino Nobile di Montepulciano, Taurasi and Aglianico del Vulture. For red meats, the same could be very effective, but other reds would be just as good (Ciró, Salento, Chianti, of course: the list is very long!). I have mentioned Amarone but in my view a distinction should be made between a young one and the long-matured version. The younger Amarone goes quite well with pork, the older is more suitable to game and especially duck and pigeon. Equally pleasant with roast pork is a sparkling red Lambrusco.

SALADS

Given the above observation concerning pickles, my recommendation is to drink only water with a salad and certainly not wine.

MUSHROOMS AND TRUFFLES

I go along with Antonio Carluccio (*A Passion for Mushrooms*, Pavilion Books, Ltd, 1989, p. 116) that it is not a good idea to drink any wine with wild mushrooms eaten on their own, since there are a few, like the Common Inkcap, which contain substances that do not blend at all well with wine and will certainly give you an upset stomach. I find that even the common Field Mushroom, if eaten on its own, i.e. without condiments, does not blend with wine of any kind.

If the mushroom forms part of a dish, in which it is not the major ingredient then, broadly speaking, the same rules apply as already set out, that is to say, one chooses the wine regardless of whether there are mushrooms in the dish. But my suggestion is to drink at most one glass; if you do not, you will certainly realize that you have gone wrong.

The Italian experts on truffles are the people from Piemonte. They are not too fussed and drink their own excellent red wines with truffles, both white and black. Carluccio suggests instead a good champagne: I am inclined to agree with him but being in favour of Italian wines, I would recommend a Franciacorta Saten (expensive, but certainly worthwhile and comparable to many Champagnes).

SWEETS

Here I would recommend a semi-sweet sparkling wine (Asti Spumante, for example), or one of Italy's sparkling gems, the red Recioto or, if one can find it, a Malvasia di Casorzo.

I am not concerned by the suggestion made by some wine writers, that sweet dishes (whether of the pudding or the 'crème brulée' type) have the ability to lessen the sweetness of the wine that accompanies them. I consider that debatable in any event; but if in doubt, opt for a 'vin santo', an Aleatico di Portoferraio or an Anghelu Ruju from Sardinia.

FRUIT (AND CHEESE)

The choice is wider and, in my view, very personal indeed. Some of us would prefer an aromatic white wine, others a rosé, or a very sweet wine with fairly high alcoholic content, others a sparkling wine. Let the reader decide, I make no recommendation under this heading. And, of course, no wine of any kind with citrus fruits: they do not mix at all well since the acid in the citrus fruits is comparable to the vinegar in the salad and the pickles.

Two general caveats. In the first place, as I see it, no wine should be drunk *with* ice cream, nor water (some might appreciate a chilled vodka), although one ought to drink a few sips of water afterwards. The reason is that the cold temperature will, so to say, anaesthetise our sense of taste, thus precluding a proper appreciation of the wine. This is why when taking ice cream seated at an Italian bar, a glass of still water is usually offered (unlikely if you are standing at the bar, where prices are lower). (I do not differentiate between milk and water ices.) In the second place, cheeses tend to complicate choice because they are so varied. From fresh to mature, from soft to hard, from gentle to strong, from goat or sheep, to cow, the choice is exceptionally personal. As a general statement I should say that, in my opinion, a sheep or goat cheese is more likely to combine well with white or rosé rather than with red wine, especially a mature strong red.

If I had to be more specific, however, I would choose a Sauvignon (unwooded) for goat cheeses, a Passito di Pantelleria for Roquefort and, with Parmigiano, sparkling wines from Emilia Romagna, say a Lambrusco Grasparossa. But I suppose that the British custom of drinking port with cheese will never easily be dislodged. . . .

More controversially, I remain convinced that only water should be drunk on top of pasta or risotto dishes and likewise, as stated, that only water should be drunk on top of or with cheese. The reason is that wine superimposed upon pasta creates a surfeit of stomach acid and, when taken with cheese, does not blend at all harmoniously with milk. (This, incidentally, is one of the reasons why I have recommended that no wine should be drunk with ice cream.)

This is so true for those who suffer from a celiac disease. They certainly cannot eat pasta in any event. Fortunately for them, there are now available many varieties of pasta made with rice. The top quality specimens of this rice pasta are, apart from colour, almost indistinguishable in taste, especially when a red sauce is used, from ordinary pasta.

In respect of rice pasta, the same considerations apply as I have set out above. I make no comment as to the sequence in which wines should be drunk, save to generally observe that apart from dry, sparkling wine, the generally accepted rule of white before red, lighter before stronger and dry before sweet, I can but endorse.

By the same token of brevity, I do not comment on which Italian wines would be suited to Chinese, Japanese, Vietnamese, Indian and other 'native' cuisines. The matter would become too complicated. For example, what wine would you drink with Chinese food? If I had to choose an Italian wine for it, I would choose a Gewürztraminer but overall I think that no wine at all should be drunk with Chinese food; preferably a beer, maybe a dry cider or some saké, but basically, only water.

The combination of flavours inherent in much native and especially Eastern cooking makes it almost impossible to choose a suitable wine, at least in my view. I feel strongly that practically no Italian wine mixes well with that kind of cuisine.

And lastly, given that some consider it, even more than roast beef and Yorkshire pudding, the English national dish, we come to fish and chips. Here I shall be provocative and say that no wine of any kind should be drunk with this dish which is much more suited to beer or cider or ideally a Guinness. The reason is that the combination of batter and cooking fat or vegetable oil of one kind or the other would preclude enjoying the wine. I openly acknowledge that under this heading perhaps I am being too Italian; so much is this so, that a dear English friend of mine, who is very knowledgeable in these matters, is quite convinced that the only wine he would drink with fish and chips is a Retsina. Maybe: but *I* cannot find a suitable Italian wine to complement this dish.

MELON AND WATERMELON

The traditional English combination of port, amongst other things, with melon is undoubtedly a most suitable one. I suggest, however, you might like to try either a Prosecco or a Franciacorta sparkling wine; even more appropriate, however, would be the Italian equivalent of port, namely the Anghelu Ruju from Sardegna.

Views differ as to what alcoholic drink best accompanies watermelon. I believe that a Marsala Vergine from Sicilia is eminently suitable, preferably though not necessarily, in its demi-sec version.

FOOD/WINE GLOSSARY

Anchovies. Definitely suitable are all dry sherries, especially a Manzanilla de Sanlucar but a dry white wine seems quite appropriate, perhaps a rosé; alternatively, a dry 'petillant' wine. Generally, I would recommend a Chiaretto del Garda, a Prosecco, a Franciacorta or even a 'brut' Lambrusco.

Artichokes. I find it difficult to recommend a wine to be drunk with artichokes but after some hesitation I have reached the conclusion that a sparkling Lambrusco *might* be appropriate.

Asparagus. I make the same comment here: the taste of this vegetable is quite distinctive and can often upset any combination with wine. Personally, I would drink water with it.

Avocado. Much depends on the condiment. If the avocado is served with crabs or crab sauce then I would recommend a light rosé. If one has it at home with a little lemon and pepper only, then a light red would seem appropriate and I would recommend a Bardolino. If it is served with vinaigrette then the same considerations apply as I have already voiced earlier on. Nevertheless, I would recommend a Grignolino.

Chocolate. Suffice it to say that one should differentiate between milk and plain chocolate and should also draw the line between chocolate as such and chocolate bars mixed with fruit, nut, mint, orange, etc. I would recommend any of the sweet wines mentioned in the text.

Fish Soups (any kind, including the bouillabaisse). The same considerations apply as I have already voiced for fish dishes generally.

Hummus. Undoubtedly here a light dry white wine is appropriate. I would recommend a Soave.

Kidneys. Not a plate beloved by many foreigners generally, but I should still say something. The flavour is often very strong, no matter how they are prepared. Accordingly, I would recommend a fairly strong wine, I find Freisa particularly appropriate or a Refosco.

Liver and Liver Paté. Again, the flavours are strong. A good solution would be a very dry sparkling wine or a rosé. I would recommend the Franciacorta Satén if you can afford it (unless one opts for a good champagne, of course) and, if money is tight, a sparkling Lambrusco.

Moussaka. A strong red is advisable, but I make no recommendation since there are so many to choose from; in any event, I would drink only water with it.

Omelettes. Not something about which I enthuse in gastronomic terms, although there are some excellent ones available in Italy and, of course, especially in Spain. Generally, I would recommend a light white wine (Arneis, perhaps) or any of our rosés.

'Asian' dishes. The combination of flavour inherent in many of what I would call generally Eastern dishes (other than Chinese), Japanese, Indian, Vietnamese, etc. is so varied that to choose a suitable wine is almost an impossible task. Furthermore, I am not sufficiently conversant with such styles of cooking.

One final comment. The Italians, possibly much to the surprise of the reader, are essentially fairly conservative people. They are certainly conservative in matters of food.

There is an old Italian saying '*moglie e buoi dei paesi tuoi*' which freely translated means that you should choose your wife from the same place where you would buy your oxen. This is by no means meant to be a chauvinistic remark and should not be taken as indicating that one should treat one's wife as a chattel, of course, but it sprang to my mind when I came to consider this particular issue of the combination of Italian wines with non-Italian food.

The reader will have noticed that I have already made the point that when it comes to sauces for pasta one should choose the wine to match the sauce. Equally, I cannot help feeling that there are certain types of wine which go better with food from the same region where the vine grows. It is essentially for this reason that I consider myself not only unwilling but also incapable of choosing a suitable Italian wine to accompany, say, chop suey or, thinking of Indian food, chicken tikka.

CHAPTER 8

OAKING IS SOMETIMES OK!

I would now like to consider an aspect of winemaking that has recently become somewhat controversial, namely, the consequences of using barrels or other containers of oak or even oak chips or staves *almost as a matter of routine*, to add to or develop the wine's flavour and quality.

On this issue, there are different views, since some, like me, maintain that oak, no matter how carefully used, *almost* always destroys the freshness and the fruitiness of wines, especially the whites, whereas others believe strongly that, except where used indiscriminately, or in the form of chips, it always improves the wine and that only oaking produces 'great' wines.

'OAKING' (maturing in wooden containers; barrels and barriques)

As for the making of wine barrels, space does not permit a detailed analysis; but essentially there are two methods of manufacture, namely the European ('French') and the American.

The European method has consisted for centuries in hand-splitting the oak (with a little help from machines) into staves which are dried in the air; the American method is to saw the oak into staves and to dry them in a kiln. The former system takes longer and is accordingly more expensive; but has the benefit of allowing the harsher tannins in the wood to leech out; the latter imparts much coarser flavours to the wine (although it is fair to say that over the past decade or so top quality American barrels have been produced in accordance with the European system). Furthermore, under the American system the staves are subjected to steam-heating; in Europe, they are normally heated over fires.

To help the reader follow the argument a little further, it may be useful to recall that there are just two types of wood containers used for storing wine. The first is the large, traditional barrel holding from 1,000 litres upwards and sometimes as much as 50 hectolitres. This container is known in Italy as a 'botte/i' and red wines have been traditionally matured in this type of container for decades. It is made of oak staves of different lengths and thicknesses which are subjected to processes that make the wood supple enough to be curved to the required shape. Usually, the thickness of the staves is 7/8 cm but can occasionally reach 10 cm. Wines of all kinds have traditionally and successfully been matured in these large barrels unless stored either in concrete containers, glass-resin or stainless-steel tanks.

The French then evolved the smaller type of barrel known as a 'barrique', which is also made of oak and of varying capacity, but customarily not exceeding 225 litres. Barriques are made with the same oak as the larger barrels but to achieve the required suppleness, the wood is heated by special treatment from fires made usually with the same oak and oak chips as the 'barrique' itself. The thickness of the strips is different: it seldom exceeds 3 cm and is often as thin as 2 cm and the length rarely exceeds 1.20 metres. Furthermore, the wood from the original oak tree is never cut by saw but is split. The system of achieving the bending of the oak strips has itself a contribution to make to the effect and taste of the wood, coarser if sawn, smoother if hand split; furthermore, the 'barrique' is toasted on its inside, if the buyer so requires.

The result of the different methodology applied to the making of the large barrel and the 'barrique', never mind the smaller size of the barrique, is reflected in the stronger oaky taste that is achieved by the latter, because it imparts to the wine a much more marked flavour (also resulting, possibly, from the knots in the wood). In this context one should bear in mind that the normal *minimum* maturation period of most wines in 'barrique' is eighteen months, rising quite commonly to two or three years for the better quality wines.

The thickness of the staves is of paramount importance: it has been calculated that the thinner wood of the barriques allows 50% of the substances that can be transferred from the container to the wine and about 200 milligrams of tannin per annum to be absorbed by the wine, if a barrique is new (the process is considerably slower if it is second-hand and reduces with the amount of usage). It is claimed that such storage improves the wine by making it smoother and reduces the chances of oxidation.

As already noted, the practice of storing wine in wooden barrels is said to have originated in Gaul. Until recent times, it was only red wines that were stored in oak, (whether American, Limousin or other types), preferably though not necessarily new, for it was felt that only reds qualified for acquiring this particular kind of distinction because of their high tannin levels. Until winemakers in the New World, especially California and Australia in the 1970s, embarked upon the practice, white wines were not normally stored in barriques. (Rosé wines seldom are.)

Hugh Johnson has observed (see his *Wine Companion*, Mitchell Beazley, London 1983, reprinted 1998, p. 27) that 'in California cooperage has become something of a fetish'. It is my opinion that the American experience and insistence in oaking white wines, which has now been common practice for nearly thirty years, deprives the drinker of the pleasure of tasting the original flavours (of fruit or otherwise) which wine itself is capable of producing. It has repeatedly been said that oaking provides the wine with more 'character': I challenge this claim. If I had to choose between preserving the purity of grape flavours and altering them because of the benefits that oaking produces, generally for reds and not usually for whites, I would always opt for purity and natural flavour; and by natural, I mean flavours that are provided by the grape itself and not by the container. (In passing, I would make the point that it is inevitable that the American system of oaking white wines produces what I can only describe as an unsavoury outcome since the variety of oak tree that grows in the USA (Quercus alba) provides a much more aromatic wood than the European versions (Holm Oak (Quercus robur) and Sessile Oak (Quercus petraea)).

There is no doubt that maturing wine in wood has a major contribution to make to its flavour. Nevertheless, it is not always easy to define what taste and smell the wine has, once it has been so matured. Put differently, with some practice it is possible to recognize, first by smell and second by taste, a wine that has acquired the flavour of the oak barrel or the barrique; but actually to describe it further by using expressions like 'it tastes of raspberries' or 'strawberries' or whatever, is not so simple for the amateur. You realize it is there, that particular oaky flavour, almost vanilla-like, but you cannot always easily relate the sensation produced by the wine to known flavours. It is quite distinctive; although after a long period of maturity, the taste imparted to the wine becomes more subtle and less 'offensive' if matured in a barrel ('botte/i'). The taste of oak tends to persist in wines aged in barrique.

The problem nowadays is that producers are in a hurry to sell their wines, (unless Regulations prescribe otherwise) so they do not allow them to mature slowly. To expedite the 'ageing process', the less respectable add to the storage vessel a large amount of oak chips or even sawdust in sacking; in that way they impart to it, over a comparatively short period, even as little as three months, a flavour which is strong, too strong, and in many cases such as to obliterate completely the tastes that the wine itself provides. Such practices are forbidden at present by Articles 42 and 43 of EEC Regulation No. 1493/99 which only allows the use of oak barrels or barriques and not any substitutes, such as oak chips, sawdust, wooden strips, etc. (It is worth adding here that concern for the reducing number of oak trees throughout the world has encouraged the European Commission recently to allow a relaxation that would result in small pieces of oak, which are only lightly burnt, to be added to wine. Indeed, there is an argument that the EEC Regulations are failing to keep up to date with new vinification techniques.)

The truth probably is that this does not matter much in many cases, because in all likelihood the wine so treated with chips was not a good wine to start with, and the vintner was trying to give it a particular kind of flavour, so strong as to ensure that nothing else could be tasted. To that extent, the practice, if the reader will forgive the pun, is a . . . . .'smoak' screen!, to hide the inferior quality of cheap or badly produced wines.

What is, or may be, objectionable in the case of red wines, becomes all the more so in the case of whites. For this, the Californians, taking their cue from the French and the Spanish, have to carry a great responsibility because they have encouraged even producers of Latin extraction in Europe to mature more and more white wines in oak, and not merely Burgundy or Chardonnay. There are now Italian and Spanish wine producers who actually boast of whites matured in barriques; I have sampled recently a heavily oaked Soave!

At this point, I am duty bound to observe that the Americans appear to have read the wine market quite correctly. In 2003, the US exported 3.58 million hectolitres of wine, representing a 29% increase on the previous year; the United Kingdom accounted for 25% of that increase since at present it takes 33% of the total USA wine market, a further mark of the solidarity between the two

English-speaking nations.

Thus, there are established separate processes when it comes to oaking wines. Producers of the better quality and proportionately more expensive type of wine will use new or little used oak barrels of good quality, especially if they wish to impart wood tannins to low-tannin wines. Extremely careful and proper maintenance of the barrels will ensure that age and constant use of such containers do not damage the wine causing unpleasant, musty odours. The result will be wines of a flavour which, although not liked by a few, will not of themselves be objectionable and will often improve on the grape. Others will employ preferably new or good used (not older than, say, five or six years) 'barriques' to flavour the wine to a greater degree; that can be problematical for those of us who do not appreciate oaked wines.

At the bottom end, as we have seen, though admittedly it is the market trend, to save money, oak cubes or oak chips are used. The cheaper the quality of the wine, the greater the temptation to add some spice to it by strongly toasting the cubes or the chips, and the skill to do so is not always available.

Skill apart, the results can be disastrous. The reader might like to know what James Halliday, an internationally renowned wine writer and judge, has to say on this particular point: 'The aroma and initial palate flavour of such oak can be attractive, but the finish is often disastrous: coarse, bitter phenolics will obliterate typically modest fruit flavour' (*A Century of Wine*, Mitchell Beazley, London, 2000, p. 58). Flippantly, one could say that, for some, oak is not. . . OK.

Flavour apart, the principal drawback of maturing wine in barriques is undoubtedly that the process of transfer of wood flavour to the wine, which can have a good outcome if carefully handled, requires such patience and expertise that it is not always successful. Using the barrique, whether for fermentation or maturing, is by no means a task for the amateur.

In my view, *heavy* (or should I perhaps say, enhanced?) oaking is a question of fashion, except perhaps in Rioja where it is almost a prerequisite. Even in Italy nowadays the requirements of a new public, which is becoming more discerning about wine, have induced conservative producers to deviate from centuries-old traditions, in order also to appease wine drinkers in other parts of the world whom we, the Italians, and the French, of course, have taught to drink wine! In fact, I do not believe that Italian wine producers wholeheartedly adopted the barrique in the certainty that their wines would improve in quality. I firmly believe that they decided to do so because they were struck by the undeniable success, on a number of world markets, of French (and Spanish) wines matured in barriques. Put crudely, they jumped onto the bandwaggon, saleability prevailing over 'purity'.

American 'culture', which has imbued European society, has elevated the oaking of wines to what I would define as a religion. Whilst this may be unpleasant in the case of reds, it becomes, in my view, objectionable for whites. Furthermore, there are clearly some wines which could or should never be *matured* in oak. Champagne is one of them, simply because of the process, obviously. (I accept, of course, that some of the better champagnes are partly matured in oak or barriques.) But there are others. Even discounting any type of sparkling wine (Asti Spumante, Prosecco, etc.), one can think of the white wine produced in the area of Canosa, in Apulia. When fresh, it strongly tastes and smells like jasmine: would one dare put it in oak? It would be a sin to overcome the flowerful scent and taste of a genuine young white wine. Examples of this type are legion.

But as fashions come, so they go. In Spain, for example, the number of producers in Rioja is increasing who offer 'vino joven', normally not matured in cask, contrary to extensive and at times tiresome national practice where, out of a total production of 3,674 types of wine (white, rosé and red) 1,735 are in fact so treated (as at 31 December 2002 – *Wines from Spain*, Editorial Paladar).

Even in Italy there are some small signs that the pendulum *may* be swinging back. We Italians owe the extensive use of the barrique, as distinct from the much more traditional, capacious oak barrels of varying dimensions, to our need to be competitive on world markets and to the possibly too strong encouragement provided by one of our leading writers on wine, Luigi Veronelli. But there begin to appear cracks in the oaking edifice. I have personal knowledge of a producer in north-east Italy whose publicity material advertises the fact that the winery is eco-friendly, inasmuch as it does not contribute to the felling of trees: *all* its wine not being oaked! The environmental benefit of *not* oaking wines should not be discounted and alternative woods (for example, chestnut and cherry) are increasingly being tested.

I am not unmindful of the fact that sensible, i.e. not exaggerated maturing of a wine, particularly a red, in oak casks, and especially so in barriques, will enable the better qualities and flavours of a good wine to come to the fore in the same manner as the addition of salt as a condiment to food will improve its taste. Similarly, I do not discount the benefits of those substances released by the wood, namely phenols, polyphenols, polymers, aldehydes and acids, all of which influence both the perfume and the colour of wine.

In the same context, one cannot deny that oaked wines often appear to grow softer with the passage of time, whether because of evaporation or because, as is the case with corks, minute quantities of oxygen are allowed to get into the wine. However, these improvements do not come about all the time as a result of oaking; quite the reverse, because often the mere fact of heavy 'wooding' can destroy a particular flavour.

At the same time, it seems to me that it is impossible to be dogmatic in this matter, since personal tastes differ. There are some wines which, if properly oaked, improve a lot. Equally, there are others for which oaking is totally unnecessary as they are sufficiently solid, smooth, 'mature' and flavourful. It is, as in many other situations in life, a matter of balance. For innovative, time and economic reasons we in Italy are now oaking far too many wines, and far too much.

One of my major criticisms of the practice of oaking wines indiscriminately is that it makes for boredom. Put it this way: in 90% of the cases where one uncorks a bottle of red nowadays, unless of course it has turned to vinegar or there is something wrong with the cork, the first whiff is that of oak. In this respect, all the wines so uncorked smell the same. The drinker is deprived of the pleasure and the expectation of sniffing something different; he may be expecting strawberries or other fruit, almonds, or whatever else the wine is capable of producing in terms of flavours and scents. But he does not get it since the initial whiff does not change much whether the wine is inexpensive or is a good quality product.

That is what is meant here by boredom. The practice may well be in keeping with what our society wants and exacts, namely regimentation, lack of inventiveness, of character and, ultimately, of enjoyment. On the negative side for Italy, it is the result of short-term thinking: it makes our wines resemble ever more those produced in other countries (especially in the New World) whereas we should, as a matter of national policy, be concentrating on the great variety of flavours which our indigenous grapes can provide.

The reader may wish to compare the wealth of indigenous Italian vines with California, a state where a mere two grapes – Cabernet Sauvignon and Chardonnay – account for a third of all wine produced there.

Furthermore, I strongly believe that there are people who would prefer to taste the wine as it is, i.e. unoaked. I know that I will be termed by some a male chauvinist; as such, I observe, not altogether flippantly, that an unoaked wine is like a woman without make-up: some men might prefer to see and taste a woman without make-up, surely, without necessarily denying all the benefits of using creams, lipstick and so on!

Sex does not seem to help in forming a view on oaking, since there are just as many women who like oaked wines in the same manner as there are others who dislike the practice of changing its original taste. I have often thought about the matter and have reached the conclusion that probably no explanation can be provided of why there is such a difference in taste; I believe that it may well be a congenital feature.

An observation I have made is that quite often where the parents do not like oaky wines, the children follow suit; but it is debatable whether this is the result of heredity, rather than of the fact that, in all likelihood, given their parents' tastes, the children started off tasting wine that was not matured in oak and developed in the same direction. I suspect it would be quite difficult to find an explanation for such likes and dislikes. I must also record that a friend of mine, who has drunk oaked wines for many years, has told me that at age sixty he grew tired of them and turned to unoaked versions!

As a general rule, wine bottles that carry a second, explanatory, label normally indicate that the wine has been matured in oak barrels or 'barriques'. However, I have recently seen in a major supermarket a 'specially selected' type of Burgundy wine where the expression 'oak matured' is actually shown in fairly large capitals on the front label. Whether this is an encouragement, as I suppose, or a warning, as one would hope, I cannot tell. . . . .

Furthermore, there are other indications that the public *may* be tiring of excessive oaking, especially of white wines. There is now (October 2007) on sale in an English supermarket a Chardonnay which displays on the bottle, quite prominently, the wording 'unoaked'!

It should not be thought for one moment that this is an idle debate and that the views of the author are idiosyncratic. Far from it.

In the Piedmontese town of Alba which is one of the major centres of wine production, if not the principal one, there were displayed recently (and there are still some to be seen), bottles of some of the best piedmontese wines produced by one of the major local viticulturists, namely Bartolo Mascarello, well known for his quality reds (Barolo, etc.).

The 'new' labels state quite clearly: 'no barrique', 'no berlusconi'!

The marketing muscle of Mascarello allowed him to combine his disapproval, well-known throughout the area, of maturing wines in barriques, with his patent dislike of the former Italian prime minister.

If an expert of such calibre can get away with making such a statement of opinion, then your author must be forgiven for his own, formed well independently of his recent finding (7 September 2004) in Alba of Mascarello's labels. (This reference should not be taken in any way as a political statement. I record the action of Mascarello purely to show that a respected producer has strong views about oaking in barriques.)

This particular, well-known vintner does no more, I believe, than to anticipate a trend which is very slowly beginning to emerge. A number of experts and many who enjoy wine are becoming somewhat disenchanted with having to taste wood instead of the grape. This is so true that nowadays some American, German and Scandinavian buyers go to Italy, especially to Piemonte, specifying that the wines they purchase must not have been matured in barriques.

Furthermore, it is conceivable that improvements in vinification techniques (thermovinification, reverse osmosis (an expensive process), etc.) resulting in the polymerization of the tannin molecules will produce a more subtle, less aggressive and, for those like me who are not too fond of that typical vanilla flavour that oak provides, much more acceptable wine.

It is also for this reason that more knowledgeable people than I maintain that it is conceivable that the pendulum is slowly beginning to swing the other way and that the days of the unqualified predominance of heavy oaking are reducing in number. *If* this is true, I add: 'not a minute too soon'.

Finally, I suggest that the man in the street would find it very useful, when looking at a wine list, say in a restaurant, to be told whether the wine has been matured in oak or not.

In South Africa, for example, it is customary to highlight this particular fact. Practically all wine lists in good restaurants there have headings like 'wooded', 'unwooded', or 'matured in oak/ barrels', or 'not matured in oak/barrels'. This is particularly useful for the visitor to the country or, indeed, even for the local layman who when confronted with a general description such as dry or semi-dry or sweet, or with the name of an estate or a wine which is not known, cannot possibly identify whether the wine is oaked or not.

CHAPTER 9

RED OR WHITE?

I am often asked by friends whether I can provide any explanation for the fact that generally speaking (although possibly not a good idea to generalize) women have a tendency to prefer white wine and champagne to red. I am not sure about the answer to that question because, as it happens, most of the women whom I know (family, friends, etc.) seem to like red more than white (I am leaving champagne out of the equation).

I have asked my GP whether there is any physiological reason why it should be so, assuming it to be true and he has advised me that he cannot think of one. I do appreciate, as he explained to me, that the liver of women metabolizes alcohol in a different way and that is why it is recommended that they should drink less than men in any event, for their liver is more at risk. But that of itself cannot explain the preference for white, assuming it to exist.

I have thought about it quite a lot and have reached the conclusion that there are probably two reasons for this. The first is that, especially when British women started drinking wine after the Second World War, the whites that were available were mainly German wines with a fairly low alcoholic content (often as low as $7°$ and seldom exceeding $11.5°$) which was possibly thought a better introduction to wine drinking than a heavy red. I accept that over the past twenty years or so the alcoholic content of white wines generally has increased in common with that of reds and rosés, but this may be an explanation.

Whilst I hesitate somewhat to proffer the first possible reason for women preferring whites, I have much greater conviction in the second one that I put forward: namely, it is established that given the same quantity (120 mls) a glass of white wine contains 77 calories whereas a glass of red contains 83 calories. Since it is common knowledge that 99.9% of Western women wish to look slim, or at least are invariably concerned about their weight, the preference for white is easily established and explained away. I hope I am right; but the difference in calories is not too significant.

It has been suggested to me that there may also be a deep-seated psychological aversion on the part of some women to liquids of a colour that reminds them of blood. I cannot tell whether there is anything in this although I am not prepared to rule out the suggestion in its entirety.

And what about regional variations? In Piemonte, for example, where the reds predominate, the culture of drinking white is not so well established. In Greece and the Greek islands, on the other hand, where the reds on balance tend to be sweetish, the position is different. In Provence, it may not even arise because of the widespread availability of rosé wines. In Germany, there are few drinkable reds but there are some good white wines, so there the choice is almost ready-made, at least if we consider locally produced wines. The same can be said of Austria and the countries fronting the Adriatic Sea.

There has been much writing and discussion as regards the consequences of gender differences when it comes to alcohol consumption but these appear to have centred on the physiological/ chemical aspects. As far as I know, little if anything has been written about the reasons why women might prefer a white to a red wine.

It is, of course, long established that because of their lower concentration of total body water, women have higher metabolic rates. For this reason, amongst others, they are more susceptible to drink in terms of its overall effect and, more particularly, to potential liver damage. Equally well established is the concept that, generally speaking, women tend to prefer wine, especially champagne, to beer. The beer belly is quite clearly a male manifestation. But more speculative is the answer to the question posed at the outset.

Another reason is that the stains of red wine are much more difficult to get rid of than those of white wines. When you are at a party, or enjoying cocktails, a woman may not necessarily be too offended by dropping some white wine on her beautiful dress but she will really get upset if you drop some red wine because no amount of salt or talcum powder or whatever will clear it.

The production and export of white wines from Australia and New Zealand, and the New World generally, is also a further proof of the fact that it is said that perhaps as many as 85% of women who drink wine prefer white to red. And, in any event, many women complain that red wine gives them headaches.

You could also argue that the colour red is more macho, and the colour white more feminine, and there is a perception of greater delicacy of taste for a white rather than for a red wine.

So, do women prefer white wine to red? The answer is a qualified yes. Qualified, of course, for a number of reasons. I start from the premise that most women are very fond of champagne. Champagne is a white wine with bubbles. For them, it is a concomitant of a smart life, a celebration, romance, success; rather like dancing, it is a prelude to fun, love and sex. For all these reasons, if no other, there is a statistical bias on the part of women in favour of white wines.

But leaving aside this aspect of the matter, it is a fact that, at least until recent times, British women were much more inclined than men to drink white wine. Statistical data are available in abundance but are not consistent, ranging from 85% preferring white wine to a mere 46%. I use the word British advisedly. I am not sufficiently conversant with the habits of women from other parts of the world to comment on them. In any event, the place from which a woman originates or where she lives may in turn colour her tastes. I know as a fact that broadly speaking – and throughout this part I will have to indulge in generalizations, because there are always exceptions – women who live in Germany and Austria tend to prefer white wine. The reason to me is really obvious: both countries produce very little drinkable red wine.

If I consider a country, Italy, which I know very well, there are regional differences. Very few women in the main producing regions for red wine (Piemonte, Emilia Romagna, Toscana) drink white rather than red; whereas in Veneto, Friuli Alto Adige and Trentino Venezia Giulia where whites predominate the position is reversed. So one must take the matter with more than a pinch of salt!

I further qualify my affirmative answer because the past ten or fifteen years have seen a greater interest on the part of women in wine generally. Until recent times, women were quite content with leaving the choice of wine to men. Today, they are the principal purchasers of wine – thanks to the immense choice found in the local supermarket. Furthermore, because of this greater interest, many more women have made the grade as either highly competent wine writers or have become masters of wine. As a result of both these factors, a shift has become apparent, in the sense, at least, that women have become more fastidious about the choice of wine, not necessarily opting for a white when an equivalent red might be more appropriate to the food with which it is associated.

But the principal reason for the shift towards red, in my view, is the fact that the last ten years have seen increasing emphasis being placed on the supposed health-giving qualities of red wine, principally because of its resveratrol content so that the more health-conscious drinking woman, who previously might have contented herself with a glass of Riesling, is more likely to go for a red.

Finally, it is worth pointing out, as a number of doctors, scientists and writers (Desmond Morris in particular, as many who know his books will confirm) have stressed, women have a significantly higher olfactory sensitivity. This is not to say that a woman has necessarily a better 'nose'; the fact that most perfume experts ('noses') are men, as anybody who has ever visited the town of Grasse in France (the European capital of perfume) will know, shows that the poor male of the species is not easily outdone. But there is no doubt of the connection with the higher sensitivity of smells for women, which reflects itself in physical, psychological and sexual manifestations, that do not apply to men.

In conclusion, I say that any difference which may have existed between the sexes in the choice of wine is now effectively reduced, if not eliminated.

CHAPTER 10

ON COLOUR, CORKS, CAPS AND STOPPERS

COLOUR

The colour of the wine is related to whether it is fermented in the presence of skins, because it is only the skins that give colour to wine. The pulp of the grape, of whatever colour it may be, produces no colour. It follows that, depending on whether one wants to obtain a red, a rosé or a white wine, there are different methods of vinification.

Red wine will be fermented on skins; the longer the fermentation period, the brighter the colour and the stronger the alcoholic content and, accordingly, the number of years for which the wine can be kept and will improve. For a rosé, the same procedure applies, but the grape juice remains in contact with the skins for a much shorter period, and as soon as the right or desired colour is obtained, the fermentation is continued without the skins.

If one is seeking a white wine, then the juice obtained from pressing the grapes is immediately stored away from the skins in containers which are of steel, if the wine is to be drunk whilst still young, or of wood if one is seeking a more long-lasting wine, or at least one with more complex flavours.

CORKS

There are different varieties of bottles, depending on the types of wine, and of stoppers and caps. The principal stopper is cork which is the outer bark of 'Quercus suber', the cork oak, found in many countries but mainly in Portugal which produces every year around 170,000 tons of cork bark – half the world's production. (It was the French monk, Dom Perignon, who gave the cork currency when he first used it for champagne.) Numbers and quality of this tree are dwindling fast: as a result, a cork stopper occasionally causes problems (nowadays, more frequently than in the past).

Cheaper wines have other methods of sealing, like plasticated cork or even a simple metal screw-on, or not, cap. No harm done there because that type of wine is not intended to be stored for very long and, indeed, the recommendation is that it should be stored upright, and drunk young. Nowadays plastic (polypropylene), silicone synthetic and lattice corks, are increasingly popular; they do not rot as easily as cheap cork and, given that cork-producing trees are becoming fewer, they may in certainly less than a decade become the norm for most ordinary wines. Wines of quality, however, will, I suppose, continue to use corks, to allow the wine 'to breathe', although one cannot rule out that one day a silicone (or equivalent) cork will be evolved capable of providing a similar performance as the natural cork.

Nevertheless, concern remains amongst wine producers for the increasingly uneven quality of cork, so much so that some have actually taken to reducing the size of the neck of the bottle so that the area of wine in contact with the cork is lessened.

Computers are taking over. There can now be inserted in corks micro chips which contain all the information that is possibly available about the wine, namely the percentages of grapes, the acidity, the dry residue, etc. which is then very easily read by a scanner giving the whole history of the wine. Probably not something that would be available in common use for the next twenty years or so because it is difficult to conceive of people going to the restaurant carrying a scanner in their pocket to read the microchip on the bottle, but of great use, apparently, for experts.

The two schools of thought concerning corks, the modernists and the traditionalists, are at loggerheads. The advantages of a bottle stopper which will not decay or deteriorate are well appreciated. Cork, especially nowadays when the quality is not so good as previously and quantities are reducing, is a kind of stopper which always carries a certain risk. It can break when being pulled out, it can crumble with the passage of time, it can give the wine a bad taste if of poor quality, it can produce customer complaints which an inert subject matter like silicone is incapable of doing.

At present in Italy, as in other wine-producing countries, there are, as is often the case, two different schools of thought when it comes to using silicone corks. The traditionalists are reluctant to acknowledge their usefulness but to show their reasonableness, are experimenting on a yearly basis. I personally know more than one producer who has set aside a few thousand bottles of high quality wine where silicone corks have been used. I was told that they would wait three or four years before forming a view.

At the other end of the spectrum, there is the more modern, usually younger, type of vintner who has taken silicone to heart, not only because ultimately it is cheaper than cork, but also because the advantages that it offers cannot be discounted.

The truth as usual will lie somewhere in between. Until a silicone cork is found that displays physical, if not, chemical characteristics which are identical to that of cork, the better wines will continue to use the traditional natural cork. The cheaper will, inevitably, use silicone.

What has to be established is an appreciation on the part of the wine buyer of the fact that a silicone cork can be as good as the old fashioned cork-type. The 'environmental' impact of using plastic/silicone corks remains to be determined; insufficient time has elapsed since their introduction and it as not been possible to answer the many questions their use will pose; for example, will there be any point, once a plastic cork is used, in storing bottles horizontally? How long will the artificial cork survive without shedding infinitesimal particles into the liquid? How long will it persist once disposed of? For all I know, it may be that in fifty years' time the world of wine will revert to using the natural product, if there is any still left. Meanwhile, however, there is no doubt that the use of the polypropylene 'cork' is spreading very fast. I recall that one of the top rosé wines of Provence is *now* being bottled with a plastic 'cork'.

I must confess that I do not like plastic corks for a number of reasons. In the first place, I am not even convinced of the common merit claimed for them, namely that they impart no taste whatever to the wine. I dispute that, I think that they can give wine an odd, unpleasant taste.

Secondly, they are more difficult to pull out than the ordinary cork. Thirdly, they are very difficult to re-use because they retain the original shape so that you have to find alternative methods of sealing a half-finished bottle. Lastly, some of them are so hard that they are awkward to release from the screw.

I suppose that the truth is that if traditionalists could be convinced that producing a good wine but using a silicone cork would not be looked upon deprecatingly by those in the know, they would be only too pleased to use plastic corks. The problem is that, for better or for worse, rightly or wrongly, most people tend to associate a 'plastic' cork with an inferior wine. Until that mentality is changed it seems to me that it will be difficult to disabuse the better producers of the notion that the only suitable 'cork' for a good, and especially a great wine, is the one derived from the oak tree.

I have wavered a lot over the last few years in trying to form a view about the development of corks made with material other than the bark of the 'Quercus suber'. I have reached the conclusion that I am psychologically affected by decades of extracting corks from bottles, smelling them, looking at the script or the images on them (the serial number of the bottling plant, the badge of the vintner, the 'bottled at the chateau or whatever' wordings). Granted that with silicone it will be no longer necessary to sniff a cork when it is extracted, I firmly believe that in ten years those who have come to wine for the first time will know no better and I suppose it is probably true to say there will be no need for them to know any better because the technology will have advanced so much that the plastic corks themselves will work in the same way as the natural product.

One final update. Some producers are experimenting even with rubber banded glass corks.

SCREW TOPS

Of course, one should not disregard entirely the screw-top bottles which are becoming more common; I should record however that, as far as I know, it has not yet been suggested that wines that are meant to be stored for longer than six to nine months could usefully be available in screw-top bottles.

The reason is that despite the claims originally made for the simplicity of this type of sealing, screw tops have their own problems if the wine is not to be drunk straight away. Screw cap wines, as they have become known, have a tendency, if kept for too long, to develop sulphidization and this is not necessarily good news for, say, New Zealand producers since 90% of the wines they sell to the UK are said to have metal caps. What happens is that the sulphides, which either exist naturally in the wine or which have been added, will always degrade and, when they do so, produce a compound called thiol which would normally be allowed to escape by the traditional cork stopper but remains in a bottle with a tight fitting seal.

It is not inconceivable that the same problem will occur with silicone corks; that is one of the reasons why, as I have stated above, many Italian producers are keeping silicone capped wines in store for two or three years to see what the effect of the cork is. That is also the reason why studies are being carried out on developing silicone corks which would allow the wine to breathe, like the natural product.

On the other hand, there is no doubt that particularly in the USA, Australia and New Zealand the screw-top method of sealing wine bottles is becoming more and more common and indeed appreciated. It has been calculated that more than half of all New Zealand wine bottles have screw tops with Australia the runner-up and the Americans trying to catch up. The debate as to which is the best method of sealing a wine bottle will undoubtedly continue for many years.

CHAPTER 11

SULPHITES AND OTHER ADDITIVES IN WINE

SULPHUR DIOXIDE (SO_2) – METABISULPHIDE

The reader may be surprised to learn that wine is not such a 'pure' product as one might be tempted to believe because of the absence of a list of ingredients.

Whilst there is still no legal requirement to show the ingredients of wine, the practice has come about of indicating that it contains sulphites (variously spelt as sulphites, sulphide, or sulphite). But wine may contain much more than that. A number of products are needed, apart from yeasts, to ensure that the wine is both presentable in colour, drinkable in flavour and capable of a minimum shelf life.

Apart from the natural addition of Aleppo pine resin that the Greeks make to their white wines to obtain Retsina, many chemicals are used for various purposes. For example:

- To obtain bubbles in sparkling wines, carbon dioxide and ammonium sulphate to stabilize the wine, in addition to a range of sulphur and potassium sulphide, bi-sulphide and meta-sulphide, potassium ferrocyanide and copper sulphate.

- To clarify the wine, gelatines, isinglass, eggshells, albumins, silicone dioxide, and the comparatively harmless bentonite and kaolin.

- To inhibit yeast growths, ascorbic and citric acid as well as potassium sorbate.

- To acidify and for general balance, tartaric acid, potassium tartrite, potassium bicarbonate, potassium bitartrate, and calcium carbonate.

Just imagine if all these 'added ingredients' should be shown on the bottle of wine. . . Admittedly, the quantities can be and mostly are miniscule and particularly now with EEC regulations they are carefully monitored and controlled. But the suspicion must remain that especially in the case of certain persons who are hyper-sensitive (Orientals, asthmatics, and so on) wine need not be such a healthy drink as most of us believe it to be. In any event, nowadays, it has become compulsory to show on all bottles of wine the wording 'contains sulphites' or 'sulphites added' or equivalent.

Wine is a reasonably natural product, if the producer is honest and if it is to be drunk immediately. If, however, it must stand even for a short period of time then it is open to the action of bacteria which will cause it to oxidize or spoil and, as a result, some cleansing agent is needed. Such an agent is sulphur (and its by-products, especially in the form of sulphur dioxide). I recall that there used to be a well-known household product claiming that it 'kills 99% of household germs': in the wine world, sulphur dioxide acts in much the same way.

In Roman times, alongside pitch and resin, sulphur was used in preparing amphorae and other vessels for wine storage, and by the fifteenth century it had become a prerequisite in Germany, laid down by law, for a preparation of sulphur powder, wood shavings, herbs and incense to be burnt in barrels before the barrels themselves could be filled with wine. It was the Dutch who, in the eighteenth century, plying their salt collection run to the estuary of the Garonne, taught or reminded the winemakers of Bordeaux to burn sulphur in barrels to sterilize them. Nothing new in this since the practice was already in existence, there being some vague references to it, not only in literature prior to the first date, 1487, when the German law on sulphur was passed, but also in Homer and Pliny.

This chemical was so effective that people even tried to use it (as copper sulphate) as a means of arresting the phylloxera epidemic which decimated Europe's vineyards from the mid-nineteenth century through to the 1920s, by which time grafting vines onto American rootstocks had saved the day.

A point often forgotten is that fermentation itself produces sulphur dioxide but that may not necessarily be sufficient and more has to be added; indeed, it could be said to be essential, at the time of bottling. The effect of sulphur dioxide on wine is, overall, beneficial. It acts as an antiseptic, a disinfectant and an anti-oxidant. It also makes wine smoother and contributes to the extraction of colour from grapes; not too significant a factor in the case of grapes like Cabernet Sauvignon but quite important, for instance, with Nebbiolo.

This ability results from the fact that sulphur reacts with oxygen and thus inhibits oxidation. In its metabisulphide form it is added to freshly picked grapes where it kills bacteria and natural yeasts. In the actual winemaking process it can assist in extracting compounds from grape skins during maceration of juice and skins.

In bottled wine, it is present in two forms, free sulphur and bound sulphur. The latter, brought about by sulphur reacting with natural compounds in the wine, is imperceptible to both nose and palate. What can occasionally be irritating by producing that typical 'struck match' odour which so readily catches the back of the throat, is the free or unbound sulphur. Rather bizarrely, perhaps, regulations concerning permitted or recommended sulphur levels (see later) usually involve calculating the combined sulphur present even though only free sulphur is likely to affect the drinker's palate or diminish enjoyment.

There has been much criticism of the use and, above all, abuse of sulphur. Indeed, the reader should be reminded that wine labels in the United States of America have carried for some time the forbidding warning 'contains sulfites' and in Australia the wine-maker has to show on the label that sulphur dioxide or 'preservative E220' has been added to the wine. This is now normal practice in Italy, where the wording 'contiene solfiti' usually appears. I suggest that any major concern such as is displayed in the USA and Australia is largely a knee-jerk reaction.

Additives and chemicals in food are fairly common and result from increased commercialization of food production and the modern habit – a bad one, of course – consequent upon eating pre-packed pre-cooked foods. Nowadays, customers are much more conscious about the use of additives and often wince when reading the catalogue of chemicals, colourants, preservatives, flavour enhancers and the like contained on the labels of most pre-packed foods; as a result, there is no doubt that a groundswell reaction against such chemical ingestion is both natural and understandable.

But to argue, as many do, that one should analyse wine into its separate constituent parts and attempt to show the result on the bottle would require the kind of label that would be totally inappropriate since science has so far isolated and identified between 200 and 220 chemical components in wine. It might be a waste of time to read on the bottle so carefully selected on the supermarket shelves that it contains 1 – isopropyl; 2 – methoxyl; 4 – methylbenzene; it may well harm one's enjoyment, although it must be admitted that there is now a tendency to pursue what I would call a compromise solution.

It is gradually becoming more common to find on wine labels, usually though not necessarily on what one might term the second smaller label an indication that not only it contains sulphites or sulphides but also citric acid. Furthermore, some bottles also show the method used in clarification: namely, bentonite, gelatine, filtration.

But this hypersensitivity, if I may say so, to the addition of chemicals to any item that is to be ingested, whether food or wine, is not necessarily a bad thing because, in the first place, it has alerted people to the risks inherent in the chemicals themselves, where such a risk is found to exist; and in the second, it has ensured that the quantities used, where strictly necessary, are kept well under control, so much so that in many cases – especially in California – no added sulphites are used in those wineries confident that all their equipment is thoroughly sterilized and the grapes are of top quality, healthy and unbruised (hand-picking essential).

For example, the Germans were always known to add too much sulphur to their wines, often as much as 500 parts per million. You could usually taste it and smell it. By the 1990s, this quantity had been halved and new winemaking technology is constantly reducing the need to add too much sulphur. There are now clear-cut rules laid down by the European Community. In Italy, the practice, regardless of the colour of the wine, is for the quantity of SO_2 to be lower than 170 milligrams per litre if the residual sugar is lower than 5 grams per litre and 220 milligrams per litre where it is higher than 5 grams. In Spain, the practice is 160 milligrams for red wines and 200 for whites. These quantities are believed to be safe, although they can be exceeded and go up to 260 milligrams per litres in sweet, rosé and white wines.

Indeed, exceptions have to be made for some wines to exceed these amounts. This is especially true of sweet wines, such as Trockenbeerenauslesen, Beerenauslesen (Germany), Sauternes, Jurançon and sweet Loire wines (France). I observe in passing that it is a pity that so far no other system has been evolved to stabilize wine and ensure that it is bacteria free (thus avoiding any possibility of a secondary fermentation in the bottle, particularly likely to occur in sweet wines) other than by the addition of sulphur.

It is often said that there are people who are allergic to sulphur and it has long been known, but remains to be established scientifically, that headaches and hangovers can, in some individuals, either be caused or aggravated by the sulphur in the wine.

I believe that there is no true allergy to wine as such, but have to accept that there are some individuals who might be termed of a high risk group, especially asthmatics, who may be detrimentally affected by wine. Where this happens, it is likely that the sulphur affects them because, in my experience (exception made for those persons of Far Eastern origin who lack a particular enzyme that would allow them to metabolize wine normally) those who claim to be allergic to wine are in all likelihood particularly allergic to the sulphur dioxide contained in it and not to the juice of the grape. Confirmation of this statement is to be found in the fact that, usually, the same people drink non-alcoholic grape juice with no ill effect.

The truth is that it is unlikely that the current low levels of sulphur in wine will cause any real damage, unless excessive quantities are drunk; much higher quantities of sulphur dioxide than in wines can be found in some salads in supermarkets and in some fast food restaurants. Equally it is true that sulphur is needed, regrettable though that fact may be. Too little SO_2 throughout the production process has the effect that wines, especially dry whites, turn towards unpleasant oxidation.

When bottled, the wine will still need protection from oxidation, which means that a reasonable level of SO_2 in the finished product is also essential. Of course, if too much is put in, not only will the high risk individuals already referred to be affected, but the excessive sulphur will be perceivable on the nose: no producer of a good product will want that. Nowadays, it is most unusual for any bottles of good wine to display obvious back-of-the-throat evidence of excessive sulphur dioxide which, in any event, under the rules already adverted to, would be illegal. Occasionally, sniffing a bottle immediately after the cork is drawn can give a whiff of sulphur, but that passes quickly with exposure to the air.

A few German wines still tend towards sulphur taint. Unfortunately, because of the sugar content in such wines being low (little sunshine, I fear) German wines, especially the cheaper ones, are fermented to 11° alcohol and then 'back blended', that is to say some sweet unfermented grape juice is added to increase fruity flavours and soften the taste with residual sugar. Therefore, for exactly the same reason that SO_2 is valuable in true, good quality dessert wines, still German wines that have such an addition of sugars require a higher level of SO_2 which causes the producer often to become over-enthusiastic and to overlook the requirements of European law.

Happily for all lovers of quality, few Italian wines display any sort of problem in this direction mainly because climatic conditions in Italy are such that, generally speaking, grapes ripen well and successfully, thus containing sufficient sugar that may be converted into adequate alcohol. As a result, a feature that is not commonly known, Italian law forbids absolutely the use of sugar to increase alcohol levels in the fermentation of non-sparkling wines, whether white, red, or rosé.

The reader ought to know that this is not the practice prevailing in many other countries of the world. Germany has already been mentioned, but the French themselves are heavily dependent upon the use of added sugar; the need to increase alcohol levels is the principal reason why much Italian wine is exported to France. (More particularly, both in Burgundy and Bordeaux it is not unusual to boost the sugar content to increase the alcohol in the wine. This procedure is known as chaptalization, after a French chemist of the Napoleon era known as Jean Antoine Chaptal.)

One further point for those who are interested in the subject matter: careful studies have shown that non-professionals with exceptionally perceptive palates can pick up SO_2 present in water at levels as low as 11 milligrams per litre; but in wine, for complex chemical reasons, this rises to around 100 milligrams per litre in red wines and 200 milligrams per litre in dry, white wines.

In conclusion, it is, of course, as I have already remarked, a great pity that we have no other way of stabilizing wine than by the addition of a chemical (SO_2); but, labelled as E220, sulphur is present in very many everyday foodstuffs; that may be no consolation for those who hanker after absolute purity of foodstuffs (very seldom indeed to be achieved) and prompts the simple, cynical suggestion: if you are worried about SO_2 levels in wine, drink less of it.

On the other hand, you might prefer drinking only organic wines, for there is no doubt that the sulphur content of wines produced organically (or biologically as they say in France and Italy) is lower. The following table may be useful:

Maximum permitted quantity of SO$_2$ allowed under EEC rules mg per litre (residual sugar content less than 5 gms per litre) 170 (if greater than 5 mgs/lt) 220	
Source: Soil Association (Great Britain)	
Red	90
White	100
Rosé	100
Sparkling	100
Sweet	250
France (Nature et Progrès)	
Red (subject to adjustment in bad vintages)	70
White	70
Rosé	70
Champagne	50
Sweet	200
Italy	
Red	60
White	70
Rosé	70
Sparkling	60

Whilst it is clear that organic producers of wine use lesser quantities of sulphur dioxide, it is equally true that the result of this reduction in SO$_2$ levels may mean needless exposure of customers to faulty wine.

PART II

ITALIAN WINES AND COMMENTARIES

AN A TO Z OF ITALIAN GRAPE VARIETIES

NOTE: Only the principal varieties are listed. The most significant and interesting are shown in bold letters.

ABBUTO

AGLIANICO. This is a vine which is to be found only in southern Italy. (Campania, Basilicata, Puglia and Molise). It has been known for over 1500 years, although it first appears in documents of the sixteenth century. It goes to making red wines and is known by various names, depending on the locality where it is grown. The wine itself can be a blended product depending on the area of production so that in Puglia it is known as Castel del Monte Rosso, in Campania it goes into the DOCG Taurasi as well as in another well-known Italian red (and rosé) which, as far as I can tell, is difficult to fmd abroad, namely Solopaca. In Molise, it is known as Molise Aglianico and in Basilicata it becomes the Aglianico del Vulture.

ALBANA. There are two theories as to why it is so called: either because it originated in the Albani hills south of Rome or, less likely, as a derivation from the Latin adjective 'albus', meaning white. This goes into making sweet wine and, depending on where it is found, it is also known as Albana di Romagna, Albana di Forli, Albana Gentile or Albana di Bertinoro.

ALBANELLO

ALBAROLA

ALEATICO. This is a black variant of the Muscat, a vine which the Greeks introduced into Italy. It is grown mainly in Tuscany but also in Campania, Lazio, Puglia and Sicilia where it is blended with local vines.

ALESSANO

ALIONZA

ANSONICA (INZOLIA in Sicily)

ANCELLOTTA

ARNEIS. This is a white grape which has been known since the fifteenth century. It is grown mainly in Piemonte adjacent to the River

Tanaro in the Roero district.

ASPRINIA

BARBAROSSA

BARBERA. This is a typical Italian black grape widespread throughout Piemonte and producing a variety of strong red wines, (Monferrato, Alba, Asti, Oltrepó Pavese). It is quite prolific but is not found in any other part of the world save in California, Argentina and other South American countries. The first reference to it dates back to 1609. Apart from Piemonte and Lombardia, there is some to be found in Campania, Emilia Romagna and Sardegna.

BELLONE/A

BELVERMINO

BIANCA DI CANDIA

BIANCAME

BIANCHETTA

BIANCO D'ALESSANO

BIANCOLELLA

BIANCONE

BLANC DE MORGEX

BOMBINO. These are both white and red vines about whose origins little is known, save that they are grown mainly in southern Italy and especialy in Puglia. Bombino is also known at times as Trebbiano d'Abruzzo and as Pagadebit (alternatively 'Stracciacambiali') in Emilia Romagna.

BONARDA. This is a black grape variety, also known as Croatina and Uva Rara. It goes into a number of outstanding Piedmontese wines such as the Gattinara, and the Ghemme, as well as others which I am not reviewing, namely Sizzano, Boca, Lessona, Fara and Bramaterra. It is fairly well known in Argentina, used for blending, especially with Malbet.

BONVINO

BOSCO

BRACHETTO. This is a fine red grape, which is used almost exclusively to produce the wine mentioned. Occasionally, especially in the Roero area, one may find a few producers who actually make a dry wine out of the Brachetto grape.

BRUGNOLA

CACCHIONE

CAGNULARI

CALABRESE

CANAIOLO. This is the principal Tuscan grape, a component of the two Chiantis. It is found almost exclusively in Toscana and in Umbria and, in both regions, a white variety is also available.

CANNONAU. This is a black grape imported into Sardegna by the Spaniards in the fifteenth century. In Spain, it continues to be known as Garnacha (in Seville, Canonazo) and, of course, as lovers of French wine well know, in France and in the old French dependencies as Grenache. It is also otherwise known as CARIGNANO, CARME-NERE, CARRICANTE, CATANESE.

CASETTA

CATARRATTO. This is a very old Sicilian vine yielding the white grapes that go into making, amongst others, the white Alcamo and Marsala wines.

CESANESE (DEL PIGLIO OR OF AFFILE)

CHIAVENNASCA

CILIEGIOLO

CIRÓ

CODA DI VOLPE. This is an old variety from Campania which goes to make both the Greco di Tufo and the Falanghina, as well as another well-known Italian wine which unfortunately is not commonly available, namely the white Solopaca.

COCOCCIOLA

COLORINO

CORTESE. This is the Italian white grape variety which most resembles Chardonnay. It goes to make one of the best Italian whites by the same name.

CORVINA. (Otherwise known as Rondinella or Molinara.) This red grape variety is the glory of the Veneto region where it goes into Bardolino, Valpolicella, Recioto and Amarone wines. There is an argument that Rondinella and Molinara are two distinct varieties.

CROATINA

DAMASCHINO

DOLCETTO. Dolcetto is a typical Piedmontese variety of red grape which is grown quite extensively. Some of it can be found in Liguria and in the Valle D'Aosta. The different varieties of wine that it produces are considered elsewhere in this guide. Notable is the fact that the bunch is usually 'Y' shaped.

DRUPEGGIO

DURELLO

ENANTICO (Probably a synonym of 'Lambrusco' (q.v.))

ERBALUCE. This grape was known to the Romans who called it 'Alba Lux', namely the 'light of dawn'. It is found almost exclusively in Piemonte but, in fact, it is believed to originate in southern Italy in the Fiano (q.v.). The Fiano wine comes from Campania and competes with the Greco di Tufo; interestingly, the Erbaluce variety is sometimes known as Greco Novarese.

FALANGHINA. This is a grape variety from Campania, well-known to the Romans. It is white and goes into a good Italian white, namely the Falanghina, although it is also used as a blend.

FAVORITA A clone of the more popular Vermentino, this grape is grown almost exclusively in the Roero region of Piedmont. It produces rather large attractively shaped green grapes which are much appreciated in the area as a table variety, hence the name 'favoured'. The wine itself (q.v.) although known since the seventeenth century, has acquired popularity only fairly recently. Its use by the locals as an aperitif in particular is spreading.

FIANO. This is a white variety that at one stage was practically extinct, but has recently been revived in Campania, in the area of Avellino, thanks to the efforts of Antonio Mastroberardino. Fiano appears in different varieties, although the principal one is that of Avellino, but there is also a Fiano from the Sannio (province of Benevento).

FOGARINA

FORASTERA

FORTANA

FRANCAVIDDA

FRAPPATO

FREISA

FUMIN

GAGLIOPPO. This is widely planted in Calabria, although it can be found in limited amounts in Campania, Marche, Sicilia and Umbria. It reached Italy with the Greeks and goes into making the most notable wine of Calabria, namely the red Ciró.

GAMBELLARA

GARGANEGA. This is a white grape believed to be of Greek origin scattered, though in small quantities, in most regions of Italy, but having found its true home in the Veneto. It goes into producing one of the best known Italian wines, namely Soave, as well as the Gambellara, Recioto di Soave and the Bianco di Custoza.

GIANNIELLO

GIRÓ (DI CAGLIARI)

GRECANICO

GRECHETTO

GRECO. Together with its brothers Grecanico and Grechetto, this is one of the most important grapes of southern Italy, mainly white but also red. It is not to be found in any other part of Italy and is, of course, of Greek origin. It produces some outstanding white wines – Greco di Tufo, Fiano di Avellino – and is fairly unique. It seems to appreciate the volcanic soil of the area. It has, however, extended as far as the Lazio region where it is known as Vignanello Greco from the name of the town near Rome around which most of it is produced. There is also a Grechetto (q.v.) wine in Umbria.

GRIGNOLINO. This is a typically Piedmontese black variety cultivated mainly in the Asti and Monferrato areas. Sometimes known as Nebbiolo Rosato or Rossetto, the wine that it produces, which is described, was much appreciated by the Italian Royal Court of Savoy because of its lightness, which married up quite well with the rather heavy cuisine of the time.

GRILLO

GROPPELLO

GUARNACCIA

IMPIGNO

INCROCIO MANZONI – A comparatively new hybrid

INZOLIA. This is a Sicilian native which goes into the making of Marsala wine. It is to be found under a different name, Ansonica, in Toscana and on the isle of Elba.

ISABELLA

LACRIMA DI MORRO

LAGREIN

LAMBRUSCO. The name is derived from the Vitis Labrusca of the Romans which produces a variety of Lambrusco wines, all quite closely related and yet with different features and growing in different areas. The resultant wine is red or perhaps, slightly rosé/cherry-coloured.

LIMASSINA

LUGLIESE

MACERATINO

MAGLIOCCO

MAIOLINA

MALVASIA. This is a grape that is grown in both the black and the white variety. It is the equivalent of the Malmsey and it is believed that it is of Greek origin. It found its way to Italy thanks to the Venetians and, indeed, it spread to the whole of the Mediterranean basin. There are many varieties. The white is to be found in Puglia, Calabria, Sicilia, Lazio, Chianti, Emilia Romagna and as far north as Friuli-Venezia Giulia and west as Sardegna. The red is found mainly in Piemonte where it goes to make the Malvasia di Casorzo, amongst others, and in Trentino Aldo Adige, although there is much red Malvasia grown in Puglia and Basilicata.

MAMMOLO

MANGIAGUERRA

MARZEMIINO. This is a variety that grows mainly in the Veneto. It is an unusual black variety distinguished by its very small size (the ending 'ino' is the Italian suffix for diminutive things) and produces a fine table wine of deep garnet red colour which some have described as having a taste of vanilla, as well as a lesser rosé.

MAMMOLO

MASSARDA

MONICA

MONTEPULCIANO. As pointed out elsewhere, this grape variety has nothing to do with the town of Montepulciano where the Vino Nobile is produced. It is now quite well established that it originated in the Abruzzo and from there, a century or more ago, it spread into Lazio, Marche and Puglia.

This variety is somewhat underrated in Italy, having so far been considered inferior to the Sangiovese (q.v.). Recent developments, however, are tending to rehabilitate it. Apart from the local wine by the same name, the grape is used in many blended wines from Lazio, it goes into the Rosso Conero of the Marche and is very common in Puglia, especially in the province of Foggia. It yields a first class black grape.

MOSCATO. This is predominantly a white grape variety but there are also black versions which are considered at length in the text and whose name has given rise to much speculation, the latest suggestion as to its etymology being that it might even derive from the Latin 'Muscum' meaning 'moss'. It is to be found extensively in Italy, from north-west to south-east and it acquires the name of the regions where it is produced, e.g. in Toscana, the Moscadello di Montalcino, in Puglia as Moscato di Trani or Moscato Reale and in Sicilia where it is known as Zibibbo. It is also the classic ingredient of the Moscato di Pantelleria. Its principal area of production, however, is Piemonte where it yields the two classic DOCGs of the area, namely the Asti Spumante and the Moscato d'Asti. In its black variety it emerges as the Moscato Rosa (Rosen Muscateller) which is well known in north-east Italy.

NASCO

NEBBIOLO. This is one of the staple grapes of Italy and produces some of its best wines (Barolo, Barbaresco, Gattinara, Ghemme, Nebbiolo). It is a strong red grape, the bunch being almost T-shaped and fairly long. It is interesting to observe that this grape was initially used to produce a sweet wine. It was only in the second half of the nineteenth century that, thanks to the effort of the then Prime Minister of Italy, Camillo Benso Count of Cavour, the situation changed and it was 'converted' into some excellent dry wines. It is a variety that has been exported successfully to Mexico, where it grows as a clone that is only available there and which, in fact, represents the foundation stone of the Mexican wine industry. The grape is also used to produce the red Roero and the wines of the Valtellina, namely Grumello, Inferno, Sassella and Sfursat.

NEGRARA

NEGROAMARO. This is another of the black varieties introduced into Italy, according to some, by the Greeks but, in the view of more chauvinistic Italian ampelographers, is indigenous to Puglia. It is certainly a fundamental grape for the region, especially in the areas of Brindisi and Lecce and is a component of one of the wines that are considered in this guide, namely the now popular Nero d'Avola.

NERELLO MANTELLATO

NERELLO MASCALESE

NERO D'AVOLA. This, too, is an indigenous vine which produces the characteristic blackcurrant-flavoured red wines which are typical of Sicilia. Indeed, this region is the only one where the Nerello Mascalese is to be found blended ever more frequently nowadays to Cabernet Sauvignon, Merlot and Syrah, whereas previously it was mainly associated with Sangiovese. It is also found in small quantities in Calabria where it is known as Calabrese d'Avola.

NOCERA

NOSIOLA

NURAGUS

OLIVELLA

ORTRUGO

OSELETA

OTTAVIANELLO

PALOMBINA

PAMPANUTO

PASCALE

PASSERINA

PASSOLARA

PECORINO

PEDEVENDA

PELAVERGA

PERRICONE

PETIT ROUGE (Despite the name which would tend to support the claim of some writers that the vine originates in Burgundy, the more likely view is that this is an indigenous variety of the Valle d'Aosta.)

PICOLIT

PIEDELUNGO

PIEDICOLOMBO

PIEDIROSSO

PIGATO

PIGNOLA/PIGNOLETTO

PIGNOLO

PINOT (Bianco and Grigio). Neither is an Italian variety, but it is mentioned here simply because of the popularity of these two Italian whites in many countries of the world.

PRIMITIVO. Considerable doubt exists as to where this black grape variety originated, but the debate is really academic since it is so obviously an Italian grape. Whether it came from Dalmatia or elsewhere, it emigrated from Italy to California where it was renamed Zinfandel. The grape is to be found in Campania where it is the main ingredient of the Falerno del Massico, as well as of the Cilento Rosato but its principal claim to glory is that it is the staple of the Primitivo di Manduria (q.v.).

PRIORE

PROSECCO. This white grape variety seems to have originated near Trieste, but it quickly was transplanted moving into Veneto. The

'Prosecco' (q.v.) is one of the better known Italian sparkling wines.

RABOSO

REFOSCO

RIBOLLA GIALLA

ROLLO

ROMANESCO

RONDINELLA

ROSSESE/ROSSOLA

ROSSIGNOLA

RUCHÉ

SAGRANT1NO

SANGIOVESE. This is one of the best known Italian black grapes, the equivalent in a sense of Pinot Noir, which goes primarily into the making of all kinds of Chianti wine, as well as into the Brunello di Montalcino, the Vino Nobile di Montepulciano, the Morellino di Scansano, the Carmignano (Chianti), the Montescudaio and the Bolgheri Sassicaia, the first 'super Tuscan' to be granted a DOC in 1994. The vine, however, is cultivated outside Tuscany quite extensively in Emilia Romagna (Sangiovese di Romagna), in the Marche (Rosso Piceno) and in Umbria (Torgiano Rosso). Small quantities of Sangiovese are to be found in some parts of the New World, especially California and Argentina, where experiments are taking place to exploit its potential.

SAN LUNARDO

SANTA ANNA

SCHIAVA

SCHIOPPETTINO

SCIANCINOSO

SEMURANO

SERRIDANO

SOMARELLO

SOMMESE

SORICELLA

SPANNA

STREPPAROSSA

SUSUMANIELLO

TASCA

TAZZELENGHE

TEROLDEGO

TERRANO

TIMORASSO

TINTORE

TOCAI FRIULANO. Despite the objections of Hungarian wine producers, who claim that the name has been appropriated from their own Tokay, this is, in fact, an Italian indigenous variety which was originally known simply as Tocai and to which the qualification Friulano was added fairly recently to appease Hungary. It is also known as Tocai Italiano. The confusion seems to have arisen because of the long-standing (ever since the year 1000) exchanges brought about by the Italian missionaries who went to Hungary and probably, as is maintained by some, by the fact that an Italian titled lady in the seventeenth century married a Hungarian nobleman and took with her cuttings of the local Italian grape. Be that as it may. The 'Tocai Friulano', which sooner or later will become known simply as Friulano so that everybody will be happy, is a component of the local Tocai but also of the Bianco di Custoza from Piemonte and of the sister wine of Soave, namely the Lugana (q.v.). For the record, there is also a fairly new Tocai Rosso, but this is undoubtedly not an indigenous variety.

TORBIANA

TRAMINER AROMATICO (Gewürztraminer)

TREBBIANO. Known in other regions of Italy also as Biancame and Procanico, this is a very typical Italian grape that goes to make a great quantity of white wines which, unfortunately for the reputation of the vine, are not always that distinguished. Its plantings are very extensive and for that reason it competes with the Spanish Airen for the first place as the most widely grown grape in the whole world. It is a staple of well known Italian wines such as (Soave, Verdicchio, Frascati) but the name is retained in the Trebbiano Romagnolo, the Trebbiano di Soave and the Trebbiano Toscano. If one were unkind one could say that its main virtue is to be distilled into either brandy, cognac, armagnac or other high alcoholic products, but this would be unfair. Attempts are now being made in Italy to rehabilitate this grape and with more modern vinification techniques it is certain, in my view, that it will produce some very fine whites.

UGHETTA

UVA DI TROIA

UVA RARA (Croatina)

UVA ROSA

VERDICCHIO. This is a very well-known indigenous Italian variety which also goes under the name of Trebbiano di Soave or Trebbiano di Lugana. Under these names it is quite common in Veneto but in the Marche the Verdicchio grape represents a substantial proportion of the overall wine production. It is a popular and versatile grape.

VERDECA

VERDELLO

VERDINO

VERDONE

VERDUZZO

VERMENTINO. Tradition has it that this white grape variety originates in Spain whence it emigrated to Corsica and from Corsica reached Italy in the fifteenth century. The grape is rather like the little girl of the curl in the middle of her forehead: when it is good, it is very good; when it is bad, it is fairly horrid. I have already made some comments about the resultant wine but it is undoubtedly a grape that cannot be ignored. Incidentally, there is also a black variety but it is scarce and is found only in Liguria and in Toscana. The Vermentino grape is very common in Liguria where it is also a component of a wine which I have not mentioned in this guide, namely the Sciacchetrá delle Cinque Terre which is a fine, strong wine, semi-dry or sweet, with a minimum alcoholic content of 17°. Whilst the grape also goes into the blends for a number of Tuscan whites, it is much more at home in Sardegna where it is supposed to have arrived in the very early part of the twentieth century, and where it has become firmly established in the northern part of the island, the Gallura.

VERNACCIA. This comes in two white varieties and one black. The black is fairly limited in scope and is the staple of the DOC Vernaccia di Serrapetrona (q.v.). The white variety goes to make the Vernaccia di San Gimignano (q.v.) and the Vernaccia di Oristano, two completely different wines, in performance and in origin. The Vernaccia di San Gimignano is said to have become established in the area round about the year 1250 and is produced over a comparatively small acreage of Toscana (less than a thousand hectares). The Vernaccia di Oristano seems to have followed a different route, since despite the fact that most historians believe that it came over from Spain, there are some who claim that it was introduced directly into Sardinia by the Phoenicians. Whichever way one looks at it, it is an important variety.

VESPAIOLO

VIEN DE NUS

VESPOLINA
ZIBIBBO

A SELECT LIST OF ITALIAN WINES AND THEIR CHARACTERISTICS

G iven the numbers quoted in the Preface, it would have been unduly cumbersome to list *all* the Italian wines circulating in the Anglo-American markets (there are said to be more than 1,000), especially since these include not only DOC, DOCG and IGT but also ordinary table wines. For example, there are over 150 Sicilian wines of one kind or the other (IGT, DOC and table wines) which can be purchased in the United Kingdom alone. The reader will no doubt appreciate that, inevitably, a selection had to be made and DOC and DOCG wines have been favoured. To the best of my knowledge all these are included in the list that follows, together with some IGTs, and a few other important wines. As a result, the listing of table wines has suffered but it is believed that a sufficient flavour is provided to enable the reader to perhaps identify types of wine and maybe even grapes and thus relate them back to the region where they originate. The author and publisher will, nevertheless, be grateful for the notification of any omissions.

Also to be borne in mind is the fact that, although a variety of grape may originate in one part of the country, it can be planted elsewhere. The most obvious present-day examples are the increased plantings of Cabernet and Chardonnay outside the original area of production (north-east Italy). So one finds a Cabernet and a Chardonnay as table wines (given the principles that have been expounded they do not qualify for any DOC appellation and probably not even for an IGT) in Sicilia, in Puglia and even in Basilicata. This is understandable: they are all areas where, because of weather conditions, the vine grows well and abundantly, and the local producers have jumped onto the bandwagon of what is fashionable.

Many plantings of Sauvignon have, over the past decade, been made in Sicilia and the resultant wines, though not great, are not to be ignored.

It must be admitted that occasionally some of these transplantings are very successful, although in the majority of cases they are almost meaningless in terms of quality.

One final matter. Whilst it is exceptionally difficult to provide an accurate estimate of what a particular wine will cost, since retailers have different pricing structures, I have tried to assist by showing a very general price band description at the foot of each individual wine description.

This is worked out as follows: (£1 = $1.85)

Band A – wines in the lowest price range up to £5 (US $9)
Band B – between £5-£8 (US$9-$14)
Band C – £8-£12 (US$14-$22)
Band D – £12-£20 (US$22-US$37)
Band E – above £20 (US$37)

AGLIANICO DEL VULTURE [DOC / Red / Basilicata]

The vines of the Vulture at times compete with those of the Aosta Valley as being amongst the highest planted in Europe.

This wine, the only noteworthy red from the region of Basilicata in the heel of Italy, is an unusual but outstanding product, and only obtained DOC status in 1971 although the Aglianico grape, one of the Greek varieties, has been around since time immemorial. Indeed, its very name is a corruption of 'Hellenico'. It is produced mainly in the province of Potenza (communes of Rionero, Barile, Venosa and Rapolla, amongst others) on the slopes of the extinct volcano Mount Vulture from vines which were most unfairly neglected for many years and were only rehabilitated by the hard work and imagination of the d'Angelo brothers. The considerable experience gained on their estate since its foundation in 1936, ultimately produced a wine whose fame is deservedly spreading at both national and international level. It has a very marked red colour, a fragrant, vinous scent and a very dry and heart-warming slightly acidic and very tannic taste which softens considerably with age, producing a colour veering towards orange.

The best description I can give of its taste, when it is not too earthy, is that it reminds one of strawberries. It lends itself to ageing (probably not more than 8-10 years) and has a minimum alcoholic content of 11.5°, rising to 14.5°. By law, it must be matured for a minimum of one year, but if the alcoholic content exceeds 12.5° and the period of maturity three years, it is entitled to be described as 'vecchio'. If matured for longer than five years it is to be described as Riserva.

Sometimes referred to as 'the Barolo of the South', it is an excellent companion to meats and hot dishes generally. Locally, it is often combined with lamb stew and small onions (or shallots) in a dish known as 'cutturiddu'.

An outstanding Aglianico, made partly from ungrafted grapes more than a hundred years old, is known as Serpico, from Irpinia in the province of Avellino, Campania. This is an exceptionally fine and strong-smelling wine, tasting of cherries and plums, although some might consider it a little too oaked. Not being produced in the original area of Basilicata it only qualifies for an IGT appellation.

There are other types of Aglianico wines made in various areas of Campania, some equally valuable; for instance, the Aglianico del Taburno made also with Piedirosso grapes (15%).

Only one DOC wine in Basilicata; but what a wine! It deserves to be number one in this List.

Band B

ALBANA DI ROMAGNA   [DOCG / White / Emilia Romagna]

This wine is produced from the grape by the same name in the provinces of Bologna, Forlí and Ravenna. It used to be said that the only good Albana came from the village of Bertinoro (there is a pun here because the name of the village is taken from the Italian expression 'to drink you in gold'). This is a well-known white, and some would say the best in the region, although the famous Luigi Veronelli is on record as saying that it is a wine 'which enjoys greater fame than it really deserves'; but he may be wrong. Indeed, there were many raised eyebrows when in 1987 it achieved DOCG status.

Undoubtedly, however, the elevation of what I would describe with some conviction as a modest wine from Emilia Romagna to DOCG status in 1987 did take a number of commentators by surprise and a famous English wine writer and Master of Wine, as well as Italian expert, went on the record as saying: '. . . this very selection has done much to tarnish the lustre of DOCG'.

Straw-coloured veering to golden as it matures, with amber reflections and an unmistakable nose of the Albana grape, its taste is dry, essentially, slightly tannic but very harmonious and, oddly enough, slightly sweetish to the palate even in the dry version. It is a full-bodied but soft wine having a minimum alcoholic content of 11.5° but more often found at 12°-12.5°. It ages well, and is available in an 'Amabile' (semi-sweet) version as well as in a fully sweet one.

There is also a 'Passito' at 15.5° alcohol and with wines subjected to light 'Appassimento', a Romagna Albana Spumante which is a golden yellow sparkling wine with a very intense flavour, sweet and a minimum alcoholic content of 15°. Non-DOC Albana wines are made in various villages of Emilia Romagna.

I should point out that there is also a white wine from Tuscany known as Albano which is not considered here. The two should not be confused.

Band C

ALCAMO   [DOC / White / Sicilia]

The Alcamo Plain in western Sicily is in reality an ocean of vines where, in addition to indigenous varieties such as Catarratto, Inzolia (called locally Ansonica) and Grillo, we find rather unusual plantings of 'northern' neighbours like Müller Thurgau and Sauvignon Blanc. This wine originates in the area of Alcamo from which it derives its name and is to be found in the provinces of Palermo and Trapani, where it is held in high esteem.

It is a blend of a variety of grapes, more particularly Catarratto

(minimum 60%), the remainder being made up of Ansonica (or Inzolia), Grillo, Grecanico, Chardonnay, Müller Thurgau, Sauvignon (to a maximum of 40%) and/or other local grapes such as Damaschino (to a maximum of 20%). It is straw coloured, not too heavily so, with greenish tinges, a very fruity, vinous nose and a fresh taste. Minimum alcoholic content 11°. It is also available as a sparkling wine. From the same general area are a rosé, a sparkling rosé, a 'novello' and a red.
Band A

ALEATICO DI PORTOFERRAIO   [IGT / Red / Elba-Toscana]

This is a fine sweet wine which may suffer in popularity because it does not appear to travel well despite its fairly high alcoholic content. It is produced on the island of Elba, about six miles off the Toscana mainland, and is made from the vine named Aleatico (probably a variant of black muscat grape), subjected to 'appassimento' either in the open air or in special buildings. Its colour varies from a strong ruby to an exceptionally deep red. It has a very marked, characteristic nose, is full-bodied with a taste ranging from the demi-sweet to the sweet.

A dessert or pudding wine, its minimum alcoholic content is 16° but it can be found at a higher level. It is a fine sweet wine to enjoy after a meal if one is fortunate enough to come across it. It lends itself to moderate ageing and not too much to chilling; in fact, a serving temperature around 13/14°C would seem the most appropriate for this mellow, friendly dessert wine.

Iron ore has been mined on Elba since the days of the Etruscans and smelting furnaces on the island have resulted in reddish iron deposits in many parts. The mining has been phased out and is now practically non-existent; because of these deposits, however, it is said that wines grown on Elba contain higher than usual, beneficial phospho ferrous and arsenious compounds.

Unfortunately, the extent of cultivation of the Aleatico grape, essentially a Muscat type originating probably on Crete, appears to be reducing.

Aleatico is a wine that is to be found in other regions of Italy, always in the sweet, high alcoholic content, liqueur-type; more particularly, there are Aleaticos of Vulture (Basilicata), Gradoli, Terracina and Montefiascone (Lazio), Monte Argentario (on land opposite the island of Giglio in the province of Grosseto, Toscana), Pitigliano (again in the province of Grosseto) and of Puglia, this last one having an alcoholic content as high as 20° which allows it to age well (up to twenty years).
Band D

ALGHERO   [DOC / Red / White / Sardegna]

Until the end of the last century the Alghero area was really a marshland. In 1899, two Piedmontese – an engineer, Erminio Sella and a lawyer Edgardo Mosca – decided that they wanted a change of lifestyle and took to viticulture. They converted marshland into vineyards and set up their eponymous firm in an area which until then had been quite unaccustomed to agricultural ventures, the coastal plain being inhospitably bleak and windswept. Nevertheless, despite the problems associated with the geographical nature of the location, their venture was quite successful.

The Alghero grouping of wines includes in addition to Torbato (q.v.) the Sauvignon Blanc known as Le Arenarie and an excellent red, Tanca Farrá. Anghelu Ruju and the Cabernet Sauvignon Marchese di Villamarina are considered separately.

These are made from a number of grapes ('recommended' and 'authorized') in the regional specifications and emerge in white, rosé, red, sparkling, Passito and liqueur version. Some of them are available either under the DOC, rather generic, label of Alghero (white and rosé); but much more worthwhile are the reds. The rosé is also first class.

Band A

AMARONE (See Valpolicella)

ANGHELU RUJU   [Red / Sardegna]

We owe this wine to Erminio Sella of Alghero fame who first experimented with vine cuttings from Portugal's Douro Valley but after many failed attempts replaced them with Cannonau, a local grape.

To produce this wine, the grapes are gently fermented to about 8° alcohol and thereafter fortified with wine alcohol up to 18° or 19° before being aged for five years in 7,000-litre oak casks. After that period of time they are bottled and released onto the market.

This is a great, though less well known than it deserves to be, dessert wine, produced from grapes of the Cannonau variety which are especially hand-picked and dried in the sun for a minimum period of one week, almost exclusively in vineyards surrounding the prehistoric town of Anghelu Ruju, about five miles north of Alghero.

It is one of the Italian answers to port wine (the other possible candidates are Aleatico di Portoferraio, Barolo Chinato, Malvasia di Casorzo, and di Castelnuovo Don Bosco, Marsala Vergine, Recioto Amarone and Vin Santo Toscano, all considered later), and it stands the comparison quite well. It is of a deep ruby red, often described as having the colour of a cardinal's robe, with an intense nose redolent of spices, mainly cinnamon, and nuts. It is a full bodied, rich, harmonious wine, having a minimum alcoholic content of 18° and more commonly 19°.

Band D

ANSONICA COSTA DELL'ARGENTARIO
                                    [DOC / White / Toscana]

The sister wine of the Ansonica from the islands of Elba and Giglio, but made on the mainland in the southern part of the province of Grosseto, in the areas of Orbetello, Capalbio and Monte Argentario, with 85% 'Ansonica' grapes and the balance consisting of various authorized others.

It is similar in every respect to the other Ansonica wine save that perhaps it is fruitier in nose and in taste, more balanced and, ultimately,

a better wine.
Band A

ANSONICA   [White / Elba-Toscana]

The 'Ansonica' grape originates in Sicily (where it is known as Inzolia) whence it reached the island of Elba and its adjacent, smaller sister island of Giglio. It is very much a local wine derived from the original Ansonica to a minimum of 85% with the addition of Trebbiano and, occasionally, Vermentino.

It is amber coloured with a very intense nose and a taste veering from the dry to the semi-dry. It has a minimum alcoholic content of 11.5° but it can reach 13°. It does not age well and a general recommendation is that it should be drunk no later than one year after it has been made.

Band A

ARNEIS (or Roero)   [DOCG / White / Piemonte]

It is not unfair to say that Piemonte, the best and top wine-producing area of Italy, is not famous for its whites. Its glories are the reds (Barolo, Barbaresco, Dolcetto, Barbera, Freisa and so on). It is probably because of this that over the past two decades serious attempts have been made to rehabilitate the region's white wines, which have certainly proved successful as far as Arneis is concerned.

This is a straw-coloured white wine with a fine intense aroma and a delicate taste, which often reminds one of Sauvignon. It may be oaked, and it has a minimum alcoholic content of 10.5°; it comes from the area known as the Langhe (q.v.) and is made exclusively with the Arneis grapes.

The Arneis was originally a poor, uneven yielder and, until recently, the quantities of this wine appeared to be reducing. The position, however, has changed. Not only has the wine become much better known, with increased plantings of a grape which started out in life as almost a runt of the litter, but the quality has improved dramatically. Some writers believe it is related to the Vermentino.

The name Arneis, derived from a Piedmontese dialect word 'arneis', is the local rendering of the Italian 'arnese' which has an ordinary meaning of 'tool' and a derogatory one of something not good, a man not to be trusted. It is first mentioned in 1478, but did not progress much until modern times.

When re-plantings of this old local grape were made after the First World War, the locals did not believe that they would be too successful because of its uneven yields; indeed, they were pleased to call it Arneis meaning something fairly rough and not too pleasant.

The name stuck, the grape continued to develop, but slowly, and it had to wait for its rehabilitation until well after the Second World War. It is now very popular in its area of production, namely the Roero hills and there are many more plantings of it. So much so that even in certain characteristic regions of the Roero, best known over decades for their plantings of Nebbiolo, such as Castagnito and others, recent years have seen the uprooting of old Nebbiolo vines and their replacement with Arneis. Fashion has an uncanny and, some might say, unfortunate habit of prevailing over tradition.

When confronted with this fact, traditionalists say that it is not that the Arneis grape is taking over, but that in reality the Nebbiolo vines uprooted were not of high quality. The fact has now received governmental endorsement because in November 2004 the wine changed denomination from DOC to DOCG.

The production area comprises nineteen communes in the province of Cuneo but vinification is allowed in a much wider area embracing a further twenty communes always in the province of Cuneo (which, incidentally, is not only the largest province in the whole of Italy, but is in my opinion the most important). They have certainly been proved right because the accolade of a DOCG was also extended to its red version (considered here under the heading Roero). Whichever way one looks at it, however, the progress made by Arneis/Roero both in its white as well as in the red versions (q.v.) has been substantial.

It is produced throughout the area surrounding Canale. It is a straw-coloured wine with amber shading, delicately grass-scented, dry and slightly bitter with a minimum alcoholic content of 10.5°. A pleasant wine, often served as an aperitif in the Langhe region. It is also available in a sparkling version.

Some 4 million bottles of it were sold in 2005, and it is variously described as Arneis or Arneis Roero or Roero or Roero di Arneis.

There is available a fairly scarce but most enjoyable red Roero (q.v.) made with a small addition (no more than 5%) of Arneis grape to Nebbiolo. There is also a sparking version of Arneis. The DOCG classification applies to that as well.

Band B

ASPRINIO DI AVERSA (or *Asprino di Aversa*)

[DOC / White / Campania]

The wines of Campania are probably less appreciated today than they were in Roman times yet it is worth remembering that the vine has been grown in this region for thousands of years.

The Asprinio grape is a typical 'Neapolitan' variety to be found in a number of communes in the provinces of Caserta and Naples. It goes to make, in a minimum percentage of 85% (the remainder being white, non-aromatic grapes), a very pleasant table wine, straw-coloured with greenish tinges, occasionally veering to golden, with an intense, pleasant nose, typically strongly fruity (some writers have identified in its flavour both apples and grapefruits) with well-balanced acidity and a minimum alcoholic content of 10.5° (more often found at 11.5°).

The grapes are grown in a particular fashion, namely vertically in what is known as the 'alberata aversana', often a selling point, which is mandatory labelling information.

This very pleasant white wine, which is also available in a sparkling version, can be found in areas other than Aversa, always in the province of Naples. In particular, that of Frattamaggiore (or 'Fratta' for short)

has been particularly well known for well over a century.
Band A/B

ASTI SPUMANTE *(See Moscato)*

AVERSA *(See Asprinio di Aversa)*

BARBARESCO   [DOCG / Red / Piemonte]

This is, with Barolo, Brachetto, Gattinara and Ghemme, one of the glories of Piedmontese reds, grown over a comparatively small area of about 500 hectares of vineyards.

It is often compared to Barolo but the two wines are quite dissimilar, although produced with exactly the same grape, one of the principal varieties in Italy, the Nebbiolo (a grape producing much tannin but from which the extraction of colour can often be problematical). The Barbaresco takes its name from the village of origin, namely Barbaresco in the province of Cuneo (although it is also produced in adjacent areas such as Neive – outstanding wines – and Treiso) but the resultant product is different in all likelihood because of the different soil. Whilst both have an alcoholic content of between 13° and 14°, the Barolo seems a much tougher wine and much more suited to very strong roasts and game. The Barbaresco on the other hand strikes one as slightly less imposing, though possibly more elegant, not only because of its lower alcohol minimum requirement (12.5° as opposed to 13° for Barolo) and lesser period of ageing (two years of which one must be in wood) four years and two years in the case of a 'Riserva' compared with the three years (of which two must be in wood) for Barolo, five and three years respectively for the 'Riserva'; but probably because it is grown in different soil on gentler sloping terrain. One could say that there are feminine and masculine differences between the two wines: these have led to Barbaresco being known in Italy as the queen of wines alongside Barolo's description as 'the king' of wines.

It is of ruby red colour veering to orange when aged, with a very marked and pleasant nose, and a dry smooth taste which reminds one of the scent of violets.

Like Barolo, it is a trifle rough when young but improves with ageing: it is not unusual to taste an outstanding Barbaresco, after five years, though it will continue to improve up to ten or more.

There is a myth that the Nebbiolo grapes produce good wines only if they are rather dark, almost inky black. This is seldom true: an honest, unblended with other grapes or with wines from southern Italy, Nebbiolo wine, is seldom deep in colour.

The Nebbiolo grape is quite versatile and, surprisingly, lends itself to blending with other varieties. In the Langhe area, it has been used to produce excellent reds which, because of the area of production and other requirements, cannot qualify as Barolo, Nebbiolo or Barbaresco. In my own personal experience there is more than one outstanding blend of 60% Nebbiolo and 40% Barbera marketed as Langhe (q.v.).

A modern school of thought believes that to respect and preserve

Nebbiolo's fruit aromas the resultant wines should rather be matured for long periods in bottles than in casks. But this view is controversial and a number of major producers of Barbaresco have, in particular since the 1980s, taken to maturing their wines in barriques, especially since they believe that in that manner they will be able to improve on the smoothness and the colour of the wine, the Nebbiolo being much higher on tannins than it is on anthocyanins that contribute to colour.

It is regrettable that the failure of Italian regulations – contrary to the French ones – actually to insist on clear-cut vineyard definitions has caused, especially after Barbaresco achieved DOC status in 1966 and DOCG in 1980, a great deal of varied planting on unsuitable sites. Whilst some quality producers (e.g. Pio Cesare) have as a result preferred to blend grapes from different sites in order to achieve a more harmonious and constant taste, there are signs that the situation is being slowly rectified.
Band D

BARBERA   [DOC / Red / Piemonte]

One of the most popular red wines in Piemonte, probably my favourite, quantitatively its first, apart from being also one of the oldest known, since there are official records of it as early as 1609 (the unofficial ones go back to the thirteenth century!). It is true to say, however, that it did not really come into prominence until the end of the eighteenth century.

It is made from the Barbera grape, a very prolific (though somewhat uneven from year to year) variety.

The Barbera grape is grown in many parts of Italy, but the classification of DOC Barbera wines is to be summarized by saying that there are broadly speaking four varieties in Piemonte and one in Lombardia.

The Barbera grown in Lombardia is known as Barbera dell'Oltrepó Pavese (q.v.). The Piemontese varieties are as follows:

1. **Barbera d'Alba**. This is an intense, tasteful red wine, ruby red when young, veering to red/violet when more mature. (Its regulatory system dates back to 23 May 1970.) It has a very marked scent of wine, with a fairly persistent aroma, and is suitable for reasonable ageing if it is produced in a good year and from good places of origin (e.g. Dogliani and Alba itself). It is, of course, produced in other areas (Barolo, Barbaresco) and there, it seems to acquire a flavour more akin to those wines.

The taste is strong and dry, the alcoholic content a minimum of 12°. When labelled 'Superiore' it has been matured for at least one year and has a minimum alcoholic content of 12.5°. It can rise to 13°-14°.

This is a superior wine, although it never seems to have made it at international level. But its potential is now being rediscovered especially considering that, if properly made, some Barberas reach their peak at ten years. The last decade has seen an endorsement of it and the reader may wish to note that whilst at the moment it is still comparatively inexpensive, it will increase in price as its producers become more ambitious for it.

Apart from the communes already mentioned, it is also to be found in Castagnito, Grinzane Cavour, Monforte d'Alba and Serralunga d'Alba and elsewhere in the area, of course. It is ideal with the local cuisine.

More bottles are produced of this wine (in excess of 10 million) than any other Piedmontese wine except Asti (in excess of 36 million) per annum.

One comment at this stage. Until recently the Barbera d'Alba was not normally matured in barriques; nowadays some of it is, though there are locally differing views as to the advisability of oaking it.

A number of producers are said to be experimenting with what I would term 'partial' oaking, that is to say blending unoaked and oaked (in barriques) wine in varying proportions (e.g. 70% unoaked, 30% oaked). In my view it is too soon to determine the success of this practice although some good results can be found.

2.   **Barbera d'Asti**. This is a slightly blended wine produced in many areas in the province of Asti. It is sometimes suitable for ageing, has a dark ruby red colour with a very marked taste of morello cherries and violets. When young, it is very dry, but it mellows with age.

This one too comes from the Barbera grape but the regulations allow up to 15% of other grapes to be added (Freisa, Grignolino and Dolcetto). It has a minimum alcoholic content of 12° but can rise to 13° and 14°.

In its 'Superiore' version it must have a minimum alcoholic content of 12.5° and minimum maturing of twelve months, of which at least six months must be in oak barrels. (Like the variety which follows, its regulatory system goes back to 9 January 1970.)

3.   **Barbera del Monferrato** (alternatively known as Barbera di Alessandria). Again, a minimum of 85% Barbera must be used to which the three other grapes previously mentioned may be added in varying percentages, at the discretion of the vintner.

The wine is dry, ruby red, veering towards a ruby orange when more mature. It is delightful when drunk young, although marked by a rather tart taste. It reaches its peak at two to three years and mellows dramatically thereafter. I would not expect it to last longer than five years.

4.   **Barbera del Piemonte**. This wine is grown in an area which overlaps the provinces of Alessandria, Asti and Cuneo, with the same grapes and in the same percentages as the one just mentioned.

It differs from the three previous varieties of Barbera because, although it has roughly the same colour and the same dryness, it also comes in a much gentler variety and is of lesser body, as evidenced by the fact that the minimum alcoholic content is 11°.

The Barbera grape is widespread throughout Piemonte where it was born and where it reaches its peak both as a simple table wine and as something more refined and, proportionately, more valuable.

In addition to the varieties that we have identified, there is a Barbera to be found in practically every district in this region. The wine is usually the same but what changes is the required minimum alcoholic content. The other varieties of Barbera are the following:

Canavese minimum alcoholic content 10.5°
Colli Tortonesi minimum alcoholic content 11.5°
Colline Torinesi minimum alcoholic content 10.5°
Colline Novaresi minimum alcoholic content 11°
Pinerolese minimum alcoholic content 10.5°

The case of Barbera provides a classic example of the extraordinary variety of Italian wines. For the record, Barbera also emerges in many 'petillant' versions (known locally as 'vivace') which, if matured for a minimum of a year, and having an alcoholic content in excess of 12.5° are entitled to be described as 'Superiore'.

Increasingly, as I have already remarked, Barbera wines are being oaked; the reader is referred to earlier comments in a previous section and if he already has knowledge of Italian wines, will see that on this issue the author parts company from a number of writers. More recently (1999), from Nicholas Belfrage (*Barolo to Valpolicella – The Wines of Northern Italy*, Faber & Faber, London, 1999, p. 295) where it is maintained that 'Barbera takes to barrique like a duck to water (barrique treatment being almost a *sine qua non* for this style of wine).' One wonders how the drinkers of Barbera managed in Italy until recent times when the practice developed of oaking it. . . . . .

Finally, it should be noted that the Barbera grape is widespread in Italy and versions of its wine are to be found as far apart as Langhirano (Emilia) and Avellino and Salerno (Campania).
Band B/C

BARBERA DELL'OLTREPÓ PAVESE [DOC / Red / Lombardia]

This wine is produced in the province of Pavia in Lombardy; a rather hilly region where the expanses of vineyards are beautiful to see.

Although the Barbera grape prevails (85%) other red grapes (not specified by law) may be added. The resultant wine is a slightly different version from its Piedmontese brethren. It is of an intense ruby red colour, absolutely clear and brilliant when young. When mature, it has a tendency to taste rather more tannic, if not acid. This wine too, is available in a 'petillant' version, but it has less body than the versions previously mentioned. Minimum alcoholic content 11°.
Band B

BARDOLINO ('Superiore' and 'Classico Superiore')
[DOCG / Red / Veneto]

A most heavily 'blended' DOCG wine produced on the eastern banks of Lake Garda, made essentially with the same grapes as the Valpolicella but the mixture that can be used (Corvina, Rossara, Negrara, Rondinella, Molinara, Rossignola, Barbera, Sangiovese, Nebbiolo, Freisa, Merlot, Cabernet Sauvignon, Teroldego and Schiava) in varying unspecified proportions is almost unique; it yields a ruby-coloured wine, very clear, bright, delicately scented.

It is a tasty dry wine, slightly, yet pleasantly bitter, veering to garnet/ cherry when moderately aged; but only moderately so, because it is at its best when drunk young. It has a minimum alcoholic content of 12° and is undoubtedly a superior table wine which must be matured for at least one year before being sold.

When grown in the original area of production (Bardolino, Garda, Lazise, Costermano, and Cavaion) it can be labelled 'Classico'. It was known to the Romans, being mentioned by Virgil, and in the thirteenth century by Dante.

The eastern banks of Lake Garda where it is grown seem to be particularly successful for this type of wine which I think is best suited to white meats. There is little doubt that the microclimate established throughout the adjacent vineyards by their proximity to sweet water is highly beneficial and has, what one might term, a moderating influence on the locally grown grapes.

Band B

BAROLO   [DOCG / Red / Piemonte]

A red wine of heavy, carmine colour, veering to orange hues when more mature, tasting of violets and roses, dry and smooth, with an alcoholic content of between 13° and 14° and an average total acidity of 7 grams. It is grown over a wide area of around 3,000 acres, on steep hills. It is traditionally matured in large barrels ('botti') but recently there has been a trend to mature much of it in barriques. I have already commented on this practice in the section on oaking and shall say no more under this heading.

The Italians have always recorded the enormous political debt they owe to the statesman Camillo Benso, Count of Cavour, who could truly be called 'the father of independent Italy'. Streets and squares all over Italy are named after him; but a different debt of gratitude is owed, for it was thanks to him that Barolo became a successful wine.

It had been known for many centuries but not in its latest, dry form. Count Cavour personally dedicated himself to his vineyards to ensure the success of this wine.

Barolo is claimed to be Italy's top wine. Indeed, Italians call it 'the king of wines, the wine of kings'. The description is not necessarily original, but indicative of the respect in which the wine is held. It is a fine wine, but at the cost of being lynched by my compatriots, I must say that it is not to everybody's taste. Its flavour is unique, as described. It is said not to have any competitors, although some say that it is on a par with another much less well-known, at least abroad, local red, the Gattinara (q.v.).

It matures slowly and should seldom be drunk young. It reaches its peak between eight and ten years, although there are some who argue that it is to be tasted at its best between five and eight years.

The problem with a good Barolo is that the bottle should be uncorked several hours before serving and it does appreciate being drunk out of a proper lead crystal glass, preferably of top quality.

There is no doubt that it acquires more flavour if this procedure is followed. Indeed, in the old days (no longer, because we are all in a hurry nowadays) it was the custom, certainly amongst those who understood the wine in its region of production, to offer the guest of honour the 'dregs' (usually one half) of the good bottle of vintage Barolo uncorked the previous day. . . . . (in Piedmontese dialect, ' '*n fund d'buta*'). The practice, however, seems to have disappeared over the past fifty years or so. Also because of the new vinification techniques aimed at producing wines with less sediment and more appealing to the young. Even for the great Barolo this can now be said to apply.

Barolo is made from the Nebbiolo sub varieties of grape known as Michet, Lampia and Rosé grown in a fairly restricted area of the Langhe centred around Barolo in the province of Cuneo (other villages where it is grown are Monforte d'Alba, La Morra, Grinzane Cavour, Verduno and Novello). To ensure quality, yield per hectare is limited (eight tons).

As a young wine, it is somewhat uncouth and the tannins do strike the palate but after five or six years it begins to acquire a smoothness and a velvety definition which combine well with its characteristic taste of violets. After that time the wine begins to change colour turning effectively to orange; one hardly notices that the scent of violets is becoming more prominent.

One would term Barolo an honest wine which can be drunk without too many concerns about the effects that may derive from having a glass too many. It is undoubtedly to be ranked amongst the top reds of the world. I cannot go so far as to say, as the Piedmontese have done, that it is the best wine in the world but there is no doubt that it is a wine which is viewed with respect and sympathy by anyone who takes an interest in matters oenological.

Those who are keen on it would do well to visit the permanent museum on Barolo wine, which is to be found in the village of La Morra where they might also dine at an outstanding local hostelry on the terrace in the centre of the village, overlooking the surrounding undulating and typically Piedmontese countryside. It is in the village of La Morra that the yearly auction sales of Barolo take place. In 2006, the most successful Barolo wines sold at auction were those of the 1999 vintage. Interestingly, 90% of those top wines were purchased by Chinese buyers. Whether their choice was made on the basis of a marked liking for Barolo wine, or because it is considered by many to be the top Italian wine, must remain a moot point.

For the record, the personality and flavour of Barolo have been so magnified that there has been current for many years a story, told repeatedly, of the very old Piedmontese vintner, fond of food and of his wine, who was taken ill and put on a fast which resulted in his getting close to death. When he felt that he was about to leave his mortal spoils, he asked for two things to be brought to him, a piece of fine cheese and a particular vintage bottle of his own Barolo wine.

His sons and the rest of the family gathered around him when the cheese and the wine arrived. The old man asked for the cheese to be passed under his nose and he sniffed it with his eyes closed. He then asked for the wine to be uncorked, poured and rested for a while on his bedside table. This was done and he waited a few minutes whilst his family stood around him, in silent expectation.

He then uttered his last words: addressing the family, who were round the bed, he said, 'You bastards: this is not the Barolo from bay 3!'.

Band C/D

BAROLO CHINATO   [Red / Piemonte]

This is an aromatic wine, exclusive to Piemonte where it was born. It is made with Barolo DOCG wine to which are added 'china calissaja' (hence the qualifying adjective), gentian, cinnamon, cardamom and about half a dozen other herbs, according to old recipes (said to be secret!), which tend to vary depending on the taste of the manufacturer.

It is available in a variety of different-sized bottles, has an average alcoholic content of 16.5°/17.5° and can be taken as an aperitif but much more often as an after-dinner drink. It is said to aid the digestion, though that may well be a selling gimmick.

It is a fine liqueur wine, one of the best and most famous in Italy. The Italian description is 'vino aromatizzato' (in the plural, 'vini aromatizzati') which is a more accurate description than the English equivalent because the normal low alcoholic content (16°-19°) of these 'vini aromatizzati' is not in any sense comparable to that of real liqueurs. What is available in England costs around £15 for 500 cls of average quality: a top Barolo Chinato retails in the UK at around £25 per 750 cls.

Barolo Chinato is a fairly unique liqueur-type wine; for those who do not mind the flavour of spices, it is a fine after-dinner drink, of some seniority since it was first 'developed' in 1895 by a chemist, agronomist and oenologist from the town of Alba called Giuseppe Cappellano: his Barolo Chinato is still available and is excellent, though expensive (Band E). It can be drunk at practically any temperature but I propound to the view that it comes into its own slightly chilled, especially in summer.

Band D

BIFERNO   [DOC / Red / White / Rosé / Molise]

By no means a common or indeed well-known wine, except in the region of production, namely the province of Campobasso; it takes its name from the local river. The vines are grown at reasonably high altitudes, around 500 metres.

Biferno Red. A pleasant ruby coloured red made from the Montepulciano, Trebbiano and Aglianico grapes with a fine nose and a fairly dry and balanced tannic taste. It has a minimum alcoholic content of 11.5° but is available also in a 'Riserva' version at 13° alcohol provided it has been matured for at least three years.

Biferno White. This comes from the same area and is produced with Trebbiano, Bombino and Malvasia grapes. It is a straw-coloured, delicately tinged in green, wine with a very pleasant aromatic nose and a well balanced taste. Minimum alcoholic content 10.5°.

Biferno Rosé. Made with the same grapes as the red, it has a minimum alcoholic content of 11.5°, a very fruity nose and a smooth dry taste. Its colour varies from light rose to light red.
Band A

BOLGHERI (*V. Sassicaia*) [DOC Red / Toscana]

BRACHETTO D'ACQUI (*otherwise known as Acqui*)
[DOCG / Red / Piemonte]

Another of the glories of the region, less known abroad than many others, made exclusively with Brachetto grapes from eighteen communes in the province of Asti and eight in that of Alessandria. These include Acqui Terme, from which the Brachetto takes its name. Up to 20% of Aleatico and Moscato nero may be added.

It is a medium bodied ruby red wine veering sometimes almost to rosé, with a delicate scent of musk and a gentle sweet taste.

It has a minimum alcoholic content of 11.5°; in my view, the more interesting version is the sparkling one, which has the same characteristics as the non-sparkling wine apart from a minimum alcoholic content of 12° but creates a delightful, persistent foam which is a pleasure to watch. Ideal drunk slightly chilled, its versatility allows it to retain charm even when consumed at room temperature. Production is small, this is not a cheap wine, often served either as an aperitif or as an after-meal drink in the better class establishments in Italy and, occasionally, abroad.
Band D

BRINDISI [DOC Red / Rosé / Puglia]

This is the area of the Negroamaro grape and of the black Malvasia to which are added other grapes like Montepulciano and Sangiovese. It produces wines of quality and in great quantity.

Brindisi Rosso of ruby colour veering to orange when mature, this most enjoyable wine has a very marked nose; it is dry, well-balanced, medium-bodied and not too tannic. Its minimum alcoholic content is 12° but 12.5° when after two years it can be termed 'Riserva'.

Brindisi Rosé. This is excellent, pinkish more or less dark, with a very fruity nose and a well-balanced taste, with a slightly bitter aftertaste. Minimum alcoholic content is 12° but usually 12.5°/13°.
Band A

BRUNELLO DI MONTALCINO [DOCG / Red / Toscana]

A wine of an intense red colour, violet-scented, dry and smooth, with an alcoholic content between 12° and 13.5° and an average acidity of 6.5 grams, this DOCG wine is one of the glories of Italy; it was the first Italian wine to receive the DOCG qualification in 1980 but was well known ever since the seventeenth century, when the Italian author Francesco Redi in his *Bacco in Toscana* defined it as the 'king of Tuscan wines'. It originates in the village, perhaps more correctly, the area, of Montalcino in the province of Siena.

Brunello is really the local name for the Sangiovese variety and is, in fact, the only wine in the world which cannot be sold before the first January of the sixth year subsequent to that when the grapes that go to form it have been pressed. Indeed, in the varieties known as *Riserva*, the stipulation is for seven years. (The runner up is the inordinately expensive Spanish red Vega Sicilia Unico, which must be matured in cask for sixty-six months before being bottled and sold.)

Because of its popularity, there has been an explosion in recent years in the number of wineries which have taken to producing it, resulting in an over-production. This sometimes makes for somewhat acid, because ultimately unripe, wines, which are not representative of the true quality of the original Brunello. A few oenologists have suggested that the time has come for blending the Sangiovese with, say Merlot and Cabernet Sauvignon, as happens with the so-called 'super Tuscans' (q.v.) Brunello ages well; it reaches maturity at about eight years and will continue to improve up to fifteen years.

As the now legendary story has it, back in 1888 Ferruccio Biondi-Santi of Montalcino, focusing on the now obvious truth that Italy's most widely-planted red grape, the Sangiovese, in reality desperately needs help, undertook what we today call clonal selection and isolated an especially favoured Sangiovese strain he called *Grosso* due to its large clusters. He also further improved on traditional regional winemaking skills by maturing his wines for considerably longer than was the custom.

The story does more credit to Biondi-Santi's public relations skills than to fact, for quality wines from Montalcino using this clone and considerably pre-dating his exploits are well recorded.

Moreover, these days a need to mature wines for long periods can often be symptomatic of clumsy winemaking. As recently as thirty years ago, before an understanding of the factors governing good winemaking was absorbed, reds that started with an excess of bitter tannin had to be held in a cellar for sufficient time for these tannins to soften. Nowadays, by inducing polymerization, we can produce wines still enjoying the valuable protection of tannin, but without the associated bitter taste.

Moreover, today's international markets are demanding fruitier wines, wines recognizably tasting of the grape(s) from which they are produced; long maturation, especially in the large 'botti' so popular in Italy, often strips the fruit before tannins are reduced. This change in world taste goes a long way to explain a current Brunello overstocking problem.

To experience the Sangiovese Grosso or Brunello as it is locally called in Montalcino, try Rosso di Montalcino (q.v.). Same wine but a shorter maturation period, hence more fruit, and a far more reasonable price.

And there is no doubt that some less than scrupulous entrepreneur-ial citizens of Montalcino, seeing the substantial sums being paid for the magic title Brunello di Montalcino, set about producing wines which officially qualified but were pale imitations of the real thing. The moral is, if you can afford to buy a Brunello, buy an expensive one; you might be disappointed otherwise.

Over the past two years or so a number of producers of Brunello have been experimenting with maturing it in French-style barriques (of Slavonian oak) for 18-24 months. This is claimed to result in a substantial improvement to the quality of the wine. Since I have not, so far, sampled one of the barrique-matured Brunellos I refrain from commenting save by reminding the reader of my observations on oaking as a general concept.

This is another break from tradition, Brunello having been matured in the large botti for as long as memory goes.

As a general rule, beware of classic wines with prices hiked by so-called exclusivity. Some are a great experience, some merely an expensive one. All this apart, Brunello is a fine wine; not cheap, though!

Suggested best ever vintage: 1997 (only 10,000 bottles).

Band D/E

CABERNET   [Red / Friuli Venezia Giulia]

Cabernet is to be found in many parts of Italy where a number of local vines are being replaced by the more fashionable Cabernet Sauvignon. There are now available a Cabernet from Toscana, as well as a Cabernet Sauvignon/Shiraz from Sicilia(!); but it is probably fair to say that the majority of the good Italian Cabernet comes from Veneto, Trentino Alto Adige (where it is often blended with Merlot or Lagrein) and Friuli Venezia Giulia.

This entry is concerned with the Cabernet from the Friuli Venezia Giulia which in the main is made either exclusively from Cabernet Sauvignon grapes or Cabernet Franc or a blend of Cabernet Franc and Cabernet Sauvignon.

We thus have a Cabernet dei Colli Orienti del Friuli, a Cabernet del Collio, a Cabernet del Piave (in the Veneto), a Cabernet del Trentino (q.v.), and three Cabernet from the Veneto, namely di Breganze, di Pramaggiore and Vicenza.

Leaving aside the exact blends of grapes, one can give a broad description of Cabernet as an excellent red wine, of garnet colour when young but turning to brick colour as it ages, which it does very well because most Cabernet mature at three years, are perfect at eight and can live quite successfully beyond that.

It has a very full nose where one can detect without much difficulty a raspberry scent. The taste is dry, initially perhaps a trifle uncouth but becoming more velvety with ageing. A harmonious wine, having a minimum alcoholic content of 11.5° for the Cabernet Sauvignon and 11° for the Cabernet Franc but rising quite commonly to 13.5°.

Once upon a time it was said that the best came from the village of Buttrio but this may no longer be true. It is wine that profits from being served at room temperature and possibly even slightly above that.

Band B

CABERNET TRENTINO   [DOC / Red / Trentino/Alto Adige]

A classic red wine of the area made from the two distinguished vines of Bordeaux, namely Cabernet Sauvignon and Cabernet Franc.

The climate and the growing conditions seem to suit these grapes in Trentino Alto Adige and there are yielded three types:

1. **Cabernet**. This is produced with Cabernet Franc and/or Cabernet Sauvignon grapes. It has a red colour, a grassy bouquet and a slightly tannic, very full and dry taste. It has a minimum alcoholic content of 11°; with 11.5° it can be sold as 'Riserva' but the versions more commonly available on the foreign markets run to 13°.

2. **Cabernet Franc**. Made with the same grapes, this has the same characteristics both in taste and aroma and within the same regulatory framework.

3. **Cabernet Sauvignon**. This is the third variety but it can be said without fear of contradiction that it does not differ too dramatically from the previous two.

All three wines are of full warm and velvety quality, admittedly tannic but by no means acid. The locals claim that, because of the length of contact with the grape skins during fermentation, these wines have also a therapeutic character and should be drunk as much as a tonic as a digestive. No comment.
Band B

CALDARO   [DOC / Red / Trentino / Alto Adige]

Otherwise known as Lago di Caldaro, in German Kalter or Kalterersee, this wine is produced in the area of Bolzano near the lake that bears the same name but can also be found in other parts of the region in the province of Trento. It obtained DOC in 1970, although known since the thirteenth century. It is made mainly with Schiava grapes (three varieties) as well as Pinot Noir and in the flat areas of the country mixed with Lagrein.

It is a wine of a ruby red colour from very light to medium, not too full-bodied with a gentle typical nose and a light almondy, fruity taste and a typical bouquet. The minimum alcoholic content is 10.5° but more commonly 11.5° to 12°. A number of German descriptions can be made to apply to it.

This wine, known to them as Kalterersee, is much favoured by the German-speaking community in the region and is produced in very substantial quantity (certainly exceeding 10m litres every year).

It will not store for very long and it is recommended that it be drunk up to three years. Despite the harsher weather conditions in the region, it is quite often served on the cool side, the lower temperature apparently suiting this kind of wine.

If made in the original area of production, that is to say, around Lake Caldaro which is south-west of Bolzano, it is entitled to be labelled 'Classico'. With 11° or more alcohol it may also be described as

'Auslese' (the Italian equivalent is 'scelto', i.e. of selected quality).
Band B

CANNONAU   [DOC / Red / Sardegna]

The wine is made from the grape variety which originated in Aragon, Spain, where it is known as Alicante or Garnacha. As a matter of fact, Garnacha is the third most widely planted grape in the world, said to cover 240,000 hectares; the first being the white Spanish Airen, reputed to extend to 423,000 hectares and competing with Trebbiano (q.v.) for first place).

The connection with Spain is of long standing and it is hardly a coincidence that one of the villages where the Jerzu version of the Cannonau wine is made is called Cardedu, which is almost identical to the locality north of Barcelona, known as Cardedeu.

The blend may include other grapes, e.g. Monica, and the wine itself is also known by another three names, depending on the area of production, namely Oliena (or Nepente di Oliena), Capo Ferrato and Jerzu. It is a solid wine, of an intense ruby colour which veers to orange with ageing, from the communes of Alghero and Sorso Sennori in the province of Sassari.

It tastes of strawberries and is quite dry with a fairly typical slightly bitter aftertaste, almost like plain chocolate. The alcoholic content is variable, starting at 12.5° and rising occasionally to 16°.

It must be matured for a minimum of seven months, but after two years, if the alcoholic content is no less than 13°, it can be called 'Riserva'. If no less than 15° it may be called 'Superiore'. It is also available as a rosé and as a dry liqueur-type wine with a minimum alcoholic content of 18° or, in sweet version, with a minimum alcoholic content of 16°.

It is an excellent table wine suitable for moderate ageing. I have sampled some fine versions of the Riserva at 14° alcohol, being no less than twelve years old. It was a favourite of the Italian writer, Gabriele D'Annunzio, who enthused over its aroma. To him we owe its description as 'nepente' to mean a drink that dispels pain and worry.
Band A/B

CARIGNANO DEL SULCIS   [DOC / Red / Sardegna]

The area known as Sulcis forms the extreme south-west part of Sardinia and comprises some seventeen communes in the province of Cagliari. It produces a number of wines (red, rosé, 'nouveau' and high alcohol sweet) and has been associated with the production of Carignano for a very long time, the locals maintaining that vine-growing in this area dates back to the Roman era.

However, the vine Carignano originates in Spain where it is still known as Cariñena, mainly in the valley of the Ebro River and more particularly, though not exclusively, south of Zaragoza. The Spanish boast that the vineyards in this area ante-date even the Romans.

The DOC Carignano del Sulcis wine must be made with a minimum of 85% of that variety of grape which produces an intensely ruby red wine, with a strong vinous, sapid, dry and harmonious taste and a minimum alcoholic content of 12°. It must be matured for no less than three months.

I have only been able to find the red variety in the UK at 12.5° alcohol, made exclusively from Carignano grapes.
Band B

CARMIGNANO (*Barco Reale di Carmignano*)
[DOC / Red / Rosé / Toscana]

Barco Reale was the name given to a rather wide hunting area used by the Medici family on hillocks not exceeding 400m above sea level.

It was classified as a DOC in 1994 and is a brilliantly coloured ruby red, dry wine, fruity and fresh, with a minimum alcoholic content of 11°.

There is also a red and a Vin Santo type but none of the three versions is easily found outside Italy.
Band B/E

CARMIGNANO
[DOCG / Red / Toscana]

It could be said that this is Chianti by another name but it is in fact a different wine produced in a very small, defined, hilly area falling within the jurisdiction of the communes of Carmignano and Poggio a Caiano (including Vinci, Capraia and Limite) in the province of Florence. This is a superior red wine which lends itself to considerable ageing; its merits have been recognized for some time since it obtained DOC recognition in 1975 and was up-graded to DOCG in 1990.

It could also be said that this wine is probably better known abroad than in Italy, despite the fact that it has a long tradition since it is grown on hills much frequented by the rulers of Florence, the Medici, who actually built villas there and established a hunting woodland preserve. In appreciation of this wine, Cosimo III granted it a 'patent of nobility', a sort of DOC.

It is made from Sangiovese (minimum 50%), Canaiolo (maximum 20%), Cabernet Franc or Cabernet Sauvignon (maximum 20%), Trebbiano, Toscano and Malvasia (maximum 10%) as well as other local grapes (maximum 10%) with a vivid ruby red colour, a very strong violet nose which seems to become more noticeable as the wine matures and a dry, full, smooth, harmonious taste with a feint bitterish aftertaste, even almost 'sparkling'. Its minimum alcoholic content is 12.5°, and minimum maturing is two years (four years for the 'Riserva'). It is sometimes referred to as Chianti (del) Montalbano.

There is a white version made in the same area from Trebbiano and Malvasia of feint straw colour and to be drunk young, but I have not seen it yet in the United Kingdom.
Band C/D

CASTEL DEL MONTE
[DOC / Red / White / Rosé / Puglia]

Those who have visited the province of Bari will no doubt have gone to Andria to see the Norman castle known as 'Castel del Monte', built by Frederick II in the thirteenth century (and possibly to visit the part of Italy that is the country's greatest producer of olive oil).

This impressive octagonal structure of whitish stone, visible from a distance, one of the most famous architectural features of the region of Puglia, gives its name to a number of excellent wines produced in Andria and surrounding districts as well as in the area of Minervino Murge always in the province of Bari.

Red. This is produced from a local grape, Uva di Troia (80%), one from the adjacent regions, Aglianico, as well as from Montepulciano with other local grapes; occasionally with up to 20% Malbech.

It is a full-bodied ruby red veering to amber when mature with a marked nose and a fairly tannic, dry taste, of blackberry and cherry. Its minimum alcoholic content is 12° rising to 12.5° with two years maturing when it becomes 'Riserva'. Also available is a 'Novello' with a lower alcoholic content, but quite pleasant and fresh.

White. This is a very pleasant, gentle and delicate white also available in a sparkling version, obtained from a mixture of Pampanino, Bombino and Chardonnay grapes as well as others; straw-coloured, gently scented and freshly tasting it is also available in a sparkling version.

Rosé. This is derived from the Bombino, Aglianico, Uva di Troia, grapes and is a delightful rosé, quite fruity in nose and in flavour. Also available in a sparkling version both with a minimum alcoholic content of 11°.

Band A/B

CERASUOLO DI VITTORIA   [DOC / Red / Sicilia]

'Cerasa' in Italian means 'cherry' and 'cerasuolo' (more correctly, perhaps, 'cerasolo') means 'of a cherry-like colour'.

It is a descriptive name for many wines to be found in southern Italy, especially, apart from Sicily of course, in Calabria (Scilla) and in Puglia (in the Murge), as well as, for instance, in the Abruzzi region (where a Montepulciano d'Abruzzo version is available bearing the Cerasuolo name).

However, the only DOC Cerasuolo is that of Vittoria which is produced in a fairly restricted area of five municipalities in the province of Ragusa, of two in that of Caltanissetta and two more in the province of Catania. It is made with the grapes of Frappato, Calabrese (Grosso, Nero and Albanello) and Nerello Mascalese.

It is a very pleasant, tasty wine of a cherry red colour (hence the name). It has a delicate vinous nose, flower-scented and a dry, rather full and harmonious taste. A medium bodied wine, it has a minimum alcoholic content of 13° rising quite often to 14°.

It is also known as Frappato di Vittoria and is available in a sweet, liqueur-style version, as well as a quite flavourful white wine, straw-coloured at first but veering to amber as it ages.

Band B

CESANESE DEL PIGLIO *or Piglio*   [DOC / Red / Lazio]

A wine produced in the municipalities of Piglio and others in the province of Frosinone from the grape known as Cesanese di Affile (90%) with the permitted addition of Sangiovese, Montepulciano, Barbera, Trebbiano and Bombino.

It has a minimum alcoholic content of 12° and is ruby red, getting darker as it ages. A very delicate nose is characteristic of the 'Cesanese' grape with a gentle, slightly bitter taste.

The principal variety is dry but there is also a semi-dry version, a semi-sweet and a sweet, as well as a sparkling.

The wine is produced in the province of Frosinone, but there is a very similar one known as Cesanese di Affile from the name of the grape used for the Cesanese del Piglio produced in certain municipalities (Affile, Rotaie and Arcinazzo) in the province of Rome, as well as a Cesanese di Olevano Romano (or Olevano Romano) also from Rome province..

The nose is rather intense but it matures and softens with age; the taste is either dry or semi-sweet, reasonably tannic. The minimum alcoholic content is 11.5° but if it rises to 12.5° and is matured for a minimum of two years it can be termed 'Riserva'.

Neither wine lends itself to long ageing and should normally be drunk within one or two years, though some exceptions can be found.

The Cesanese del Piglio wine could be said to have been in the doldrums since the 1950s; recent years, however, have seen what I would term its rehabilitation, well deserved for what was for decades, especially prior to the Second World War, one of the staple reds in the area surrounding Rome.

Band B

CHARDONNAY
[DOC / White / Trentino Alto Adige / Friuli Venezia Giula]

Until recently, Italian *Chardonnay* wine did not qualify for any approved denomination and was sold as an IGT. There are, however, wines that are entitled to a DOC or an IGT which are made with 'Chardonnay'. These are commonly called by that name followed by the denomination of origin so you can have a Chardonnay Trentino, a Chardonnay delle Venezie, or a Chardonnay Collio (also known as Collio Chardonnay. . . . .), which may be either DOC or IGT.

There are plenty of Chardonnay table wines, which do not qualify for an approved denomination in any event. These I shall not be considering.

1. **Chardonnay Alto Adige** or **dell'Alto Adige** or **Südtirol** or **Südtiroler** (DOC). This is a yellow/green delicately fruited dry and full-bodied white wine, having a minimum alcoholic content of 11° which can also be found in a slightly yeasty tasting sparkling version, very dry or medium dry.

2. **Chardonnay Terlano** or **Terlano Chardonnay** (IGT). Made almost exclusively with Chardonnay grapes (90%) to which may be added other white grapes from the locality, it is only available as a dry, yellow/green wine with a delicate fruity nose and a fairly full aftertaste.

3. **Chardonnay Valle Venosta** (IGT). This has similar characteristics to the Terlano Chardonnay.

4. **Chardonnay Trentino**. This wine is to be found in the DOC area of production of Trentino wines; it is straw-coloured and delicately scented, with a smooth, almost woody taste and a minimum alcoholic content of 11°. When this rises to 11.5° and the wine has been matured for two years it can be termed 'Riserva'.

5. **Valdadige Chardonnay** (IGT). A wine produced with a minimum 85% of Chardonnay grape, the balance being represented by non-aromatic recommended and authorized white grapes.

Straw coloured with a minimum alcoholic content of 10.5°, freshly tasting and quite harmonious, it comes also in a slightly sparkling version with a minimum alcoholic content of 11°.

6. **Carso Chardonnay** (DOC). This wine is produced in the Carso area, namely the south eastern tip of Friuli Venezia Giulia bordering on Slovenia, which includes a number of communes in the province of Trieste.

It is straw-coloured and delicate, with a minimum alcoholic content of 11°.

7. **Chardonnay Colli Orientali del Friuli** (DOC). It is a straw-coloured delicately scented and reasonably tasty wine with a minimum alcoholic content of 11°.

8. **Chardonnay Collio** or **Collio Chardonnay** (DOC). This is produced in the Collio, in the province of Gorizia, exclusively from Chardonnay grapes.

It has a delicate nose and is harmoniously dry, fairly full-bodied wine. It has a minimum alcoholic content of 11.5° which, when raised to 12° and with two years' maturing, entitles the wine to be called 'Riserva'. It is probably one of the most popular and best Chardonnay wines.

9. **Chardonnay Friuli**. A DOC wine obtained almost exclusively (90%) from Chardonnay grapes, it has the same features as other Chardonnay from this area. It is also produced in a sparkling version.

And to think that, say, thirty years ago, one could probably find only one or two Chardonnay wines in the whole of north-east Italy!
Band B

CHARDONNAY TRENTINO
[DOC / White / Trentino Alto Adige]

Straw-coloured with a delicate characteristic taste, a typical Chardonnay with smoothness and occasional woody aftertaste. The same specifications as for the Sauvignon Trentino (q.v.).

For those who like Chardonnay wines, it should be recorded that there are now available oaked north-eastern Italian versions which in my view are comparable, if not superior to the New World Chardonnay wines which have become so popular.

Band B/C

CHIANTI   [DOCG / Red / Toscana]

Chianti is an area between Florence and Siena which is the oldest officially defined wine-growing area in the world. It was established by Cosimo III di Medici, Grand Duke of Tuscany in the eighteenth century, the wine-growing characteristics of that particular part of Tuscany being recognized quite early. One had to wait, however, until the beginning of the twentieth century for a proper definition, not only of the area as such, but also of the nature of the wine, the first editorial demarcation for Chianti dating back to 1932, DOC being granted in 1967 and the up-grading to DOCG occurring in 1984.

There cannot be much doubt that this is the best known Italian wine; it is the red DOCG wine that is produced in greatest quantity in Italy. More than 150,000 hectolitres were produced in 2003; of these, two-fifths were sold in Italy, the remainder abroad. In terms of alcoholic drinks, it is to Italy what Guinness is to Ireland, Scotch Whisky to Scotland and saké to Japan.

For those who are interested in statistics, the following may be a useful reminder. When the 'Consorzio per la Difesa del Vino Tipico del Chianti' (the 'Consorzio') was set up, it had thirty-three producer members. The numbers have steadily grown and membership now exceeds 600, at least 250 of whom bottle under their own labels.

Furthermore, the members themselves produce more than 80% of all the wine that qualifies for the Chianti Classico DOCG and come in all sizes, from small operators to major industrial enterprises.

The present annual production of Chianti Classico is around 30,000 tons and has remained reasonably constant over the past few years. This corresponds to 45m bottles, a major effort bearing in mind that the relevant production area does not exceed 7,000 hectares.

The principal importers of Chianti Classico recorded for the latest year for which statistical information is available namely 2002 are, in order of importance: USA 32%, Germany 20%, Switzerland 17% and United Kingdom 12%. The other nations noted for their importation of Chianti are (alphabetically): Austria 1%, Canada 6%, France 1% and Japan 4%.

It is also the Italian wine, which, because of its popularity, is most subject to 'falsification'. Varieties crop up at regular intervals all over the world, more especially in the United States and Canada, two countries which have no cause whatever to be proud, as far as the Italians are concerned, of their disrespect for food and wine authenticity as well as for their almost non-existent protection of denominations of origin or geographical descriptions, generally; but that is a different, sad story.

It can fairly be said that of all Italian wines Chianti is the most universally acceptable. It is popular with all classes of drinkers. For the record, however, there is at least one well-known Englishman who does not agree with this statement. Forgetting about the times when he used to imbibe more than necessary and ignoring completely that on one occasion (see Boswell's *Life of Johnson* aetat.54 – 1763) his biographer records that he and Dr Johnson sat up until one or two o'clock in the morning when they had 'finished a couple of bottles of port' with his friend Boswell, Dr Johnson is recorded (*Boswell's Life of Johnson*, Wednesday, 7 April 1779) as saying '. . . . . Florence wine I think the worst; it is wine only to the eye; it is wine neither while you are drinking it, nor after you have drunk it; it neither pleases the taste nor exhilarates the spirit'. I am quite fond of Dr Johnson's 'sayings', with many of which I agree, but on this occasion I am, of course, bound to part company from him. Chianti remains a popular wine and its popularity is due to a number of factors of differing degrees of importance.

The principal one is that in 1902, thanks to Baron Bettino Ricasoli, the Chianti area was the first to organize itself into a 'Consorzio' and later on adopted distinguishing marks (the black label with a cockerel or a 'putto'), that provided uniformity and controls.

More important, however, is the fact that the straw-covered flask with which it is associated is a regular feature of Italian restaurants (genuine and artificial) and is a common portrayal in films. The discerning buyer should be made aware of the fact that a fair quantity of Tuscan red, normally labelled as Toscana Rosso, is now sold in the one-litre flasks. Clearly, advantage is being taken of the popularity of the container, where the wine cannot qualify for the official Chianti label.

Admittedly, there are practical reasons why the rather fragile flask is nowadays used much less than the bottle but it is of considerable seniority since wine flasks were first produced in 1265 in the town of San Gimignano. There is an aura of pleasantness, almost of charm about the Chianti flask which has made it the subject of historical studies. One of the biggest producers of Chianti, Ruffino, in November 1993 went on the record with the rather astonishing assertion that the straw cladding for the 'fiasco' was invented by Leonardo da Vinci and, indeed, that it can be identified in some of his drawings.

When the atomic battery was 'discovered' at Chicago University, its pioneer Dr Eugene Wigner and his colleague Enrico Fermi, together with others who had assisted in the experiment, celebrated the event by uncorking a flask of Chianti and then proceeding to append their signatures on it. (I am not too fussed about that and will now go on to consider the wine, rather than its containers.)

First of all, one should note that there are two types of Chianti available on the market: Chianti and Chianti Classico. Both are DOCG wines and both are produced in Tuscany but in different areas. They are fairly similar in terms of vine and technical requirements with a minimum alcoholic content of 11.5° for the former and 12° for the latter.

Chianti has a vivid red colour which takes on brick-like tinges as it matures, and some experts claim to be able to detect also yellowish reflections. It smells as wine should, occasionally offering a violet scent which becomes more refined with the passage of time.

It is a dry, harmonious, slightly tannic wine which, more often than not, is subject to what is known in Italy as the 'governo'. This means that as soon as the initial fermentation stops, slightly dried grapes are added to provoke a second fermentation. This is said to give the wine greater character and allows it to develop a marked smoothness as it matures.

Before it matures, however, and when drunk soon after vinification, it can be even very slightly sparkling. It is often consumed after six months but the better wines do not reach maturity for at least two or three years, and age well.

Now onto the differences.

1. **Chianti.** Is derived from the Sangiovese grape in varying percentages from a minimum of 75% to 100%. The producer is allowed to add a maximum 10% of black Canaiolo, a further maximum 10% of Trebbiano Toscano (white) and/or Malvasia and other black grapes.

Its alcoholic content varies. It is 11.5° for the Chianti produced in the Colli Aretini (province of Arezzo), in the Colli Senesi (province of Siena) and in the Colline Pisane.

It has a minimum of 12° alcohol if it is produced mainly in the areas of Colli Fiorentini, in Montespertoli and in Rufina (province of Florence).

If matured for at least a year subsequent to that in which it is produced and with a minimum of three years in bottles, then, provided it has a minimum alcoholic content of 12°, Chianti can be termed 'Riserva'.

For some areas, with whose names we shall not trouble the reader, the minimum requirement is 12.5°. The distinguishing mark of the 'Consorzio' is the 'putto' or cherub.

2. **Chianti Classico.** There's a slight variation here as regards the grapes used. Chianti Classico is derived from the Sangiovese grape in the percentage of 75-100% but the producer may add Canaiolo Nero, maximum 10%, Trebbiano Toscano (white) and/or Malvasia, maximum 6% and other red grapes, maximum 15%. The fluctuations are minimal but apparently do have an effect on the quality of the wine. Chianti Classico is made in the original Chianti production area.

These matters are mentioned for the sake of the record, especially because Chianti is such a well-known wine. For the average drinker, I suggest that the differentiation between Chianti and Chianti Classico (apart from the wording on the labels. . . . .) is difficult to detect.

Chianti Classico are undoubtedly wines which represent Italy well abroad. What should be borne in mind all the time, however, is that the Chianti Classico area is quite distinct from the areas that produce the 'simple' Chianti. The distinguishing mark of the 'Consorzio' is the black cockerel. Furthermore, the yields per hectare vary.

Apart from that consideration, Chianti – as distinct from Chianti Classico – can also come from a number of areas outside the traditional 'classical' districts. So the reader will find on the market the following types of Chianti:

Chianti dei Colli Aretini, Chianti dei Colli dell'Etruria Centrale, Chianti dei Colli Fiorentini, Chianti Montalbano, Chianti delle Colline Pisane, Chianti Rufina, Chianti dei Colli Senesi made in the provinces of Arezzo, Florence, Prato, Pisa, Siena and, lastly, in a very small area known as Rufina which is to be found north-east of Florence.

There are differences between these various wines; for example, the Rufina Chianti is very scented but rather thin, the Montalbano Chianti will not always age well, the Chianti from the Colli Fiorentini is not quite so distinguished, perhaps, as the others, although this, too, is designed to be drunk young save in its 'Riserva' version which will probably stand eight years' maturity; that made in the province of Arezzo is considered by some to be less satisfactory. All these are very much matters of opinion, for the wine is always a Chianti wine. The Chianti of the Colli Aretini is a softer version, with a marked scent, but in most varieties to be drunk fairly young.

The Chianti Classico on the other hand is produced in the central area of Toscana, south of Florence, in a number of villages steeped in history and part of the Italian oenological scene. Depending on taste, one may prefer a Chianti Classico to the other. Are the wines originating in Gaiole in Chianti better than those coming from Greve in Chianti? Are those from Castelnuovo Berardenga to be preferred to those of Castellina in Chianti? And what about Barberino Val d'Elsa or Radda in Chianti or, indeed, Panzano?

There is probably no single answer to these questions and the reader who is really interested in Chianto Classico will have to experiment. Most varieties are available abroad.

Alternatively, he could do worse than take a trip through the undulating Tuscan countryside where he can shop around, not only for wine, but also for olive oil since, as in many other parts of Italy, the vine and the olive tree normally go hand in hand.

Finally, for the reader of a literary bent, a reminder that references to Tuscan wines go back 500 years. Lorenzo de' Medici who, when he was not a statesman and patron of the arts, was also a poet, refers to it in his poem *I Beoni* (the drunkards) which he dedicated to his drunken friends. Another Italian poet, Francesco Redi, wrote a charming piece by the title 'Bacchus in Tuscany' where he describes and eulogizes the antics of Bacchus and friend Ariadne who, burning with love for each other, partake of the red wine when celebrating their love accompanied by nymphs. Most Italian schoolboys with a 'classical' education recall with pleasure how, according to Redi, Bacchus and Ariadne would go hugging each other right up to the town of Brindisi. The pun is that the noun 'brindisi' means a 'toast (in wine)' (accent on the first syllable, please!)
Band C/D

CHIARETTO DEL GARDA   [IGT / Rosé / Veneto]

This is one of the best known Italian rosé wines, 'created' in 1896 at Monica del Garda, originally with grapes of the Marzemino variety, the same that go to make the local red.

It is one of the few Italian rosé wines deserving of attention and has been described as being among northern Italy's better rosés. It is an extremely pleasant wine, produced in the same area as the Bardolino (q.v.) with the same grapes, of a cherry colour, which when aged turns to garnet. It has a very delicate scent. It is dry, very slightly bitter, fruity and lively. It has a minimum alcoholic content of 10.5° and is also available in a sparkling version.

Band A/B

CIALLA

The name includes in a generic sense a number of wines such as Picolit, Ribolla Gialla, Verduzzo, Refosco dal Peduncolo Rosso and Schioppettino. These will all be dealt with under separate headings. The important thing to note is that they are all wines produced in a well-defined area which includes the town of Cialla and, generally speaking, tend to be very fruity.

CIRÓ   [DOC / Red / Calabria]

The principal wine in the area of Calabria comes in red, white and rosé versions and originated in the old Greek town of 'Krimisa' or 'Kremisa', now no longer in existence.

Calabria is the region in the western toe of Italy, surrounded for the most part by sea. It is there that the Greeks created one of the oldest definitions of Italy, namely 'Enotria' meaning the land of wine. They found that their own vines grew very well in Calabria and even today some of the other principal grape varieties in this region are considered to be of Greek origin. I have in mind the Gaglioppo, the Greco (white and red), the Mantonico and the Piedelungo. There is also much Trebbiano as well in the area where Ciró is produced, which consists in the main of the communes of Ciró and Melissa in the province of Catanzaro.

In oenological terms Calabria has been one of the most neglected regions of Italy but over the past ten years a number of other grapes, like Cabernet, Merlot and Syrah have been planted and the quality of the wines produced there has improved dramatically, so much so that other types of wine are coming to the fore, such as the Greco, produced as a white wine which almost competes with the original Greco from Campania.

The red Ciró is a wine suitable for long ageing of ruby red colour which, like many other Italian wines, changes to orange with age, coming into its own after seven or eight years.

It is made in the main from the Gaglioppo grape, with the addition of Trebbiano and Greco.

It is a dry wine, which has to be matured for a minimum of eight months and has a minimum alcoholic content of 12.5°, rising to 15°. If produced from grapes originating in the communes of Ciró and Ciró Marina it can be termed 'Classico' but with a minimum alcoholic content of 13.5° it can become 'Superiore'. The 'Superiore' matured for a minimum of two years is entitled to be called 'Riserva'.

Ciró has a pleasant dry taste, warm and velvety as it matures. It is a full bodied wine which ages well.

I do not believe that the white version of Ciró is available in the UK but there is here a 'rosato', having a minimum alcoholic content of 12.5°, which is quite pleasant, though not outstanding.

There are other wines in Calabria, of course, such as Savuto, Lamezia, Melissa, Donnici, Pollino and at least half a dozen more, which are not considered here.

Band B

COLLI BOLOGNESI [DOC / White / Red Emilia / Romagna]

These DOC wines originate in the hills around Bologna and elsewhere in its administrative area as well as in a limited number of communes in the province of Modena.

White This is made with Albana and Trebbiano grapes and is a more or less gently straw-coloured, dry vinous wine occasionally petillant. Minimum alcoholic content 10.5° but usually available at 13.5°.

There is also a Colli Bolognesi Sauvignon made totally with grapes of the same name and having a minimum alcoholic content of 11° rising occasionally to 15°.

It is a much more smooth, subtly aromatically flavoured white, which comes in a dry, semi-dry and sparkling version. [See PIGNOLETTO]

Red There are broadly three varieties made respectively with Barbera, Merlot and Cabernet Sauvignon grapes, having the characteristics of the grape from which they originate. The minimum alcoholic content is 11.5° but it can rise to 15° for all three types. The three reds are dry but the Barbera is also available in a sparkling version.

With a minimum maturing of three years the Barbera and the Cabernet Sauvignon can be called 'Riserva'.

Band B (Whites)
Band C (Reds)

COLLI DI CONEGLIANO [DOC / White / Red / Veneto]

White This is a reasonably low alcohol (minimum 11°) dry, straw-coloured white wine, pleasant enough, produced in the province of Trento in twenty municipalities.

It is a blend of white Pinot and/or Chardonnay for a minimum of 30%, Incrocio Manzoni for a further 30% and a prescribed maximum 10% of Sauvignon and/or Renano Riesling. It is aged for a mere five months and is available also in a sweet version having a minimum ageing period of one year and a minimum alcoholic content of 16°.

Red This is a dry, full-bodied, vinous product made with a blend of Merlot (maximum 40%), Cabernet Franc, Cabernet Sauvignon and Marzemino in no less than 10% for each variety, plus a minimum of 10% Incrocio Manzoni.

It is produced in a number of municipalities in the province of Treviso and starts out in life with a minimum alcoholic content of 12°. It must be matured for no less than two years before being put on the market.

This is possibly less well known than its white version, although in my view probably more worthwhile. Reasonably tannic, it retains its aroma even after several years' maturity.

Band B/C

COLLI EUGANEI   [DOC / Red / Veneto]

This wine is produced in the province of Padova from grapes of Merlot, Cabernet Franc, Cabernet Sauvignon, Barbera and Raboso in varying percentages. It is ruby red with a typical vinous nose and a dry, but occasionally not so dry, taste, smooth and delicate. It has a minimum alcoholic content of 11° and as usual with a minimum ageing of two years and 12.5°, it can be termed 'Riserva'.

A wine of great antiquity, it was much appreciated by the poet Petrarch who justified, in the fourteenth century, the purchase of a house at Arquá (now known as Arquá Petrarca) by saying that he liked the wine of the locality!

Band A

COLLI LANUVINI   [DOC / White / Lazio]

This pleasant, unassuming white wine is produced in the general localities of Genzano and Lanuvio in the province of Rome and it takes its name from the hills in one of two areas of production. It is made with the two staple vines of Lazio, namely the Trebbiano (30%) (both Verde and Giallo) and the Malvasia Bianca (70%) following a practice which, it is said, was established by the Etruscans. It was certainly well-known to the Romans.

It is a more or less gently straw-coloured dry wine, vinous in taste, fairly pleasant and smooth, with a minimum alcoholic content of 11.5°. It is also produced in a slightly less dry version. It should be drunk young. It certainly does not lend itself to any kind of ageing.

Band A

COLLI ORIENTALI DEL FRIULI
                [DOC / Friuli / Venezia Giulia / Red / White / Rosé]

The past few years has seen an increase in the export of wines coming from this area, in the three types, all produced in the province of Udine with a number of grapes without any specificity either of the grape varieties or the blend or the percentages in a blend.

Red This is a pleasant, dry, well balanced wine, of intense red colour turning to brick when aged. It is sapid with a pleasant aftertaste. It is made with local red grapes.

White This, too, has a minimum alcoholic content of 11°, is a straw-coloured, delicately scented, gentle wine, usually tasting of almonds.

Rosé Again, a minimum alcoholic content of 11°, a dry, pleasant, fresh wine, cherry-coloured and an extremely pleasant nose.

The general description Colli Orientali del Friuli includes a number of wines which are dealt with separately (such as Picolit, Ribolla Gialla, Verduzzo, Refosco dal Peduncolo Rosso and Schioppettino) as well as others not specifically dealt with in this guide such as the Istrian Malvasia, the Pignolo, the Rosazzo and the Tazzelenghe.

Under the same heading also fall Cabernet, Cabernet Franc, Cabernet Sauvignon, Chardonnay, Pinot Bianco, Pinot Grigio, Riesling, Sauvignon, and Tocai Friulano.

Band B/C

COLLI PESARESI   [DOC / Red /Rosé / Marche]

This all embracing DOC description covers wine produced in a large area in the provinces of Pesaro and Urbino, in something like thirty municipalities.

The grapes used are very numerous indeed. For example, the white is made with varying percentages of Trebbiano (known locally as Albanella), Verdicchio, Pinot Bianco, Pinot Grigio, and even Pinot Noir, Riesling, Chardonnay, Sauvignon and a variety that grows successfully in the locality, namely Biancame.

The locally produced Rosé (known as 'Rosato' or 'Rosé') is pleasant enough, made with the same grapes as the red.

Red This is made with a minimum of 70% Sangiovese to which are added other local grapes, especially Montepulciano d'Abruzzo. Of ruby red colour, it is a pleasant, reasonably dry, vinous wine, having a minimum alcoholic content of 11° but more commonly sold at 12.5°.

The variety known as Colli Pesaresi Sangiovese is a more substantial wine made with a minimum of 85% Sangiovese and an average alcoholic content of 12.5° (minimum 11°).

Some version of the red are emerging which do NOT comply technically with the DOC specifications in as much as they are made with 60% Montepulciano d'Abruzzo and 40% Cabernet Sauvignon.

These wines are much more substantial (alcoholic content 13.5°) and normally matured in barriques, which, the producers claim, give them a more 'international' character!

CONEGLIANO-VALDOBBIADENE   [DOC / White]

(See PROSECCO)

CONERO   [DOCG / Red / Marche]

A very recent addition to the DOCG classification that is produced in a fairly restricted area fronting the Adriatic coast in the province of Ancona.

This wine, whose name is derived from the Monte Conero which is at the apex of the production area, is obtained from the grapes of Montepulciano (minimum 50%) with the addition of Sangiovese and Cabernet Sauvignon.

It is a fairly dry, ruby red wine, with a pleasant nose, good body and a vinous taste, with a minimum alcoholic content of 12.5° and maturing

period of two years.
Band C

CONTESSA ENTELLINA   [DOC / White / Red / Sicilia]

An outstanding Sicilian white wine is produced at the Vigna di Gabri by the firm of Donnafugata. Donnafugata is sometimes said to be the name of a well-known castle in the locality and it means 'the woman who escaped', derived from a story (factually incorrect) of a wife who was kept prisoner there! . . . . . and finally managed to get away. In reality, it is a word of Arab origin.

It is a fairly novel wine since it was first produced in 1987 out of 100% 'Ansonica' grapes, and it takes its name from the small town in the province of Palermo. Nowadays, this grape is prescribed for at least 50% of the production, the balance being made up with many others (such as Catarratto, Grecanico, Sauvignon, white Pinot, Grillo and even Chardonnay).

Like many southern Italian wines, the grapes are harvested at the end of August and fined for at least four months in bottle to achieve an average alcoholic content of 13°. It is dry, but smooth and at times it tastes almost slightly sweetish. This is why, in all likelihood, its intense aroma reminds me, at least, of candied peel, especially citrus. It has a pleasant, strong nose and a very aromatic aftertaste.

The Contessa Entellina DOC also covers red and rosé wines made with Syrah and/or Calabrese grapes (50%), the balance being non-aromatic red grape varieties. The red wines from this part of Sicily age quite well, but few are available abroad.

Band B/C

COPERTINO   [DOC / Red / Rosé / Puglia (Salento)]

There are very few tourists to Italy who are aware of the existence, in its south-eastern tip, of one of the most beautiful cities of which Italy can boast.

Lecce vies with Naples and with Noto, in Sicilia, as being the capital of Italian baroque architecture. Anyone who visits it could travel not too far to the town of Copertino where, with the grapes of Negromaro (70%), Malvasia (Nera of Brindisi and of Lecce), Montepulciano and Sangiovese, are produced the following wines:

Copertino Red. This is a ruby colour veering to orange as it matures with a marked nose and a dry slightly bitter taste. It is a smooth strong-bodied wine with a minimum alcoholic content of 12° which rises to 12.5° when it has to qualify as 'Riserva', a very fine version.

Copertino Rosé. This is a very pleasant, unexpectedly so perhaps, rosé wine of basically salmon colour veering at times towards a light red. A marked nose, dry, smooth, herb-like taste with a slightly bitter aftertaste. Its minimum alcoholic content is 12° but quite often it goes well above that.

Band B

COPERTINO   [IGT / Red / Puglia]

Certain other non-DOC versions of this wine have become available. It is made mainly in the town of Copertino but also elsewhere in the provinces of Lecce and Brindisi from Negroamaro grapes (80%) and others, especially local Malvasias.

It is of an intense ruby red colour veering to orange when mature. It has a strong vinous nose and a dry, smooth taste. The minimum alcoholic content is 12° but if matured for two years and with 12.5° alcohol it can be termed 'Riserva'.

Band A/B

CORTESE (*dell'Alto Monferrato*)   [DOC / White / Piemonte]

Cortese is a dry, white wine which, in a sense, is of mixed origin. The vineyards that produce it are to be found mainly in what is known geographically as the Alto Monferrato which, of course, is in the region of Piemonte but is very close to Liguria, as witness the fact that its main area of production is practically on the border with Liguria and the village which is the centre of the production area is called Novi Ligure, even though it is in Piemonte.

So much is this so that in the whole of the locality they speak Piedmontese dialect, but with a ligurian accent and, when it comes to gastronomy, extensive use is made of the Genoese 'Pesto' which is hardly at home in Piemonte. In fact, a more correct description of this wine would be a Bianco Cortese di Gavi, rather than as per heading.

It should not be confused with the Cortese dell'Oltrepò Pavese which originates in the province of Pavia in Lombardia and is a fairly similar wine, nor with the Gavi (q.v.) a DOCG wine (which should more accurately be described as Cortese di Gavi). Cortese is also produced in the communes of Gavi, Serravalle Scrivia, Arquata Scrivia and Tortona in the province of Alessandria.

It is made from the grape of the same name which yields a yellow/greenish clear wine with a delicate scent and a dry, fresh but perhaps slightly acidy flavour. It is a wine with a minimum alcoholic content of 10° which seldom exceeds 12°. It cannot be kept for too long but it is quite suitable for a two to three-year ageing.

Band B

CORVO   [IGT / Red / White / Sicilia]

The possessions of the Duke of Salaparuta at Casteldaccia in the province of Palermo are well known. Even though the estate itself is not extensive, in 2003 it produced just over 14m bottles. Partly from grapes obtained from local co-operatives, it produces a number of wines of which the red and the white are particularly well-known in England where they became firmly established in the early 1960s. The grapes used are Nero d'Avola, Perricone, Nerello Mascalese, Grillo, Inzolia and Frappato.

Corvo Rosso The red version is produced by traditional methods of vinification and matured for two years in Slavonian oak prior to bottling. It is made with Nero d'Avola, Perricone and Nerello

Mascalese grapes, has a bright red colour veering with age to greater intensity. It is flavourful, dry and yet smooth and quite sapid. Its normal alcoholic content is 12°. It reaches its peak at about five years and I would not expect it to last much beyond eight.

Corvo Bianco This is a very successful, strongly-coloured white wine made with Inzolia, Catarratto and Grecanico grapes. Its alcoholic content seldom exceeds 11.5°. It is a useful white, smooth, dry and vinous.

Band A

CUSTOZA (or *Bianco di Custoza*)   [White / Veneto]

This is another much blended Venetian white produced in approximately the same area as Bardolino, that is to say in the southern part of Lake Garda in the province of Verona, mainly in the communes of Custoza and Sommacampagna. It results from a mixture of Trebbiano (maximum 45%), Garganega (maximum 40%), Tocai (maximum 30%) and Malvasia, Riesling, Pinot Bianco and Chardonnay.

It is a straw white wine with a greenish tinge, delicate, with a very fruity, highly scented and slightly aromatic nose. Of medium body, it has a pleasant slightly bitter taste. Minimum alcoholic content is 11°. It does not really lend itself to maturing and should be drunk quite young.

It is also available in a 'Superiore' style with a minimum alcoholic content of 12.5° but broadly with the same features, save that it has tendency to veer to golden colour as it matures, as well as in sparkling version; there is also a Passito with a minimum alcoholic content of 15°.

Band A/B

DOLCETTO   [DOCG / DOC / Red / Piemonte]

The grape that gives its name to this wine is one of the most important varieties in Piemonte, if not in Italy. It is produced extensively over a wide area of the Langhe, mainly on hills and sometimes even on sandy soil. 'Dolce' in Italian means sweet, but this wine is certainly not that! It is, in fact, smooth but quite dry.

It takes its name from the flavour of the Dolcetto variety grape which is exceptionally sweet and, perhaps unusually for a winemaking grape, can also be savoured as a table variety. It is found principally in the provinces of Alessandria and Cuneo, and comes in seven varieties, all capable of being differentiated one from the other.

The wine is rich in anthocyanins, but not too tannic for the simple reason that it is not left to ferment for too long on the skins. The consequence is that the colour of a young Dolcetto is very intense but does not last long. It is an established fact that as wines mature their colour depends more and more on the amount of tannins and less on anthocyanins.

1. **Dolcetto d'Acqui** DOC. It derives its name from the commune of Acqui in the province of Alessandria and has a minimum alcoholic content of 11.5°; when matured for one year and of 12.5° gradation it can be termed 'Superiore'.

It is a dry wine, with a vinous and slightly bitter taste. Of an intense ruby red colour, it veers to brick red when mature.

2. **Dolcetto d'Alba** DOC. This takes its name from the town of Alba in the province of Cuneo, at the heart of the wine producing district, and is considered by some to be the best out of the seven varieties. Its taste almost reflects the undulating countryside where the grapes are grown, but it is difficult to identify. It is tannic, though not too much, vinous, occasionally sharp but does not recall any fruit or flavour one can think of. In fact, it has what can only be called the taste of wine, subtle but incapable of definition; so much so that when one of the leading Italian wine writers tried to describe its aroma, he confined himself to using the adjective 'subtle'! (Luigi Veronelli). Other wine tasters claim they can detect a scent of violets.

It is of ruby red colour, which changes to violet when swirled in the glass and has a very good body. Minimum alcoholic content is 11.5° rising to 12.5° for the 'Superiore' variety but, over the past ten years or so, stronger types of Dolcetto d'Alba have emerged of between 13° and 14° strength.

In its better versions, and in good years, it lends itself to some limited ageing reaching its peak at between three and four years, occasionally drinkable even at six, though certainly not beyond.

Many bottles are produced of this wine (in excess of 9 million).

3. **Dolcetto d'Asti** DOC. This version is produced in the hills around the town of Asti and is, in effect, a variation, if one can put it that way, on the Dolcetto d'Acqui in every respect.

4. **Dolcetto delle Langhe Monregalesi** DOC. Again, from the Dolcetto grape, grown on the hills flanking the river Tanaro in the province of Cuneo, produced mainly in the communes of Alba, Fossano and Dogliani. The wine is of a vivid ruby colour, dry, of medium body, with slight aftertaste. Minimum alcoholic content of 11° which when rising to 12° allows the term 'Superiore' to be used.

The wine can be drunk when very young and matures quickly. Perfect at two years, it ages fast. It is of ruby red colour if grown in sandy soil, and garnet red if grown in chalky soil.

Like the Dolcetto d'Alba, it is difficult to classify its flavour. It is a very dry wine but not offensively so because it leaves a subtle, almost sweet, aftertaste. A generous wine, although perhaps lacking in refinement.

5. **Dolcetto di Diano d'Alba** or Dolcetto Diano d'Alba DOC. This is produced exclusively in the hills of Diano d'Alba in the province of Cuneo and is in practically all respects similar to the other types of Dolcetto except that it has an almondy taste.

6. **Dolcetto di Dogliani** DOCG. Dogliani is also in the hills and this wine originates there.

It is similar to the Dolcetto d'Alba in most respects but I have not so far seen it with a higher alcoholic content than 13.5°. In many versions it is to be preferred to that of Alba as smoother and more flavourful:

this is a judgement that I formulated in 2003 and I am pleased to report that it appears to have been vindicated because in 2005 this particular variety of Dolcetto has obtained a DOCG.

7. **Dolcetto di Ovada**. From the town of Ovada in the province of Alessandria, it is produced almost exclusively in the communes of Ovada and Acqui Terme. There, Dolcetto has a very intense ruby colour and is comparable to the Dolcetto di Diano d'Alba.

N.B. Dolcetto is produced in other areas of Piemonte, the grape being quite versatile, but the alcoholic content varies. For instance, in the area south of Turin (e.g. Pinerolo) a very pleasant Dolcetto is produced with a minimum alcoholic content of 10.5° which, in other respects, resembles its seven brothers previously considered.
Band B/C

ELBA   [DOC / White / Red / Toscana]

It is rumoured that when Napoleon Bonaparte was exiled to the isle of Elba he spent some of his time trying to learn about viticulture. Hardly surprising since in ancient times Elba was called 'Insula Viniferax', namely an island where the vine abounds. In fact, ever since Roman times, but especially during the reign of the Medici, viticulture on Elba was one of the primary activities of the locals who initially relied on autochthonous vines but later, during the Napoleonic Wars, also imported some cultivars from France.

The wine production on Elba is not very great but the red and white under the denomination of origin Elba are in their own way worthwhile wines.

Elba White. This is made with Trebbiano grapes, (known locally as Procanico) 50% minimum, Ansonica (q.v.), and Vermentino grapes to a maximum of 50% and other grapes to a maximum of 20%. It is a pleasant lightly straw coloured wine, delicately scented with a minimum alcoholic content of 11°.

Elba Red. This is made with Sangiovese grapes, locally known as Sangioveto (the same that goes into the Brunello di Montalcino, for example), to a minimum of 60%, the balance being made up with red and no more than 10% white grapes. It is a medium-bodied ruby red dry wine with a minimum alcoholic content of 11.5°. Much more interesting are the white Ansonica (q.v.) and the Aleatico (q.v.).
Band A

ELORO (*v Nero d'Avola*)   [DOC / Sicilia]

This is a comparatively new DOC which acknowledges the giant strides made by the Sicilian wine industry, especially with a view to escaping from the usual high alcoholic content wines.
Band A/B

ERBALUCE DI CALUSO (*Otherwise known as Caluso*)
[DOC / White / Piemonte]

As observed elsewhere, the region Piemonte is not particularly well known for outstanding whites, but this is certainly one of them. It is produced exclusively with grapes of the same name from vines in thirty-three communes in the province of Torino, two in that of Vercelli and three in that Biella; a beautiful sight in autumn, when both the leaves and grapes take on an especial copper hue.

It is a brilliant, straw-coloured wine with a pleasant nose and a very dry and typically fresh taste. It has a minimum alcoholic content of 11° and is also available in a sparkling wine version with a minimum alcoholic content of 11.5°.

The sparkling version, as far as I can tell, is not available outside Italy, nor is its 'Passito' edition, a beautifully golden colour, sweet wine with a minimum alcoholic content of 17° and a minimum maturing of four years (five for the 'Riserva').

Band B

ESINO   [DOC / White / Red / Marche]

This wine has only recently begun to be exported and, as far as I could find out, only in its white version. It is made with no less than 50% Verdicchio grapes in its white version and no less than 60% of Sangiovese and Montepulciano in its red. It is produced in the provinces of Ancona and Macerata.

It is a lightly straw-coloured, dry wine, reasonably fruity and fresh tasting with a minimum alcoholic content of 10.5°. There is also a sparkling version. The red is similar in minimum alcoholic content, ruby coloured, fairly dry, vinous tasting. Pleasant enough, but not outstanding.

EST! EST! EST! DI MONTEFIASCONE [DOC / White / Lazio]

A white wine produced in the province of Viterbo from the Trebbiano and Malvasia grapes, also available as sparkling, straw-coloured, brilliant, with a slightly aromatic nose and a typical persistent, sapid taste. It comes in dry, semi-dry or sweet versions, with a minimum alcoholic content of 10° and a maximum usually of 12°.

It has been famous since the twelfth century and is tied to a very old and probably boring story of how Bishop Giovanni Defuk, part of the retinue of the Emperor Henry V, had asked his valet, Martino, whilst on their way to Rome from the north, to precede him and identify as he went along the better quality wines in the various hostelries.

It was agreed that when Martino found a wine which pleased him particularly he would mark on the door of the establishment the word 'Est', Latin for 'here it is'. When Martino, however, got to Montefiascone, on the shores of Lake Bolsena, he sampled the local wine and found it so exquisite that he wrote 'Est' three times. . . . .; the Bishop having sampled it, he remained and died there. His tomb is still said to exist and in abundant years tradition has it that a barrel of wine should be emptied over the tombstone. Charming, probably naïve and

maybe even spurious, but a mark of appreciation centuries ago for a wine which is now perhaps less popular, and possibly even less worthwhile, than it was.
Band A/B

ETNA   [DOC / White / Red / Rosé / Sicilia]

White Produced mainly in the province of Catania from Carricante and Catarratto white grapes (in percentages respectively of 60 and 40 and with a permitted addition of Trebbiano and Minella, up to a maximum of 15%) this is a golden-straw-coloured, vinous, dry wine with a minimum alcoholic content of 11.5° (12.5° for the Superiore version). The production zone is fairly extensive covering more than twenty communes.
Red This is produced in the same area as the white with grapes of Nerello Mascalese (80% minimum) and Nerello Mantellato (20% maximum). It is a ruby red, dry, full bodied, harmonious wine with a minimum alcoholic content of 12.5°, although some versions may reach 14°.
Rosé Same rules as for the red. Lightly coloured tending to ruby. A pleasant and surprisingly successful summer wine.
Band B

FALANGHINA   [White / Campania]

This is a straw-coloured white wine produced almost exclusively in the province of Benevento, more particularly in the area that used to be known to the Romans as the 'Samnium' ('Sannio'). It is made from the grapes of the same name. It is a fine wine, which claims to be a competitor for Greco di Tufo (q.v.) and Fiano (q.v.). It is also a wine with an ancient lineage since not only was it known to the Romans but it (the grapes) went into one of their top wines, the Falernum (see Falerno).

It has a typical slightly acidic nose, quite fruity at times; a dry taste and a minimum alcoholic content of 11° (though more normally marketed at 12.5°; I have also seen a version at 13°). It is available in sparkling form and as a 'Passito'.

Straw coloured, often yellow/gold with greenish hues, it has an extremely pleasant after-taste. This wine is becoming more popular than it has been for quite some time, both in Italy and abroad.
Band B

FALERIO (otherwise known as *Falerio dei Colli Ascolani*)
                                          [DOC / White / Marche]

This is a fairly recent new wine, which dates back to 1956 and obtained DOC recognition in 1975. It is produced in the province of Ascoli Piceno, a well-defined area containing some seventy-three municipalities and extending over 2,000 square kilometres.

According to specification, the grapes used are Trebbiano Toscano (maximum 50%), Passerina (maximum 30%) and Pecorino (maximum 30%). In some versions a Malvasia is added.

It is a gently straw-coloured wine, only lightly aromatic, dry, with a slightly acidic after taste. Its minimum alcoholic content is 11.5° but is normally available at 12.5°.

The advertising blurbs for it state 'it is pleasantly scented, with overtones of acacia and peach'. I must confess that I do not detect these overtones, but there it is.

It is a wine to be drunk only very young, quite suitable as an aperitif. The locals tend to serve it with the well-known Ascolana type of olive, a native speciality.

Band A/B

FALERNO (DEL MASSICO)   [DOC / Red / White / Campania]

Probably the most respected and appreciated wine made popular by the Romans (Falernum) who called it 'the wine of the emperors', but its history is said to go back nearly 3,000 years. (Falernum is mentioned by Emperor Marcus Aurelius in his 'Meditations' [Book VI, 13].)

'Vinum Massicum' – taking its name from Mount Massico – continued to be known long after the Roman Empire had disappeared. In his book *The Evolution of The Grand Tour* (Frank Cass, London, 1998, p.106) Professor Chaney records that travelling through Italy southwards towards Naples, Richard Lassels adverts to the fact the Massico mountain was 'famous anciently for Vinum Massicum'.

The Roman writer Lucius Annius Florus records that round about the year 318 BC a tribe known as 'Falerna' started developing land at the foot of Mount Massico. The area soon became known for its fertility and, of course, for the production of wine.

It was derived from the Aglianico grape, mainly, and at that time was produced on land bordering Campania and Lazio. The Romans were exceptionally fond of it. Pliny described it as austere, yet sweet and smooth; Ovid termed it a 'godly epithet'. Horace said that it was a wine that burned and, perhaps going over the top, Martial termed it 'immortal'.

They liked it particuarly because with it they made their honeyed wine called 'mulsum'. We have forgotten about honeyed wine, of course and the spicing of table wines with herbs and resins can be said to have remained only in Greece (see Retsina). Nowadays, it is made with the Aglianico grape with additions of Piedirosso (both reaching 80%), the remainder made up of Primitivo and Barbera.

It has a very marked ruby red colour, bright, a distinctive and intense nose and a very warm harmonious, almost hot, taste, with a pronounced hint of strawberry. It is a very well balanced wine with a minimum alcoholic content of 12.5° and a minimum maturing of one year – two if it is to be labelled 'Riserva'.

One of its central areas of production is the village of Mondragone, but it is to be found also in the areas of the Campi Flegrei (Naples) and of Formia (Latina). The red lends itself to ageing. Some versions do not reach their peak until five years; I have sampled a twelve-year old Falerno which was in excellent condition. It is a well-known table wine which the locals enjoy drinking with wild duck.

A white Falerno, made principally with the Falanghina grape, is also produced in the municipalities of Pozzuoli, Bacoli and Cuma in the province of Naples. A 'Primitivo' variety is made with a minimum alcoholic content of 13°.

Band B/C

FAVORITA (*See Langhe – Langhe Favorita*)

FIANO DI AVELLINO   [DOCG / White / Campania]

This is one of the great Italian whites from Campania, produced mainly in the communes of Atripalda, Candida, Lapio and Serino. In addition to the Fiano grape, an ancient variety now not so common (indeed, one could say that it is becoming scarce), there are blended Greco and Coda di Volpe grapes, the same as are used for the Greco di Tufo, and there is added here the Tuscan Trebbiano. The blend produces a wine with a very intense nose and a pleasant, fairly characteristic taste; a very dry wine, which often hits the palate as slightly less than smooth. The minimum alcoholic content is 11.5° and its colour is lighter than that of Greco di Tufo. Nowadays, it is more likely to be found in the 12°/12.5° gradation, given the general trend to increase the alcoholic content of wines. There is also a growing tendency to make it with 100% Fiano grapes.

It is often awkward to describe the taste of Fiano; the addition of Trebbiano does give it a particular flavour which occasionally reminds one of the Muscat grape, and at times, of nuts. (It makes a most enjoyable sweet sparkling wine, unfortunately not normally available outside Italy.)

It is a superior white which lends itself to moderate ageing. A fairly outstanding version of it, oaked!, is known as Campanaro. It is eminently suited to fish dishes and there are some who say that it is to be preferred with trout.

The Fiano grape was certainly known to the Romans who, some believe, called it 'Appianum', from the name of the vine, 'vitis apiana', thus described because its sweet grapes attract bees ('api' in Italian). Frederick II is said to have been fond of it.

Band C

FRANCIACORTA   [DOCG / White Sparkling / Lombardia]
                          [DOC / White Dry / Lombardia]

In the region of Lombardia known as Franciacorta, squeezed between the provinces of Bergamo and Brescia, (technically, the plain south of Lake Iseo, which stretches from the River Oglio to Brescia), an area, incidentally, well known for its haute cuisine, is produced one of the sparkling glories of Italy, Franciacorta.

This is made with a blend of Chardonnay, Pinot white and Pinot black grapes and is fermented in bottles. It is a straw coloured wine of greater or lesser intensity with gentle variations towards either the green or the golden.

It has a fine, smooth and delicate nose with a fresh, harmonious taste. It has what I would call a flowery bouquet, often reminiscent of violets. With a minimum alcoholic content of 11.5° it must be matured in bottle for at least eighteen months. The bubbles are fine, not too intense and rather slow moving. An outstanding sparkler, in my view Italy's best.

The fermentation method for this product is said to be complex, with a slow re-fermentation in bottle following the original one. The whole wine industry of the area has as its capital the small town of Erbusco which the locals call 'city of wine', known for wine production since at least the fifteenth century.

This whole area in the province of Brescia has many associations; it may be worth recalling that the fast road that joins Brescia to Turin, another city with surrounding countryside is best known for wine production, is called 'The motorway of the wine'. (The reader might like to know that it is not unusual in Italy to identify motorways by what I would term practical/artistic descriptions: thus we have the 'motorway of the sun' running from Milan to the south, the 'motorway of the flowers' running the length of the Italian Rivera from Ventimiglia to La Spezia. The former because theoretically at least there is more sun in the south than in the north of Italy, the latter both because of the oleanders which beautify the central reservations and also because of the greenhouses and hothouses, the heart of the Italian flower industry).

Franciacorta also comes in a sparkling rosé version (with a colour of varying intensity) resulting from a 15% use of black Pinot grapes.

It is also produced exclusively with Chardonnay and Pinot Bianco grapes (that is to say, without Pinot Nero) in a version which was formerly known solely as Cremant but is now more popularly known as Satén. This is an outstanding sparkling wine: the sugar content is lower than usual (18 grams per litre or thereabouts) which allows it to develop a lower carbon dioxide pressure than its brethren (4.5 bar) and only comes in a Brut variety. Its taste is very smooth indeed, produces very fine bubbles and an attractive foam.

This wine can be termed the 'Italian Champagne' and it is certainly worth listing below the seven available versions of it:
1. Zero dosage, i.e. with no sugar syrup added. Dry.
2. Extra Brut dry with a maximum sugar content not exceeding 6 grams/litre.
3. Brut also dry but with a higher sugar content, not exceeding 15 grams/litre.
4. Extra dry follows the description. . . with a sugar content ranging between 12 and 20 grams/litre.
5. Dry (sec) somewhat less harsh on the palate but still fairly dry with a sugar content between 17 and 35 grams/litre.
6. Demi-sec medium dry with a sugar content ranging between 33 and 50 grams/litre.
7. Saten as described above, with a maximum sugar content of 15 grams/litre.
There is also a Franciacorta DOC still white wine, made with

Chardonnay, Pinot Bianco and Pinot Nero. This is a straw-coloured wine with green tinges, dry and sapid, having a minimum alcoholic content of 11° but usually sold at 12.5°, and despite the fact that its sparkling 'brother' is much more fashionable, is still to be considered as the most important white wine in the area. Such is the commonly held view. I differ slightly, in this sense. Whilst it is true that in its immediate impact the flavour is not too reminiscent of Chardonnay (which as far as I am concerned is a very good thing) I find that the aftertaste is somewhat difficult to define. Put differently, whenever I drink it I am always left slightly dissatisfied. It is almost impossible to fault it, of course, since it is well made, well balanced and reasonably flavourful. And yet, it often tastes almost unfinished, giving the feeling that the initial promises of the first sip are not being kept. But perhaps I am being over-fastidious.

Band E (Sparkling)

Band C (Dry)

FRASCATI
[DOC / White / Lazio]

Most people have either heard of or enjoyed a white Frascati, a staple wine in Italian restaurants abroad and in all the trattorie and pizzerie of Lazio. Its nutty flavour is quite unique and in its DOC (1966) version it is produced almost exclusively in the province of Rome (communes of Frascati, Grottaferrata, Monteporzio Catone and Montecompatri). Famous since Roman times, especially in the Middle Ages and in the fifteenth to nineteenth centuries.

It is a mixture in varying proportions of a number of grapes and it is the most popular of the wines in the area surrounding Rome known as the 'Castelli', namely the castles.

It emerges from essentially the Malvasia and the Trebbiano grapes, with many additions and has an alcoholic content varying between 11° and 12.5°. Straw-coloured, brilliant, often golden, one can sometimes taste in it the volcanic nature of the soil on which the grapes are grown, though another explanation of its astringency may be the fermentation process. A wine that should be drunk young and, *pace* all foreign restaurateurs, does not really travel well. It comes in three versions, dry, demi-sweet and sweet.

There are also sparkling varieties, and the sweet Cannellino is a most pleasant summer wine.

Band A

FREISA
[DOC / Red / Piemonte]

This wine is derived from the grape of the same name which is an indigenous, typical variety of the region where it is fairly widespread. The variety was first identified in 1875; it appeared to be resistant to the scourge that had affected vines in Piemonte (oidium which started in 1852) and proved also fairly resistant to the subsequent infestations of peronospera (1880) and phylloxera (1894).

A tough vine, the grapes of which yield between 10° and 12° alcohol and which, in all the varieties mentioned, provides a lovely ruby colour, good, highly tannic nose and a very dry taste.

Easy to store, but slow to mature, most wines are fairly acidic and some of them require blending with other grapes such as Barbera, Nebbiolo, Bonarda and Neretto. It is normally produced in two types, one dry which starts off as a fairly uncouth wine, but softens as it matures; the other a much less dry wine, almost sweetish, with a lower alcoholic percentage and more often than not, also sparkling.

The main varieties are:

The Freisa of Pinerolo in the province of Turin, a youngish, happy wine, with a minimum alcoholic content of 10.5° and made with 85% Freisa grapes, blended as above.

The Freisa of Asti which has a minimum alcoholic content of 11° and is also blended in the proportions previously mentioned.

The Freisa of the Langhe which has a minimum alcoholic content of 11° but is made exclusively with Freisa grapes and that of Chieri similar in content and in grape variety. Both these are brilliantly coloured wines with a mixture of aroma between raspberries and violets. I especially like the former. In smaller quantities, and less known, there is a Freisa of Alba.

Freisa is available also in a slightly sparkling version. A most enjoyable wine, especially with some of the Piedmontese specialities like 'bollito misto' (assorted boiled meats) for which some Piedmontese villages are particularly well known (e.g. Carrú). Freisa should be drunk young: it will not keep well much beyond three to four years.

The Salerno School of Medicine, to which reference has already been made, laid down that alcoholic drinks should be 'fortia, formosa, fragrantia, frigida, frisca (freely translated, strong, full-bodied, fragrant, refreshing and fresh)'. It is obviously a coincidence that like the *Freisa* wine, all these qualities start with a letter 'f'.

Band A/B

FRIULI GRAVE (*See Grave delle Friuli*)

GAMBELLARA [DOC / White / Veneto]

Originating in the village by the same name in the province of Vicenza (geographically as well as historically halfway between Vicenza and Padua) and made with a minimum 80% of Garganega (locally known as Gambellara) grape (the balance can be made up at will provided the grape is not too aromatic; Trebbiano di Soave and Trebbiano Toscano being commonly used), this is a versatile wine available in three versions:

1. **Gambellara Dry** is of varying colour (straw yellow to light gold), and of a very marked scent and taste, which, whilst originally dry, often seems to be semi-dry. This slightly bitter, medium-bodied white wine has a minimum alcoholic content of 10.5°, which when produced in the original area, and entitled to be classed as a 'Classico', must increase to 11.5°.

2. **Gambellara Recioto** is made with the same grapes that, however,

have been subjected to the 'appassimento' process (q.v.). Its colour is the same as its dry brother, but the scent is much stronger and fruitier. It tastes as a sweet wine should, either semi-sweet or truly sweet, flavourful but, again, with a slightly bitter aftertaste. Its minimum alcoholic content must be 12° and it is also available in a slightly fizzy version.

3. **Gambellara Vin Santo.** This wine, too, is sweet, the Garganega grape being subjected to the 'appassimento' process. However, it is a much more solid wine. It has a strong amber colour and is heavily scented. It must be matured for a minimum of two years, have an alcoholic content of at least 14° but is more often available in higher gradations.

There are some who maintain that the dry Gambellara is not easily distinguishable from Soave and there is an element of truth in that, save that the prescribed minimum of Garganega grapes in Soave is 70% as distinct from the 80% in Gambellara; it thus allows the added Trebbiano and Chardonnay grapes to provide their own flavourful input. One's taste buds will determine what conclusion is to be reached on the issue of the two wines being similar. What is certain is that Gambellara is not produced in quantity, possibly also because the grape doubles as a table fruit.

Band A/B

GARDA (*Garda Classico – Garda Colli Mantovani*)
[DOC / White / Red / Rosé / Lombardia / Veneto]

The area surrounding Lake Garda straddling Lombardia and Veneto is one of the most ancient wine-producing locations in Italy and yields some fine white, rosé (see Chiaretto del Garda) and red wines. The whites have a minimum alcoholic content of 10.5°, rising to 12.5° more usually and the reds a minimum of 11°, rising to 13°.

The whites are made with a blend of Trebbiano, Chardonnay, Sauvignon and Riesling (Renano and Italico). The rosé with a blend of Merlot, Rondinella, Cabernet, Sangiovese, Molinara and Negrara, the reds essentially with Cabernet (whether Cabernet Sauvignon or Cabernet Franc). All the wines that fall under the Garda DOC can be labelled with the name of the grapes that go to produce them provided the minimum quantity used is 85%.

We thus have:

For the whites, Chardonnay, Cortese, Pinot Bianco, Pinot Grigio, Riesling, Riesling Italico, Sauvignon, and Tocai.

For the reds, Barbera, Cabernet, Cabernet Sauvignon, Corvina, Groppello, Merlot and Pinot Nero.

Chiaretto and Marzemino are dealt with separately.

These are sound, pleasant wines, by no means outstanding but eminently drinkable.

A number of rosé versions of a wine produced in this area, which have tended to utilize a blend of grapes different from the traditional one, have recently been exported. For example, there is a Garda Rosé which is a blend of Marzemino, Sangiovese and Barbera grapes, produced by one of the best known houses in the area. A fine rosé, of course, but not in my opinion worth the price tag, especially when a reasonable 'chiaretto' (q.v.) can be found at about half the price.

Band B/C

GATTINARA (*also known locally as Spanna*) [DOCG / Red / Piemonte]

Another of the Piedmontese top reds, which some Italian wine writers consider even superior to Barolo (q.v.) and Barbaresco (q.v.). This is a wine produced in a well-defined area in the commune of Gattinara (province of Vercelli) on the hills going from Vercelli towards the area known as Valsesia, with Nebbiolo (Spanna) grapes and a very small addition of Vespolina and Bonarda. It was known in Roman times, its name said to be derived from the Latin 'Catuli Ara', i.e. Catullus's altar.

It is worth noting that a number of good Piedmontese wines also use the Bonarda grape which, in fact, comes to Piemonte from the Oltrepó area. In the Gattinara it can be added in a ratio of up to 10% but although the quantity is modest, it does have an impact on the wine's flavour.

Its nose is quite perfumed ranging between roses and violets, its colour ruby red, its taste dry with a slightly bitter aftertaste which, like the wine's roughness, improves with ageing. It will age quite well up to ten or fifteen years, if not more.

With an alcoholic content ranging between 12.5° and 13° (minimum 12.5°) it must be matured for at least three years except for the 'Riserva' type which must have a minimum of 13° and a maturity period of at least four years.

The wine is quite flavourful and when it starts to mature (at about five years) one can also detect some raspberries amongst the fruity flavours. It really improves a lot with ageing.

The problem with Gattinara is that the area of production is as limited (about 500 hectares) as the quantity produced. The net result of this is that one should be very careful in purchasing it and, as has often been suggested, one should first taste and then buy.

Band C/D

GAVI   [DOCG / White / Piemonte]

Gavi is a very pleasant white wine considered by some to be the best Piedmontese white, and is otherwise known as Cortese di Gavi (the technical description). It is available both in Italy and abroad in two versions, namely a Gavi and a Gavi di Gavi (or Gavi dei Gavi or Gavi del Comune di Gavi).

What all this really means is that there is a Gavi produced in ten communes in the province of Alessandria, one of which is Gavi (hence the name of the wine). That actually produced in Gavi is a Gavi di Gavi which is inevitably a more expensive, usually, though not necessarily, better wine.

It is a perfectly clear straw-coloured white wine with a more or less delicate and rather typical nose, a dry fresh and harmonious taste, derived from the local Cortese grapes. The minimum alcholic content is

10.5°. Most of what is exported is of at least 11°. There exist also sparkling versions.

There are conflicting views about Gavi. It does appear that it takes a couple of years to mature in the bottle. Accordingly, it is maintained by some that it will improve if matured for longer.

I believe that this is probably not correct. The wine is acidy enough, admittedly, but somehow it seems to me to be lacking in body and therefore may not emerge quite so successfully from a longer period of maturation. In any event, demand for it outstrips supply so most of it is sold when it is still quite young. A fine wine, nevertheless. Recently, it has been produced also in a sparkling version which is proving reasonably successful. This is not quite a 'Brut' variety but it is, nevertheless, dryish and serves as a fair substitute for the numerous types of Prosecco offered in Italy as apéritif. Prices appear to vary. This is a particularly fruity version of the Gavi wine, lightly straw-coloured, pleasant, of moderate (12.5°) alcoholic content.

It often reminds me of some of the better versions of the Spanish 'cava'; it has the same versatility and, as a result, I am fairly confident that it could be usefully employed, not merely as an aperitif, but throughout a meal. As far as I have been able to ascertain, it is not normally available outside Italy.
Band B/C

GEWÜRZTRAMINER (see Traminer)

GHEMME   [DOCG / Red / Piemonte]

A superior red which lends itself to considerable ageing, it derives its name from the small town of Ghemme whose origins are dated back to the tenth century.

On the morainic hills in the communes of Ghemme, Romagnano Sesia and Sizzano, in the province of Novara, is grown a Nebbiolo grape which is locally called Spanna. It goes to make this fine wine in a minimum percentage of 75% to which are added some Vespolina and Uva Rara (maximum 25%). In passing, one observes that the specification refers to Uva Rara which is nothing else but a Bonarda, a variety that is anything but rare in the locality since it grows on many sites; be that as it may.

This is a ruby-coloured, clear wine with dark red reflexes; a typical, elegant, fine fruity nose. Its taste is dry, sapid with a very pleasant, almost harmonious bitterness. It has a minimum alcoholic content of 12° and must be matured for a minimum period of three years, twenty months of which in 'barrique' and nine months in bottle. With a minimum alcoholic content of 12.5° and minimum maturing period of four years (twenty-five months of which in 'barriques' and nine months in bottles) it can be termed 'Riserva'. An uncommon but very fine red, sometimes available in 'fancy' bottles, it will age well; it reaches its peak at about eight to ten years but will last quite well up to fifteen to twenty years, and at times more.
Band C

GRAVE DEL FRIULI (*or Friuli Grave*)
[DOC / White / Red / Friuli-Venezia Giulia]

The area of the Grave del Friuli which falls within two provinces, Udine and Pordenone, is similar both in name and type of soil (stony/ sandy) and countryside to the French area of the Gironde known as 'Les Graves', close to Bordeaux on the left bank of the River Garonne.

In the central area of Friuli astride the River Tagliamento in the provinces of Udine and Pordenone, there are produced a number of wines of quality, white, red, rosé, Chardonnay, Pinot Bianco, Pinot Grigio, Riesling, Sauvignon (q.v.), Tocai Friulano (q.v.), Traminer (q.v.) and Verduzzo (q.v.), Cabernet, Cabernet Sauvignon, Merlot, Pinot Nero and Refosco dal Peduncolo Rosso (q.v.).

The wine takes its name from the alluvial Friuli plain which the locals in their own dialect have for many, many years called 'Grave'.

The DOC classification covers two areas, namely the Grave del Friuli and the Grave Isonzo, both areas where the grapes mentioned above are cultivated. Many of these wines, some of which are treated individually, also come in sparkling versions.

Many of these are produced in other areas of Friuli, as the reader will no doubt appreciate. Good, reliable wines, grown on fertile alluvial soil by over 8,000 producers. They are mentioned solely for the sake of completeness since many of them, other than those separately recorded, are not easily available outside Italy.

Band B

GRECANICO   [IGT / White / Sicilia]

A wine that is becoming more widely known outside Italy, it is made in many parts of Sicily (Alcamo, Sclafani, Menfi, Belice and Sciacca areas) with grapes bearing the same name, usually in a minimum percentage of 85% plus others authorized in the different areas.

It is of a very pale yellow colour veering to greenish, has a delicate, pleasant and smooth perfume and tastes of fruit. It is dry and light, yet with some body. The minimum alcoholic content varies from area to area, starting at 10.5° and rising to 11.5°.

Band A

GRECHETTO   [IGT / White / Umbria]

The Italian diminutive might tempt the reader to think that it has some connection with the Greco (either of Campania or from Calabria). Not so: the Grechetto is a native Umbrian grape which is fairly common in the region and which is also used with Trebbiano and Malvasia in the production of the classic white Orvieto (q.v.) and the Torgiano Bianco, a white version of the popular red (q.v.).

It is a fairly delicate (alcoholic content 11.5°) yellowish/straw-coloured wine, pleasantly dry, velvety, with a fruity taste, occasionally slightly nutty and with a somewhat marked bitter aftertaste. Apart from its useful and obvious combination with fish and white meat, it is often served locally as an aperitif.

Band A

GRECO DI TUFO   [DOCG / White / Campania]

Produced in the area north of Avellino (communes of Tufo, Atripalda, S.Paolina, Altavilla, Irpino, Lapio, Montefusco and Mercogliano) with grapes in the main of the Greco variety (85%) with additions of Coda di Volpe as necessary, this is undoubtedly one of Italy's best white wines.

The Greco grape, as its name implies, one of the oldest varieties in the Italian peninsula, originates in Thessaly (Greece). The vine was first planted on the dark grey, almost black soil on the slopes of Mount Vesuvius, where it became known as Lacrima Christi (q.v.). It produces wine of golden bright yellow colour which does not lose much if aged for up to, say, a maximum of five years, but I feel it is best consumed fairly young.

It has an alcoholic content of between 12° and 13° and a fresh, dry, velvety taste, very hard to describe and typical of the Greco variety. It is an outstanding white, particularly good with fish, known for years in the locality but beginning to acquire notoriety throughout the world. It is one of my favourite Italian whites for fish dishes.

It vies with the other white wines from the locality, the Fiano, (q.v.); awkward to say at times which is to be preferred. It is beginning to find its way abroad where it manages to perform quite well; but it is difficult to beat when drunk anywhere on the Amalfi Coast, especially, I would suggest, at Ravello.

It should be noted that other versions of the Greco wine exist; one, produced in Gerace (Calabria) made of Greco grapes mixed with Trebbiano. Others, like Greco di Todi (Umbria), Greco di Ghemme (Piemonte) or even the red version from Catanzaro (Calabria) are by no means to be disregarded. A fine wine indeed!
Band C

GRIGNOLINO   [DOC / Red / Piemonte]

A charming name for a very old grape (recorded as early as the late sixteenth century) which, whilst yielding a delightful wine, is not too productive and for that reason is almost being phased out.

There are two main types:
Grignolino d'Asti, cultivated in the hills surrounding Asti, made from the Grignolino grape to which are added minor quantities of Freisa. It is a friendly, almost effeminate wine of a bright ruby colour, delicately scented, not too dry, with a slightly bitter and persistent aftertaste. The colour is very clear and the alcoholic content is in the range of 11-12°.

It grows on sandy soil typical of the area which, in the tertiary era, was covered by the Adriatic Sea. Traditionally, before planting a vine the local peasants went looking for fossils of shells because it was believed that only there was to be found suitable sandy soil for this particular variety of grape. Even today, shells can be seen amongst the rows of grapes.

It is a wine to be drunk fairly young since it begins to spoil after three or four years.
Grignolino del Monferrato Casalese is produced in the area of Alessandria

and the only difference from that of Asti is that sometimes greater quantities of the Freisa grape are added. Same colour, veering to orange when slightly older, but more tannic in taste. Apart from this, it is very similar to the Asti version.

Band B

GRUMELLO (*See Vatellina Superiore*)

INFERNO (*See Vatellina Superiore*)

INZOLIA   [White / Sicilia]

The Inzolia grape is used fairly extensively throughout Sicily but it is in the province of Agrigento that the wine bearing the same name as the grape is produced. It is a light (minimum alcoholic content 10.5°) straw-coloured white wine with a very marked fruity nose and a pleasant taste. Over the past few years it has begun to appear on the foreign markets.

Band A

ISCHIA   [DOC / White / Campania]

Ischia is the sister island of Capri and, with the much smaller Procida, it forms a cluster opposite Naples. It is less well known than Capri but to many, is to be preferred. Of volcanic origin with hot springs and spas throughout, it has been producing wine for at least 1,500 years. Initially, the Greco grape was used, which is fairly widespread in Campania and other parts of southern Italy, in any event; but over the centuries others were introduced, especially Biancolella, Forastera and Coda di Volpe for the whites and Guarnaccia and Piedirosso for the reds.

The white Ischia wine is produced mainly with Forastera and Biancolella grapes (85%) and with other white grapes. It is of straw colour, varying in intensity, with a very pleasant nose and medium body. The taste is dry, yet harmonious. The minimum alcoholic content is 10.5° and for the 'Superiore' 11.5°.

It is also produced in a sparkling wine version which is often served in the local bars when one asks for a Prosecco.

Band A

ISCHIA   [DOC / Red / Campania]

The red Ischia is of a gentle ruby colour, not too scented, dry, medium-bodied and fairly tannic. It has a minimum alcoholic content of 11° and must be matured in bottles for at least three months. It is made with Guarnaccia, Piedirosso and other black grapes.

The volcanic nature of the island is not easily detected in the whites but it is very marked in the reds of Ischia, which emerge as perhaps less exciting than they might be expected to be, despite being of good, medium body and properly tannic.

The principal communes for wine production are Forio, Lacco Ameno, Casamicciola, Piedimonte (which is also an alternative name for the Piedirosso grape), Barano and Buonopane.

Ischia wines have been recognized since the sixteenth century as
having the same therapeutic virtues as the springs and baths for which
the island is otherwise famous. I cannot vouch for that. . . . . .
Band A

LACRIMA CHRISTI DEI VESUVIO (*See Vesuvio*)
[DOC / Red / White / Rosé]

LAGREIN
[Red / Rosé / Trentino Alto Adige]

This wine is not that well-known in Italy except in the north-east where
it originates, grown on the hills near Bolzano, formed in prehistoric
times by the river Talavera.

It is derived from the grape of the same name and it is available as a
red and a rosé. The red is very often matured in oak casks and is a wine
with a considerable depth of colour, of an intense ruby, fruity, dry,
pleasant and smooth with a minimum alcoholic content of 11.5°. When
matured for at least two years, starting from 1 January subsequent to
the vintage year it can be called 'Riserva', when it often rises to 13°. It
has a roundish body and a scent of violets and is also known as Lagrein
Scuro (locally, Lagrein Dunkel).

In addition, there is a rosé to be drunk quite young, resulting from
the skinless working of the Lagrein grape (Lagrein Kretzer), having a
pink colour and a fairly typical bouquet of vanilla. It is usually quite
tasty, fresh and slightly sparkling. The colour is a gentle ruby with
salmon pink variations (some writers have described them as fuchsia
shadings. . .). A light wine, harmonious, with a minimum alcoholic
content of 11°, grown quite extensively in the province of Bolzano, like
its red counterpart. It ranks amongst Italy's best rosé wines.

When it originates from the commune of Gries it can be called
Lagrein di Gries (Grieser Lagrein or Lagrein Aus Gries), a description
that applies both to the red and to the rosé.

There seems to be some doubt as to how the grape acquired its
name. One theory is that the name comes from 'Lagarra' which was a
Greek colony famous for its wines. Another school of thought
challenges this origin although it seems to be incapable of providing an
alternative. The dispute centres on the fact that there is no recorded
evidence for 'Lagrein' in the Trentino area until the seventh century
when it was, or so it is said, originally cultivated by the monks in
Bolzano and no real evidence of substantial production until the
twentieth century.

We should not be troubled by these historical and terminological
problems. The Lagrein grape goes into a number of combinations such
as the Alto Adige Cabernet-Lagrein, the Alto Adige Merlot Lagrein and
the Vallagarina Lagrein. The Lagrein variety is fairly popular in Trentino
Aldo Adige and goes into much blending either with Cabernet or
Schiava grapes. Indeed, there is some evidence that the extent of the
plantings of this variety of grape is becoming greater, probably at the
expense of Schiava.

It is noteworthy amongst other reasons for the fact that it is trained along trellises reaching as much as eight metres in span.

Band B

LAMBRUSCO   [DOC / Red / Emilia Romagna]

In addition to Chianti, this is the most popular Italian red wine that the British public, eager to imbibe something different from beer, got to know after the Second World War.

It was a somewhat unfortunate choice, because the quality of the Lambrusco regularly imported into the UK and the USA until recent times has been anything but consistent and, in many cases, very poor indeed. 'White' and 'pink' versions of it were produced especially for some supermarkets; slightly 'sparkling', sweetish, of low alcoholic content. Not a nice drink which, above all, represented a rather inadequate introduction to Italian wines, to the detriment of their reputation generally. Inordinate quantities of the same type of drink were imported in the 1970s and 1980s into the USA: which did not help much, either.

The main variety of grape used is the Lambrusco, an ancient grape probably known to the Etruscans, with Ancellotta and Fortana (this latter one known locally as Uva d'Oro) as well as Malbo and indeed, in some of its still versions, the useful addition of Sangiovese, Merlot, Cabernet Sauvignon and Marzemino. (There exist numerous subvarieties of it, scattered throughout Italy.)

Lambrusco is made in the provinces of Modena and Reggio Emilia in Emilia Romagna, in so many communes of production that they are hardly worth listing. It is a very useful wine, having a minimum alcoholic content of 10.5° and seldom exceeding 12.5°. It comes in either a red or a rosé version, still but more often sparkling, dry, semi-dry or sweet, of a rather bright red colour, tending to violet in colour and, surprisingly, also in taste.

Always pleasant to the palate in its better versions, it is very versatile in its combinations with food. Apart from being used as an aperitif, especially in its sparkling versions during the summer months, it is a staple drink for the local cuisine with dishes such as the 'Zampone' (or 'cotechino') with lentils and other specialities, all from the locality, such as prosciutto, parmigiano and mortadella but it also combines easily with fish, especially trout. It should normally be served at below room temperature and some of the sparkling varieties benefit from being served at the same temperature as sparkling wines generally.

The best known are: Lambrusco di Sorbara (thus called from one of the villages of production), Lambrusco Grasparossa di Castelvetro (which derives its name from its reddish stalks as well as a local village), Lambrusco Reggiano (produced in the province of Reggio), Lambrusco Salamino (which is said to be called in this unusual manner because of the thin shape of its bunches which are said to resemble salamis..) and Lambrusco Salamino di Santa Croce.

My recommendation is that if you have to drink Lambrusco, try and avoid the very cheap versions, especially since standards have improved dramatically over the past decade: there are now excellent, fairly inexpensive Lambruscos to be found, but it is still a fact that the best Lambrusco is not exported.

A personal note. I am enthusiastic about drinking Lambrusco with roast duck. A slightly sparkling, lightly chilled Lambrusco Salamino di Santa Croce is an ideal companion at any time of the year but especially in spring and summer.

There is also a white version of Lambrusco.

Band A/B

LANGHE – LANGHE FAVORITA

[DOC / Red / White / Piemonte]

'Langhe' is an all-embracing description to cover something like ninety-four municipalities in the province of Cuneo.

Le Langhe identifies an area approximately bounded to the west by Cuneo, to the north by Asti, to the east by Acqui and to the south by the adjacent region of Liguria, with some of the best vineyards and the most beautiful countryside in this part of north-west Italy.

It is an area which is not geographically defined with precision, between the rivers Tanaro and Bormida. It is the oenological and, some say, gastronomic jewel of Italy, brilliantly cheerful in spring and with magical hues in autumn, illustrated at length by the writers Beppe Fenoglio and Cesare Pavese. This is the area of Barolo, Barbaresco, Barbera and Dolcetto, of truffles and hazelnuts. Well worth a tour, by the way, to appreciate the labyrinth of hills, hillocks and road bends around which nestle some of the most important and valuable vineyards of Italy. Touristically, the little villages are all gems.

The DOC description 'Langhe' is very wide because it covers both red and white wines. It includes wines produced there such as Nebbiolo, Dolcetto, Freisa, (reds), Arneis and Chardonnay (whites). In fact, there are at least two Langhe Chardonnay (oaked) which are excellent and quite capable of competing both with the Chardonnay from north-eastern Italy, as well as those from the New World.

White Favorita, however, is in a class of its own at least in the sense that it is produced exclusively with the grape known as Favorita (a relation of Vermentino) and in a fairly limited area. It is first mentioned in 1676, in the family records of the Counts of Roero. The grape variety is exceptionally prolific, the bunch being beautifully shaped and abundant, with strong, bright, green/golden fruits. It is also used as a table grape.

It is a delicate straw-coloured wine, not too scented but pleasant, of a dryness that is not offensive, with a slightly bitter aftertaste redolent of fresh hazelnuts for which the whole area is well known.

According to regulations it must have a minimum alcoholic content of 10.5°. In reality, given the tendency to increase the alcoholic content of wines generally – a tendency nowadays common throughout the world – one is more likely to find Favorita at 12.5° alcohol. The overall production, however, is not substantial.

Red The DOC Langhe is a fairly new one and its reds are now becoming more popular. It is said that it came about to assist those vintners who also produce other DOC wines but want to experiment with grapes that are new to the region (for example, the famous or infamous Chardonnay) and new blends which would be outside the scope of DOC specifications, especially those covering wines such as Barolo and Barbaresco made from single variety grapes.

Since there are no restrictions on the grapes used in the new Langhe DOC either for red or for white wines, this appears to be a contradiction of the DOC concept which, as observed, aims above all at ensuring the compatibility of tradition with consistency and quality.

There may also be other consequences, if one had a suspicious mind, namely that with the disappearance of the specificity of the DOC label, there may be a temptation for the less scrupulous vintner to use the 'new' grapes or blends of grapes even in their own DOC wines, especially in bad years where different grapes may perform to varying standards.

I hasten to say that there are some outstanding Langhe reds. I have tasted in Italy a first class Langhe made with 60% Nebbiolo and 40% Barbera grapes.

Band B

LISON-PRAMAGGIORE   [DOC / Red / White / Veneto]

The name identifies an area which includes Pramaggiore in the provinces of Venice, Treviso and Pordenone, the new DOC created in 1986 incorporating a number of older ones (such as Tocai Lison). The grapes used there vary depending on the type of wine that is produced. The principal wines of the area are:

Red
Merlot grape up to 70% – 12°
Cabernet grape – ruby red 11.5°
Cabernet Franc grape – ruby red 11.5°
Cabernet Sauvignon grape – ruby red 11.5°
Malbec grape – ruby red 11.5°
Refosco dal Peduncolo Rosso (q.v.)

White
Chardonnay grape – 11°
Tocai grape – straw-coloured 11° but produced in many areas
Pinot Bianco grape – straw coloured 11°
Pinot Grigio grape – amber coloured 11°
Riesling grape – straw coloured 11°
Sauvignon grape – straw coloured 11°
Verduzzo grape – amber-coloured, flower scented 11° but also available in a sweet version

Band A/B

LOCOROTONDO   [DOC / White / Puglia]

The visitor to that area of Puglia straddling the provinces of Bari and Brindisi which is known as Locorotondo, usually only goes there because of the Trulli, the conical stone-roofed buildings unique to this region and to be found almost exclusively in the town of Alberobello, where they are used as dwellings. They date from the Stone Age and are all protected as national monuments.

The same visitor, however, may not be aware of the fact that in the locality and especially in the whole of the areas of Locorotondo, Cisternino and Fasano, there is a well-known white wine obtained from a blend of many grapes (Fiano, Bombino, Malvasia, Verdaca, etc.) which is very pleasant indeed.

It has a colour which is primarily greenish, occasionally light straw and a very delicate nose. The wine is dry but is extremely easy on the palate and has a minimum alcoholic content of 11°. Some versions, perhaps rather irritatingly, emerge tasting of gooseberry.

Band A

LUGANA   [DOC / White / Lombardia / Veneto]

An interesting wine, one of a few so-called inter-regional DOC classifications. The area of production straddles the regions of Lombardia and Veneto, in the communes of Rivoltella, Pozzolengo and Peschiera. The locals consider it more a Veronese (Veneto) than a Lombard wine.

The main area of production is south of Lake Garda, on flat lands which go from the province of Brescia (Lombardia) right up to that of Verona (Veneto). It is made from a variety of Trebbiano (90%) known locally as Lugana, an autochthonous vine, as well as other non-aromatic white grapes (10%).

The Trebbiano used in the Lugana is known as Veronese or Lugana and is grown at the southern end of Lake Garda. This is an unusual Trebbiano, since it has been suggested that the reason why it differs from the Tuscan Trebbiano is that it is a relative of the Verdicchio (q.v.) from the Marche.

It is a white wine with a yellow/greenish colour when fresh, veering to a golden colour when ready for bottling. It is often compared to Soave, but it is much fruitier and more full-bodied, often slightly less dry than Soave.

It has a pleasant delicate nose and a fresh Trebbiano-like taste with a minimum alcoholic content of 11°, rising to a maximum of 13°. It often reminds me of New Zealand Sauvignons, sometimes tasting of apples and of honey. The stronger Luganas lend themselves to fair ageing. When aged, the wine retains its fine scent and taste, though losing some of its brilliancy.

It is interesting that many producers show on their bottles the suggestion that the wine should be drunk when fairly young: that is somewhat odd because I know as a fact that many will comfortably reach 10/12 years.

It is a very fruity wine, of greater body and more intense colour than the better known Soave (q.v.). It is smooth and much appreciated by those who like a dry wine that does not hit the palate too harshly. Occasionally tangy, it often produces a not unpleasant salt-like effect, which is quickly offset by its delightful flavour.

The Lugana of Sirmione is well known but quantities have suffered; as a result, other Trebbiano-based whites from the Lugana district have become much more successful.

In passing, the reader should be reminded of what a delightful place Sirmione is, beautifully located on Lake Garda. Well apart from the town and the well-known castle, an oddity from the area is the yellow (rather than red) water melon; it is delightful to see the two colours, red and yellow, when at the height of summer water melon is displayed for sale by the shores of the lake.

Band B

MALVASIA DELLE LIPARI   [DOC / White / Sicilia]

This is one of the delightful Malmsey-type wines produced on Lipari, one of the seven Aeolian Islands in the province of Messina.

The grape bears the same name and produces a golden, lightly-coloured wine when young, which veers to a strong golden colour when matured, reaching its peak between three and eight years.

It is a pleasantly aromatic wine having a minimum alcoholic content of 11.5° which is available in two types, namely:

Passito with a minimum alcoholic content of 18° and a maturation period of no less than nine months.

Liquoroso with a minimum alcoholic content of 20° and a maturity period of no less than six months.

The taste of the Malvasia delle Lipari is very marked. Its aroma is reminiscent of the tamarind, a plant which grows abundantly also in Sicilia and the adjacent Calabria.

MALVASIA DI BOSA   [DOC / White / Sardegna]

It is said that the grape from which this wine originates is the result of an arrangement that the Venetians made in the thirteenth century with inhabitants of the Peloponnese to export the sweet wines that were being produced at the time in that area of Greece.

After having traded with Crete, they, or the Byzantines, brought this particular variety to a number of locations in the Mediterranean starting from Venice where the wine itself became so popular that at the time and for perhaps a couple of centuries thereafter, there were a number of wine shops ('osterie') in Venice which concentrated on selling this particular kind of malmsey wine and for that reason were known as 'malvase'.

This wine is produced in fairly limited quantities ('officially' there are only two or three producers) in a number of territories in the island of Sardinia but, more particularly, in the area surrounding the town of Bosa in the province of Nuoro.

It is a golden, almost amber-coloured, intensely aromatic white wine with a delicately bitter aftertaste, having a minimum alcoholic content of 15°.

In its 'liqueur' version, sweet or dry, it must have a minimum alcoholic content of 17.5° and be matured for no less than two years, when it acquires a more marked flavour and aroma.

Its intense aroma, both in the sweet and the dry version, makes it a wine which is somewhat difficult to combine with food. The most that can be said is that it comes into its own with puddings, sweets and tarts. More appropriately, perhaps, I would suggest that it almost qualifies as a 'meditation' wine.

Band C/D

MALVASIA DI CASORZO (*d'Asti – otherwise known as Casorzo*)
[DOC / Red / Piemonte]

The Malvasia grape is quite widespread throughout the region. It produces sweet wines with a not-too-high alcoholic content but outstanding bouquet; and yet, Malvasia wines are much neglected in Italy. This is particularly true of the wine I am considering here, perhaps because it does not lend itself to ageing and is at its very best when drunk quite young.

Strangely, the village of Casorzo, which is 23 kms from the main town of Asti, once had more than 3,500 inhabitants but now claims only a mere 697 (so much so that one gets an eerie feeling walking through it since it is mostly uninhabited; there is neither a restaurant nor even a bar). At one time, it had a Protestant community made up of migrants to the USA who had returned home. There was a belief that even as recently as the end of the Second World War, the inhabitants of Casorzo had a lower than average height, which may be another reason (supposedly!) why there are so few people living there today. Who knows!

The village is 670 feet above sea level and overlooks a pleasant, fertile plain.

It should not be forgotten, of course, that Malvasia is to be found in Friuli Venezia Giulia, Lombardia, Basilicata, Sardegna, Calabria, Lazio, Emilia Romagna, Toscana, Liguria, Sicilia and Puglia. In other words, it recurs in most of the Italian wine-producing regions.

What is true is that this DOC Malvasia is produced in a very confined area (Casorzo, Grazzano, Alta Villa and Vignale).

Casorzo is made from the black Malvasia (minimum 90%) which is also known locally as Casorzo with the addition of Freisa, Grignolino, Barbera and other local grapes in the provinces of Asti and Alessandria, sometimes grown at 700 metres above sea level. It has a rather complex vinification because in the first place the must, with no stalks, is partially fermented to about a third of its initial sugar content and then fermented again off the lees, and decanted; it then undergoes a series of final fermentations which, coupled with centrifugation and refrigeration, make it a fairly expensive wine to produce, the fermentation process lasting one year. Minimum alcoholic content 10.5°.

The wine is of a clear, cherry ruby red colour, an exceptionally fragrant, aromatic nose and a very sweet taste, but its alcoholic content is low (10° to 11°). It has a very marked personality and it is probably a pity that it is not so well-known as it deserves to be. It is also available in a sparkling and a 'Passito' version.

It must be recorded, however, that the locals themselves have a rather ambiguous attitude towards it. Some say that it is much too sweet, others that it lacks personality. Because it is produced in fairly small quantities by a limited number of vintners joined in co-operatives and also because it does not last too long (indeed, it is often recommended that it should be drunk within the year) it seems to have become rather a difficult wine to find and not too many drinking establishments, even in the general area of production, stock it as an after-dinner drink or possibly even as an aperitif. In my view, its popularity has suffered a lot in recent years. It is undoubtedly a typical dessert wine quite suited to dry fruits, nuts, some pastry and ice-cream, especially fruit ices; but it does not blend at all well with any kind of citrus fruit.

A fairly similar wine is the Malvasia di Castelnuovo don Bosco (q.v.)

Band C

MALVASIA DI CASTELNUOVO DON BOSCO
[DOC / Red / Piemonte]

Produced with a different type of grape called Malvasia di Schierano in the province of Asti in what is known as the 'Basso Monferrato', to this grape there is added, though not all the time, only the Freisa, up to a maximum of 15%.

The difference between the Malvasia with Freisa and the Malvasia (100%) is that the latter is much darker and more heavily scented; the other features of the two wines, however, are the same. It is a cherry-red wine, fragrant, sweetish, I was about to say a pudding wine: very pleasant, considered by some suitable also with fruit and ice cream.

This wine, too, is produced following a special vinification technique which, it is said, ensures that it retains the fragrant aroma of the grape from which it originates. It has a minimum alcoholic content of 10.5°, comes also in a 'petillant' version and as a proper sparkling wine with a minimum alcoholic content of 11°.

As noted, there is of course plenty of Malvasia in Italy, the grape being widespread and sometimes growing almost wild. Three more are entitled to a DOC classification, namely the Malvasia delle Lipari (Lipari is one of the Aeolian Islands near Sicily), the Malvasia di Bosa, an outstanding dry/sweet white wine with a minimum alcoholic content of 15° and the Malvasia of Cagliari with a minimum alcoholic content of 14° for the wine and 17.5° for the wine/liqueur.

But many other Italian regions produce Malvasia, hence the Malvasia del Collio, del Friuli, dell'Oltrepó Pavese, del Vulture, di Catanzaro, di Brindisi, di Gallipoli, di Grottaferrata (Lazio), di Maiatico (Emilia), di Toscana, di Rapolla (Basilicata), di Trani (Puglia), and even one (Passita) from Pietraligure in the province of Savona (Liguria).

These wines tend to be drunk in the same locality as they are produced.

Band C

MANDROLISAI
[DOC / Red / Rosé / Sardegna]

It is not easy to find either version of this fine wine outside Sardinia, but it deserves mention. Both wines are produced in the provinces of Nuoro and Oristano from a fairly uncommon local grape, known as 'bovale sardo'.

Both types have fairly similar specifications, namely no less than 35% of bovale sardo, Cannonau in the range 20-35%, Monica similarly, with a remainder of other unspecified grapes not exceeding 10%.

Red This is a very brightly ruby-coloured wine, veering to brick red when aged, with a very pleasant, vinous and typically persistent nose and a full, dry taste with a very slightly bitter aftertaste.

The minimum alcoholic content is 11.5° and if matured with a minimum of 12.5°, it can be termed 'superiore'. To qualify, it must be matured for a minimum of two years, twelve months of which in oak 'botti'.

Rosé This is cherry-coloured, made with the same grapes as the red, with a very pleasant nose and a fairly smooth, sapid, typically Sardinian taste. It comes in a minimum alcoholic content of 11.5°.

Both wines are cultivated at fairly high altitudes, around 750 metres above sea level. The combination of fresh air and outstanding wines is said to contribute to the longevity of the local population.
Band C

MARCHESE DI VILLA MARINA [Red / Sardegna]

This is to be classified as one of Italy's (Sardinia's actually) 'new' wines. It is made on the island, where the prevailing red grape is Cannonau, from 100% Cabernet Sauvignon vines that were planted many years ago by the long and well-established firm of Sella and Mosca (founded over a century ago).

It was felt by Messrs Sella & Mosca that the local soil and weather conditions would be conducive to the creation of a wine that it would be difficult, at first taste, to relate back to Cabernet Sauvignon grapes which here seem to have acquired different characteristics.

It is a full-bodied and yet not heavy, dark red wine, with a marked fruity nose and a long, smooth, velvety aftertaste. It has no prescribed minimum alcoholic content as it falls outside any classification of either the IGT, DOC or DOCG type; typical, however, is 13.5°.

As I have endeavoured to explain, these classifications relate to long-established wines from well-known, tried and approved grapes. This wine could not possibly qualify and, in a sense, it falls in the same category as the 'super Tuscans', for it was made *ad hoc* by vintners who, in any case, have had an extensive experience in planting and grafting new vines.

It has only one fault: like the 'super Tuscans', it is expensive; but it is mentioned here, somewhat outside the scope of this book, as a further example of what Italy can do in the wine world when it sets its heart to it. A first class red.

For the record, the wine takes its name from a Piedmontese nobleman, who was made Viceroy of Sardegna in 1810 by Victor Emmanuel the 1st of Savoy.
Band D/E

MARSALA   [DOC / White / Sicilia]

A wine which is very dear to the heart of the Englishman since it was in 1773 that there sailed to England on the HMS *Elizabeth* from the port of Trapani in western Sicily, a shipload of sixty barrels of wine to which alcohol had been added so that the rigours and the delays of the journey could be taken care of.

The word 'Marsala' is of Arabic origin coming form 'marsh-el-Allah' (literally, God's harbour) and is related to the port at Marsala, which was well-known for years.

There is a romantic story behind the discovery of Marsala wine by John and William Woodhouse, young merchants from Liverpool who certainly had not gone to Sicily to buy wine, but on a venture to find raw material for the manufacture of soda.

When they realized how close the local wine was to the similar type of wines that were well-known in England, namely those emanating from Portugal and Spain (mainly port, madeira and sherry) they thought that it would not be too difficult to exploit the situation and they set up a base to attract producers of Marsala wine and also make some, but principally to export it.

Interestingly, about a century earlier in 1678, it was again two Englishmen who contributed to the creation of a wine that was to become famous. Having just bought wine from some monks in Portugal, they tried to determine how best to ship it back to England so that it would remain in good condition; they decided to add a little brandy to each of the casks and that was how port came about, although it is fair to say that port is probably much more successful with the British than it is with the native Portuguese themselves who seem to prefer drier, lighter types of wines as an aperitif or a dessert drink.

Initially, the 'new' Marsala wine came to England but gradually it spread to other parts of Italy, especially southern Italy which was then part of the Kingdom of Naples.

The Woodhouses were anything but slow and their major undertaking was a supply contract of Marsala to the English fleet in the Mediterranean. This was not too difficult because at that time one Horatio Nelson was in charge of the Mediterranean fleet. Nelson had already been honoured with the title of Duke of Bronte, a small town in the province of Catania in eastern Sicily on the western slopes of Mount Etna and now exceptionally famous for its special variety of pistachio nuts.

Nelson had earnt the title by his action in protecting the then King of Naples, Ferdinand IV, in 1799 during a revolt by the Neapolitans inspired by the French (an historical event which has caused much writing, also because of the hanging by Nelson of one of the participants in the 'Revolution', Admiral Caracciolo).

With the dukedom went some 16,000 hectares of land, quite a nice manor house and an ancient abbey church. Nelson was very proud of this gift although it would appear that he never managed to visit his property which descended through his elder brother and was ultimately sold in 1981 to the Local Municipality.

The fact that Marsala wine was being supplied to the English ships in the Mediterranean contributed to its popularity, especially after the death of Nelson at Trafalgar and it can be stated unhesitatingly that, subsequently, there was nothing to stop a number of English noblemen and wine merchants from developing the local wine into something which has become known the world over.

Marsala is produced in the whole of the province of Trapani (except Pantelleria) in the municipalities of Marsala, Mazara and Castelvetrano from the Catarratto, Grillo, Inzolia, Damaschino and Nero d'Avola grapes to which is added etyl alcohol or wine Eau de Vie (and, if appropriate, cooked or concentrated must obtained from other grapes within the area of production). Some vintage Marsala is made exclusively from a single grape variety, normally Grillo.

There are very many types of Marsala wine depending on how long they have been aged. 'Fine' – one year; 'Superiore' – two years; 'Superiore Riserva' – four years; 'Vergine/Soleras' – five years; 'Vergine/Soleras Stravecchio' or 'Riserva' – ten years.

The wines come as dry, semi-dry and sweet and, depending on the sugar content, they are of golden, amber or ruby colour; all have a characteristic nose and aroma, smooth and generous to the palate. The essential impact of the wine's flavour is that of burnt sugar (caramel); all of them display this feature to a lesser or greater degree and, in my view, it adds to the smoothness of the product.

The alcoholic content also changes depending on the type, starting at no less than 17° with the ordinary Marsala and no less than 18° for the better quality wines.

It is matured in barrels and lends itself to fairly long ageing (in excess of fifteen years). It is so popular that additions have been made to the sweet wine like egg, almonds, coffee, in order to produce slightly more palatable versions. Apart from these rather fanciful combinations, it is worth noting that a good quality, dry Marsala Vergine is an outstanding apéritif or 'digestive' drink. It will stand comparison with the best Sercial Madeiras, Oloroso sherries, and with port.

The popularity of Marsala seems to have suffered somewhat after the Second World War but has picked up of late. Italians have always looked upon it as a tonic and especially the version with 'added eggs' was until recently a routine 'medicament' during times when it was felt the body or the mind needed some cheering, especially during periods of convalescence.

Band C to E

MARZEMINO   [Red / Trentino / Alto Adige]

One of the most characteristic wines of the area produced from the Marzemino Gentile grape, which is a fairly unusual variety distinguished by its very small size (the ending 'ino' being one of the Italian suffixes for diminutive things). It produces a fine table wine of deep garnet red colour and although the village of Isera, near Rovereto, is considered its natural home, it is made in many other districts in the area and especially in the Vallagarina.

Left to mature with the skins it becomes a fine, robust yet delicate table wine of deep garnet red colour with what some have described as a fruity aftertaste of vanilla and a fairly pleasant flavour, not unlike that of violets. It lends itself to some ageing, has an alcoholic content range between 11° and 12° but it is not produced in great quantities. If matured for longer than two years it may be termed 'riserva'. One would call it an aristocratic wine. There is also a sweet, sparkling version.

Opera lovers may recall that Lorenzo da Ponte, the librettist of Mozart's *Don Giovanni*, immortalizes Marzemino since it is the last wine that Don Giovanni drinks (see the last scene of the opera when he encourages Leporello to 'pour the wine' which is an 'eccellente Marzemino').

Band B

MENFI [DOC / Red / White / Sicilia]

This is a comparatively late newcomer to the DOC classification (1995). The area of Menfi, however, has been well-known for wine production over many years. Some wines from it do not qualify for a DOC as such (for example Inzolia – q.v.); others are quite widespread and have been finding their way into foreign markets.

So we have a white Menfi made with a maximum of 75% Inzolia, Chardonnay, Catarratto and Grecanico, the balance with other non-aromatic white varieties; there is also a Vendange Tardive ('Vendemmia Tardiva') white made with Chardonnay, Catarratto, Inzolia, Ansonica and Sauvignon, but nothing else, also subjected to light drying; finally, a Menfi red made with Nero d'Avola, Sangiovese, Merlot, Cabernet Sauvignon and Syrah, up to a maximum of 70%, the balance from other local red varieties.

The wines from this area are usually quite reliable. The whites are fragrant, dry and straw coloured with a minimum alcoholic content of 11°. The reds are fine, good bodied examples with reasonable tannins and a minimum alcoholic content of 11.5° and the Vendemmia Tardiva wines are excellent specimens with a minimum alcoholic content of 15°.

Band A/B

MERLOT [DOC / Red / Trentino Alto Adige / Friuli Venezia Giulia]

1. Trentino Alto Adige

Made in the province of Bolzano, covering an area controlled by thirty-four municipalities collectively referred to as Alto Adige or Südtirol, it is vinified with usually 90% of Merlot grape which can also be mixed with Cabernet and Lagrein. It is a ruby-coloured, dry and fresh wine with a pleasant, almost grass-like nose. Minimum alcoholic content 10.5° but more commonly 11° or 11.5°, depending on the area of production; when matured for at least two years it can be termed 'Riserva'.

2. Friuli Venezia Giulia

It is also produced throughout the Friuli areas (Carso, Colli Orientali, Collio, Friuli Annia, Aquileia, Grave and Isonzo).

I have indicated the minimum alcoholic content according to regulations, but it must be recorded that nowadays most of the Merlot originating from these areas emerge with an alcoholic content of 12.5° as a minimum and more commonly of 13°. In the Trentino area there is also a rosé version (Merlot Kretzer).

Of course, Merlot is to be found in other parts of Italy. There is an excellent IGT Merlot known as Merlot delle Venezie produced in the Veneto region; furthermore, the same Veneto Merlot is now being blended with Cabernet Sauvignon to provide an indifferent house wine in many English pubs.

Band A/B

MONFERRATO　　　　　　[DOC / Red / White / Rosé / Piemonte]

Monferrato, an area of undulating countryside and a centuries-old winemaking tradition, produces large quantities of outstanding wines from Asti Spumante to Grignolino. Its 'smallholdings' yield wines of such variety as to be able to satisfy most tastes.

More specifically, however, the DOC Monferrato covers some 100 municipalities in the province of Alessandria and just as many in the province of Asti. It is an all-embracing DOC description within which the following are the more important wines:

Monferrato Red – dry, bright red, pleasant, minimum 11° alcohol

Monferrato White – straw coloured, dry, minimum 10° alcohol

Both the above wines are made from a number of different local grapes.

Chiaretto – this is a very pleasant ruby red, but more often rosé wine made with a minimum of 85% 'Barbera' grape plus a number of others ('Bonarda', 'Cabernet Sauvignon', etc.). Dry, minimum 10.5°.

Dolcetto – produced with a minimum 85% of grapes of the same name, similar to the other DOC *Dolcettos* (q.v.).

Freisa – again produced with a minimum of 85% grapes of the same name, this is a ruby red, pleasant, dry wine, minimum 11°.

Cortese (Casalese) – made in the area of Casale with a minimum 85% of 'Cortese' grapes. It is an extremely pleasant straw-coloured light wine with greenish effects. It is only lightly scented but a fairly definite nose. It is dry, sapid and with a slightly bitter aftertaste with a minimum alcoholic content of 10.5°.

Band A

MONICA DI CAGLIARI　　　　　　　[DOC / Red / Sardegna]

The 'Monica' grape originates probably in Spain, possibly in Portugal and is widespread throughout Sardinia. The wine, which is produced in the province of Cagliari and must be matured for a minimum of eight months, is of a number of types:

Sweet. This is a ruby red wine veering to orange as it ages with an intense and at the same time gentle nose and a sweet, almost velvety taste. It has a minimum alcoholic content of 14.5°.

Dry. This is the same wine in a dry version which must be matured for a minimum of nine months but after two years may be termed 'Riserva'.

Liqueur-type. Another version of the same wine but its nose and taste is somewhat more refined and overall it emerges as more flavourful, possibly because of its higher alcoholic content, 17.5°. The minimum ageing is nine months but, again, after two years it can be termed 'Riserva'. It is not an easy wine to find outside Italy.

Band C/D

MONICA DI SARDEGNA   [DOC / Red / Sardegna]

Like its counterpart at Cagliari, this is also made with Monica grapes but quite commonly there are added other white grapes. The result is a brilliant ruby red wine, which also has a tendency to veer towards the orange as it ages.

It is available in two versions, either dry or semi-sweet and is pleasant in both versions which have a minimum alcoholic content of 11° and must be matured for no less than six months. The dry version is normally matured for at least a year and must have a minimum alcoholic content of 12.5° but is more commonly found at 13°. If it complies with these two requirements it may be termed 'Superiore'.

There is also a sparkling version of both, which is reasonably scarce outside Italy. Monica di Sardegna is considered to be a lesser wine by comparison with the Monica di Cagliari although they both originate from the same grape.

Band A/B

MONTECARLO   [DOC / White / Red / Toscana]

There appears to be no connection whatsoever between the principality of Montecarlo and the commune in Tuscany, in the province of Lucca which, together with grapes from the adjacent areas of Altopascio, Capannori and Porcari, produces a number of excellent wines on the hills that surround the small town of Montecarlo. Its produce was much appreciated both by the Medici families as well as by the various wine bars of Florence.

Montecarlo Bianco. This is made with the grapes of Trebbiano, Pinot Bianco, Pinot Grigio, Vermentino, Sauvignon, Semillon and Roussanne. The possibly unusual blend produces a brilliant white wine, straw-coloured or golden, more or less, with a very delicate nose and a harmonious flavour. Minimum alcoholic content is 11°, often rising to 12.5°.

Montecarlo Rosso. This, too, is a blend of many grapes (Sangiovese, Canaiolo, Ciliegiolo, Malvasia, Cabernet Sauvignon, Cabernet Franc, Merlot and others) and is produced in the same area, both with white and red grapes.

A brilliantly-coloured wine, of vivid ruby red, strong vinous nose and a dry sapid taste, which reminds one of 'Côte du Rhone' wines. It has a minimum alcoholic content of 11.5° rising to 13.5°. When matured for a minimum of two years it can be called 'Riserva'. It improves in smoothness but changes colour slightly to amber. From the same area comes a Vin Santo (q.v.).

Band A/B

MONTEFALCO   [DOC / Red / Umbria]

The younger brother of the better known Sagrantino di Montefalco (q.v.) is produced in the same area, namely the commune of Montefalco in the province of Perugia, as well as a few surrounding areas.

It is available also in a white version but the red one is produced from Sangiovese, Sagrantino and other red grapes with no stated percentages.

It has a vivid ruby colour with a vinous nose, good body and a pleasant taste. It must be matured for a minimum of eighteen months and it has a minimum alcoholic content of $12°$ but more usually $13°/13.5°$.

Once the minimum is raised to $12.5°$, if the wine has been matured for more than two-and-a-half years it can be termed 'Riserva'.

Band B

MONTEPULCIANO (see *Vino Nobile see Nobile di Montepulciano*)

MONTEPULCIANO D'ABRUZZO – (*Colline Teramane*)
                                   [DOCG / DOC / Red / Abruzzo]

The 'Montepulciano' grape was introduced into the Abruzzo region of Italy in the early 1800s and soon proved its worth. It is planted throughout the provinces of L'Aquila, Chieti, Pescara and Teramo and, together with a maximum addition (15%) of other black grapes, it goes to produce this, one of the latest Italian reds to receive the accolade of a DOCG in 2003.

Until that time, Montepulciano d'Abruzzo wines were not considered by many to be of a very high standard and could be purchased reasonably cheaply. So much so that over the years it was the wine preferred by some Italian restaurateurs as their own offering of 'house wine'. The recent upgrading of a special version of it to DOCG will inevitably change the situation.

It has a strong ruby red colour, sometimes violet and veering to orange when matured. There is a strong vinous scent and a dry, lightly tannic sapid flavour. It must be matured for a minimum of five months and have a minimum alcoholic content of $11.5°$. The 'Riserva' version must be matured for a minimum of two years and have an alcoholic content of $12°$.

An interesting statistical fact: the province of Chieti is second in the league of those producing wine in Italy (the first is Trapani, in Sicily). It can boast of 17,500 hectares of vineyards producing four million hectolitres of wine, which corresponds to 89.4% of the total production of the Abruzzo region and, quite a substantial figure, to 7% of overall Italian wine output.

DOCG Band C
DOC Band A/B

MONTEVETRANO   [Red / Campania]

This is one of the many 'new' wines of Italy, a blend of Cabernet
Sauvignon (60%), Merlot (30%) and the balance made up of Aglianico;
one purely French grape, one Italianized French grape and a native
Italian variety! The blend has proved quite successful producing a wine
with a dark ruby colour tending to violet, an intense fruity, especially of
blackcurrant, nose and a smooth taste with marked but exceptionally
refined tannic notes. Alcoholic content: 13.5°.

Band E

MORELLINO DI SCANSANO   [DOC / Red / Toscana]

The wine is said by some to take its name from the Italian 'mora' which
means 'blackberry'. It is not too easy to detect a taste of blackberry,
although psychologically, if one knows this origin of the wine's name,
one may end up by associating that taste with this beautiful ruby red,
dry wine produced mainly in the municipality of Scansano in the
province of Grosseto. Another tradition is that it takes its name from
the 'morello' cherry. This is more likely because there is certainly more
than a hint of cherry in the Morellino which, surprisingly, started out in
life as a sweet wine resulting from 'appassimento'. Burton Anderson
suggests the name is derived from the original hue of this wine. Tasting
notes apart, however, it would appear that the name Morellino came
about by way of association with the 'morelli' horses which are plentiful
in its area of production.

Nowadays, the grape used is still Sangiovese (85%) together with
other recommended grapes (e.g. Alicante, brought to Toscana by the
Spaniards in the seventeenth century) which yield a wine that matures
quite well, turning to a very dark red colour and changing nose and
flavour, becoming almost perfumed. Its colour, a bright red when
young, tends to garnet when aged.

It is a warm-hearted wine, extremely pleasant, not too tannic with a
minimum alcoholic content of 11.5°. When it reaches 12° then, if
matured for a minimum of two years, one of which at least must be in
oak barrels, it can be termed 'Riserva'.

Much of it available today has an alcoholic content of 13.5°-14°. The
wine, despite its maturation process, does not taste at all oaky.

This is not a wine that is commonly known abroad: but it represents
a worthwhile experience for those who wish to know more about
Tuscan wines than just the more obvious ones mentioned in this book.
Indeed, I would go so far as to say that Morellino di Scansano is a very
good example of the much criticized versatility of the Sangiovese
grape.

It may well be that the proximity to the sea and the relative sea
breezes have some effect on the vine but I have no hesitation in saying
that, were it not for the fact that people used to refer to it as 'similar to
Chianti' and thus perhaps look upon it as an inferior wine, the
Morellino di Scansano would be a typical Tuscan product of high
quality.

Band C

MOSCADELLO DI MONTALCINO   [DOC / White / Toscana]

Available in three versions, it originates in the same production area as
the better known Brunello. It is a wine which has a long tradition, made
with white Moscato grapes with the addition of a maximum 15% of
other white grapes. Straw-coloured, delicate, fresh, quite aromatic and
sweet, it comes in a minimum alcoholic content of 10.5°.

It is also available as a very pleasant, lightly sparkling wine and, when
produced by the well-known 'Appassimento' process, also in a 'vendage
tardive' type which must be matured for a minimum of a year and with
a minimum alcoholic content of 15°. This is an unusually pleasant wine,
much less known abroad than it deserves to be.

Band C/D

MOSCATO D'ASTI *(Asti or Asti Spumante)*
                    [DOCG / White / Sparkling / Piemonte]

A well-known wine writer, E. Penning Rowsell, termed Asti Spumante
'the success wine of Piedmont'. A perfectly justified description of what
is probably the most popular sparkling wine in the world, as well as
Italy's most widely exported, grown over an area of about 10,000
hectares, stretching over fifty-two communes from the Langhe to the
Monferrato. There are about 6,500 producers of this wine, all members
of the Consortium created in 1932.

It is derived from the Moscato grape. This is not exclusively an
Italian variety. It goes to make wines of varying sweetness, which are
known by different names (Muscat de Baumes de Venise in France,
Samos in Greece, or Moscatel – as an adjunct to dried fruits and nuts
or to end a meal – in Spain and Portugal).

It is said to be one of the oldest grape varieties known. It is believed
to be originally a Greek variety which the Romans adopted and called
'uva apiana' (from the Italian word 'ape', meaning bee: apparently bees
are attracted to its sweetness). Whilst it is true to say that it is cultivated
in many parts of the world, the modern Moscato originated in Italy and
is grown nowhere more profitably than in Piemonte. (A useful variant
of it, Zibibbo, is extremely successful in Sicilia and surrounding islands,
especially Pantelleria.)

Indeed, it is of venerable antiquity. Whilst all writers agree on its
antiquity, they do not necessarily concur on the etymology of the word.
There are those who maintain that we find the first reference to it in the
term 'muscatellum' in 1511 from which one derived 'moscado'; one
finds an equivalent in the French 'moscadet'.

Others claim that the name is derived from the Roman 'mustaceum'
which was a little cake made up with flour and sweet wine distributed to
parents and friends of the bride (rather like the almond confetti of
today). They rely for this origin on the Latin poet, Juvenal, who claims
that one should not marry a woman who had had too many previous
sexual experiences because one would then waste the 'mustacea'
(Satires VI 202). ('Mostaccioli' are still sold in most parts of southern
Italy, and in Rome.)

It is only fair that I should record that the English nineteenth century traveller and writer, Norman Douglas, was of the opinion that the 'Moscatel'-type of wine ('Moscatellone'), which he found in Calabria, originated in the 'Maskat' of Asia Minor and that the local development of this sweet wine in that particular region is owed to the Arabs.

As far as Piemonte is concerned, it is a matter of record that the 1511 reference already quoted occurs in a document known as the 'La Morra Statutes'. La Morra is one of the many attractive villages scattered around the area where some of the best Italian wines are made. This particular statute required that anyone planting a new vineyard had to cultivate the Muscat grape in a ration of one to five with other varieties.

However, the effect of the La Morra Statutes extended beyond its original region, because it is recorded that in 1597 the Duke of Mantua requested cuttings of Muscat vines from the vineyards of another Piedmontese village, Santo Stefano Belbo. A further historical reference to it is the comment by a Spanish captain (unnamed, apparently) who happened to be in Canelli, the heart of the Moscato-producing area, in 1616. He defined the wine as 'Muscadello delicatissimo' (most delicate musk wine). It is from there that the Muscat spread to most other countries in the world.

In Italy the Moscato grape is found in no less that twenty-four wines, two of which are DOCG wines: (Moscato d'Asti, Asti Spumante) and nine DOC (Moscato di Pantelleria, di Trani etc). The origin of these sparkling wines is in the natural white Moscato, which is available either as a still wine or slightly re-fermented, naturally. One could say that this was the father of the new flavourful sparkling wines which now prevail throughout the world. There are two Italian specialities:

Moscato d'Asti or **Moscato d'Asti Spumante**. This is made with the Muscat grape, has a fairly dark straw colour and an impressive, fruity characteristic aroma. It is suitably sweet, though not excessively so, delicate and produces a fine white froth: it is fizzy rather than sparkling.

It is a much underrated dessert wine which seems to come into its own once a year during the Christmas holidays when great quantities of it are sold to be enjoyed with the seasonal 'three P's': 'pandoro', 'panettone' and 'panforte'.

A brilliantly clear wine with an average alcoholic content of 7° (but occasionally as low as 5.5°) rising to 11°, it is the classic dessert wine to be served very chilled and is produced in many districts in the provinces of Alessandria, Asti and Cuneo. It is sealed with ordinary corks, since it is bottled under fairly low pressure; and should be drunk young, usually within no more than a year. Its dry version has a minimum alcoholic content of 11°; there is also the 'Passito', which is an exquisitely tasting wine.

Moscato d'Asti is the staple of Asti Spumante if it is utilized no later than 30 June subsequent to the year in which the grapes were gathered.

Asti Spumante. This is the better known product having a natural amber colour, bright, with a characteristic scent and flavour and white froth. It is fermented naturally either in autoclave or in bottle and its alcoholic content varies from 6° to 12°.

It is produced in the same districts as Moscato d'Asti and benefits from being served almost icy (this is a matter of taste, of course, but the difference in the serving temperature of the Moscato d'Asti and the Asti Spumante is quite significant for those who are interested in this type of wine).

I maintain that the Moscato d'Asti should be served lightly chilled whereas the Asti Spumante should be served almost icy.

Apart from the Moscato wines mentioned separately (Asti or Asti Spumante, Moscato di Trani and Moscato di Pantelleria), the reader might like to be reminded that Moscato is made in Italy, as in many other wine-producing countries, (this means effectively most temperate countries where the grape is cultivated and more specifically, Australia, France, Greece, North America, Portugal and Spain) in practically every area where the Moscato grape is planted.

Some of the other varieties of Moscato available in Italy, though not necessarily abroad, having a DOC are as follows:

Moscato di Cagliari (Sardegna)
Moscato di Noto (Sicilia)
Moscato di Sardegna
Moscato di Siracusa (Sicilia)
Moscato di Sorso-Sennori (Sardegna)
Valcalepio (province of Bergamo)
Moscadello di Montalcino (Toscana)
Moscato di Pantelleria
Moscato di Trani (Puglia)

These are the, if you like, officially recognized Moscati. But Moscato as a sweet wine, flavourful but often with low alcoholic content, also appears under the following labels:

Moscato dei Colli Euganei
Moscato dell'Oltrepó Pavese
Moscato del Salento Bianco (up to 17°)
Moscato del Salento Rosso (up to 17°)
Moscato del Vulture (up to 16°)
Moscato di Barletta (up to 16°)
Moscato di Canelli
Moscato di Chambave (up to 17°)
Moscato di Cosenza (up to 15°)
Moscato di Montalcino
Moscato di Segesta (up to 15°)
Moscato di Strevi
Moscato di Tempio
Moscato di Terracina

Finally, the reader might like to know that there is in the Asti area a still wine made from Moscato grapes: it is the fairly scarce Loazzolo and takes its name from the town where it originates.

Band A/B/C

MOSCATO DI NOTO [DOC / White / Sicilia]

According to official publications this wine is said to have been created in the early nineteen thirties at Noto, a charming baroque small town in the province of Siracusa. (There is, in fact, also a Moscato di Siracusa which is produced slightly further north and which is not to be confused with that of Noto.) The area of production includes Noto, Pachino (where the new DOC Eloro applies – wines not available in the UK, save for Nero d'Avola (q.v.) and Avola). According to historians, however, this is no more than a variant on the sweet wine which Pliny called 'Haluntium'.

Made with 100% white Moscato grapes, it comes in three varieties:

1. **Ordinary (or natural) Moscato**. This is a golden yellow wine, slightly aromatic with the usual Moscato flavour, having a minimum alcoholic content of 11.5°.

2. **Sparkling**. This is similar to the natural Moscato, save for the fizz.

3. **Liqueur type**. This is a particularly enjoyable golden muscat-flavoured wine, sweet and smooth with a minimum alcoholic content of 22°.

As a generalization, all three are produced in fairly limited quantities and have been described as rare gems that deserve to be better known.

When, in July 1943, the British troops who had landed in Sicily reached the town of Noto, the local officials celebrated their arrival in the town hall by offering them in champagne glasses the Moscato di Noto.

Band C/D

MOSCATO DI PANTELLERIA
[DOC / White / Pantelleria (Sicilia)]

Otherwise known as Passito di Pantelleria, it is the result of an 'appassimento' either on the vines or after they have been gathered, of the Zibibbo, a variety of Muscat, grape.

It is of an amber/gold colour, exceptionally fragrant both in nose and in taste, the Muscat flavour hitting the drinker immediately with its sweet aroma. It is an exceptionally smooth wine and has a minimum alcoholic content of 15°.

Following the same 'appassimento' method, there is also made a Passito di Pantelleria which has a minimum alcoholic content of 20° and when fortified rises to 21.5°.

There are other wines from Pantelleria, namely a Pantelleria Bianco, a Moscato Dorato, a Moscato Spumante and a Zibibbo Dolce. The Passito di Pantelleria is a fine after-dinner drink, but it is not easily found.

Band C/D

MOSCATO DI TRANI [DOC / White / Puglia]

Trani is a small town in the region of Puglia, known in the main for its wine and for its outstanding cathedral.

The origin of this wine is lost in the mists of time. What is known is

that as far as human memory goes, it has been grown along the
Adriatic coast of Puglia from Barletta in the north to Bisceglie in the
south and has crossed inland to cover ground in the provinces of Bari
and Foggia.

It is not to be confused with the red wine of Trani which, during the
early 1900s – simply because it was produced in great quantities –
became the cheapest wine to be sold in Italian 'osterie'. So much so that
the 'osterie' where this type of wine was dispensed, actually had the
name 'Trani' showing on the outside.

Moscato di Trani is a fine, not inexpensive, naturally sweet wine of a
heavily golden colour, an intense scent of flowers and a sweet, though
not sickening, gentle flavour. It has a minimum alcoholic content of
14.5° and must be matured for a minimum of five months. It is quite
suitable for reasonable ageing (up to ten years).

It is also available in a much heavier version which is to be matured
for a minimum of one year and have a minimum alcoholic content of
18°. It is made with dried grapes.

Band C/D

MOSCATO ROSA (*Rosenmuskateller*)
[Rosé Friuli-Venezia Giulia (Trentino/Alto Adige)]

This is one of the most fanciful wines in the region, usually sold in tall,
odd-shaped, thin bottles. It is made with the Muscat grape and it has a
gentle ruby colour, a pleasant and delicate nose and a sweet taste which
is perhaps less marked than the Moscato wines from other regions of
Italy.

It has a minimum alcoholic content of 12.5° and is also available as a
'Passito' with a minimum alcoholic content of 16°. It is produced both
in Alto Adige and in Trentino. It should be served chilled.

Band C

NEBBIOLO   [DOC / Red / Piemonte]

'Nebbia' in Italian means 'fog' and this wine is so called (the name first
appeared in the thirteenth century) because the grapes are picked late,
at the time of Italy's Indian summer.

In passing, one should observe that this can produce rather odd
results, for if one has a bad vintage either in Piemonte or in the rest of
Italy, but then the sun that shines in October and November is
unseasonably hot, one will find that wines made with Nebbiolo grapes
have a good year whereas the remainder of the Italian wines have a bad
one.

(Clearly, one should never underestimate the significance of the
weather. In 2003, for example, because of the very high temperature
throughout Italy, France and Spain, the vintage started early, often in
mid-August, at least in Sicily and Tuscany.)

There are many Nebbiolos which take their name from the area in
which they are produced. The principal one is the Nebbiolo d'Alba but
there is a Nebbiolo from the hills of Novara (known as Spanna), there
is one from the hills traversed by the River Sesia in the provinces of

Vercelli and Biella, also known as Spanna, and there is one from Monferrato.

Nebbiolo is a fine wine of ruby red colour, turning somewhat to amber when mature. It was officially acknowledged as a DOC in 1970.

This wine bears the same name as the grape which also goes into the top Italian reds of Piemonte. It is a wine that, like Barbera, is to be found in many of the wine-producing areas in this region. It is found in the Canavese, in the Colline Novaresi, on the hills adjacent to the River Sesia (in the provinces of Vercelli and Biella), and also in the area of Cuneo province, better known as the 'Langhe' (q.v.) and, most abundantly, in the classic wine-producing districts of Alba and its surrounding area.

It is usually made with a minimum of 85% Nebbiolo grapes to which may be added other varieties. It is a ruby red wine with a typical nose and flavour which remind the drinker of violets. It is dry, full-bodied and fairly smooth, having a minimum alcoholic content of 11° to 12°; many types reach 13° and even 14° alcoholic content. It goes from dry to very slightly sweet, always full-bodied and quite harmonious. Its attractive ruby red colour veers to orange with maturity. Although often used as a table wine, it reaches maturity at three years and its peak at six.

Over the past ten years or so Nebbiolo grapes have been blended with Barbera varieties to produce wines which, whilst not qualifying for the official DOC label because not made in accordance with the Nebbiolo wine specification, are still excellent products. The blend is proving quite successful, so much so that some producers maintain that it is an improvement on the original which, as recorded, must contain a minimum of 85% Nebbiolo grapes.

It is available in three versions. A dry one, a sparkling, pleasantly aromatic version and a dessert-type wine, sweet and delicate to be served not chilled, but slightly below room temperature.

Band B/C

NEGROAMARO   [Red / Puglia]

This wine is becoming fairly popular with foreign buyers. It is produced generally in various territories in the province of Lecce with grapes of the same name in the minimum percentage of 85%. These are supplemented with the black Malvasia of Brindisi, the black Malvasia of Lecce, Montepulciano and Sangiovese in accordance with local rules.

It is of a bright ruby red colour, veering to brick as it matures. It has the characteristic flavour of the Negroamaro grape, which is quite marked but still pleasant; harmonious with a pleasant slightly bitter aftertaste. It is a full-bodied wine with an intense vinous taste and a minimum alcoholic content of 12°.

There is also a 'Riserva' version (minimum alcoholic content 12.5°, minimum ageing two years of which at least six months in wooden barrels).

Band A

NERO D'AVOLA (*Eloro, Nero d'Avola*)   [DOC / Red / Sicilia]

This has recently become well known in the UK and elsewhere. Its ancestor, the local, pure red available in the production area between Pachino and Siracusa (with an average alcoholic content of 14-15° but occasionally reaching 20°) became very popular with the British troops soon after their landing in Sicily on the 14 July 1943. Throughout July and August of that year they much appreciated the wine made available to them by the local population, which was often served chilled. More than one private was heard to remark that it was a very good substitute for whisky.

It is a strong red (minimum 12°) made from grapes of the same name, grown in the municipalities of Noto, Pachino, Portopalo and Rosolini in the province of Siracusa, as well as at Ispica in the province of Ragusa. The grapes used are Nero d'Avola to make up the prescribed minimum 90% of grapes; the remaining 10% is left at the discretion of the vintner; but one should record an increasing tendency to use exclusively Nero d'Avola to achieve a distinctive mono-varietal wine.

It is a full-bodied wine, vinous, dry, reasonably fruity, which I think sometimes tastes of almonds. This is probably a psychological reaction to the fact that I know, as many others do, that the area of Avola is also famous for its almond production.

More correctly, one should refer to the whole of this area, i.e. the south-eastern tip of Sicily where the Allies landed during the Second World War (Capo Passero and Pachino, to be precise).

The wine is not at all heavily tannic, despite its consistency and alcoholic content and lends itself to fair ageing. It has only recently been raised to DOC status in 1994 and should be more correctly described as Eloro, Nero d'Avola.

There has recently been a rehabilitation of wines from Sicily, which slowly but surely are becoming better known, not only in Italy but abroad. But Nero d'Avola appears to be making very fast progress towards much greater success: it was nominated Italy's wine of the year in November 2004, under its 'Chiaramonte' label. This is an IGT wine made with 100% Nero d'Avola grapes, partially matured in barriques for six months.

During the last ten years Nero d'Avola has become effectively the most produced Sicilian grape (red wines) at the same time as the white variety of Inzolia has almost taken over in Sicily.

It blends most successfully with Cabernet Sauvignon, Merlot, Sangiovese and even Syrah in IGT versions.
Band A/B

OFFIDA   [DOC / White / Red / Marche]

The area of the Marche on the Adriatic sea is slowly gaining in popularity for its wine production, which is fairly ancient: remnants of Vitis vinifera found in the province of Ascoli Piceno, have been traced back to the Iron Age. From the same region and more specifically from the commune of Offida, come two fine whites, which recently one has been able to purchase outside Italy.

1. **Passerina**. Made with a minimum 85% of grapes of the same name this is a gently straw coloured wine, dry, sapid and pleasant. It has a minimum alcoholic content of 11.5°. The same grapes, when subjected to the 'Appassimento' procedure, yield an excellent sweet wine (Passito) as well as a *vino santo*.

The wines are similar having a minimum alcoholic content of 11.5° but the period of maturing in oak is different; eighteen months for the former, thirty-six for the latter. A sparkling wine is also made with the same Passerina grape.

2. **Pecorino**. Another white from the same area but made with grapes of the unusual name Pecorino, (not to be confused with the well-known Italian cheese!). Here again the minimum quantity of stated produce is 85% but the minimum alcoholic content of this wine is slightly different, namely 12° (although it is often sold at 13.5° alcohol).

It is a pleasantly flavourful, solid, white dry wine, straw-coloured with green tinges. With an initial nose almost gooseberry-like, its attractive taste is somewhat reminiscent of Viognier. It is matured for at least six months in bottles and is, in my opinion, a classic example of what comparatively little known, indigenous Italian grapes can produce.

The linguist might like to know that it takes its name from the Italian 'Pecora', meaning sheep, since it is claimed that in ancient times the sheep that grazed freely among the vines appeared to be exceptionally fond of the particular grape.

3. **Offida Rosso** – This is a very successful, pleasantly scented wine to be consumed reasonably young (although there is a 'Riserva' version that will last up to five years). It achieved the DOC qualification only in 2001 and in the intervening period a number of substantial improvements have been made to a wine made with the Montepulciano and Sangiovese grapes in varying proportions, of a ruby red colour, harmonious, dry and quite full-bodied. Minimum alcoholic content is 11.5°.
Band B

OLTREPÒ PAVESE   [DOC / Red / White / Rosé / Lombardia]

A hilly area in the province of Pavia well known for its grapes, gives its name to some good wines. Apart from the Barbera (q.v.) it produces a great number of wines, some of them DOC of varying types, white, red and sparkling (as far as I have been able to ascertain the only two available outside Italy are a Pinot Nero and a sparkling Pinot).

The white Cortese is dealt with separately. Also available in the area is a very fine Riesling.
Band A/B

ORMEASCO   [DOC / Red / Rosé / Liguria]

When, as one of the four sea-faring cities of the Mediterranean, Genoa ruled the Tyrrhenian Sea, the wines of Liguria were much better known than they are at present. They travelled to many places by sea – though not by land, since communications were more difficult.

There are essentially two versions of this wine, although a white is also being made.

Red. This is made with 95% 'Dolcetto' grapes in the provinces of Genoa, Savona and Imperia. It comes in a 'superiore' version which must be matured for at least one year but otherwise is usually fairly drinkable quite young. It is of a red ruby colour with a pleasant dry vinous taste and a slightly bitter aftertaste. It has a minimum alcoholic content of 11°.

Rosé. This, too, is made with 95% 'Dolcetto' grapes subject to a particular vinification in the same area as the red and is normally matured for a minimum of twelve months. It has become gradually more popular over the past ten to fifteen years.

It is a coral-shaded, dry, extremely pleasant wine which the locals normally drink either as an aperitif or as an after-meal drink, especially with dry fruits or sweets.

This rosé comes essentially in two versions. A darker than usual variety of rosé which is often ruby coloured, almost veering occasionally to violet, with a nutty taste.

A slightly lighter rosé made in the hills at altitudes between 500-700 metres which is extremely fruity, with a pleasant nose and a marked taste of raspberries. I cannot help feeling that the anticipation provided by the nose and taste is slightly marred by the bitterish aftertaste. Whether this is due to the method of vinification or to the fact that the grapes for this version of the wine are picked when slightly unripe, I really cannot tell. Both have a normal alcoholic content of 12.5°.

That produced in the part of the Italian Riviera west of Genoa is known as di Pornassio (from the name of the principal production area) whereas that produced in the area east of Genoa is known as Ormeasco Sciacchetrà, although I have seen the rosé of the western riviera referred to alternatively as di Pornassio and Sciacchetrà. To complicate life, the former, if produced in particular areas, is also referred to as Ormeasco Riviera dei Fiori.

BAND B

ORNELLAIA – *a 'Super Tuscan'*   [Red / Toscana]

This wine takes its name from the winery owned by Marquess Ludovico Antinori, one of Tuscany's premier vintners, called 'Tenuta dell'Ornellaia' in the commune of Bolgheri (province of Livorno). Its history starts in 1981 when Ludovico Antinori selected the vineyards out of the ninety-one hectares owned by him, where he planned to plant the vines of Bordeaux (Cabernet Sauvignon, Merlot, Cabernet Franc and Petit Verdot) which, after taking advice, he considered would be most suitable.

The reader should bear in mind at this stage that until the late 1960s, Bolgheri was not known as a wine-producing area and only supplied table wines. The French vines then planted were to revolutionize the Italian wine scene. Sassicaia (q.v.) was born, which subsequently got a DOC, and other wines in whose footsteps followed Ornellaia, a blend of Cabernet and Merlot.

A great wine in its own right which has opened the way to other wines (see for instance Masseto from the same winery) with a marked taste of blackberries and blackcurrants. It is a full bodied wine with a very smooth tannic taste. The alcoholic content is 13.5°.

Band E

Masseto

The seven hectares where this wine is produced are at the heart of the Ornellaia estate halfway between the sea (which the vines actually face) and the old road which goes from Bolgheri to Castagneto Carducci. The vines grow at 120 metres above sea level on clay/sand/stones.

Masseto started life in 1986 as a mere Merlot and not much of it was bottled. 1987 was its first year when 6,500 bottles were produced and since then it has gone from strength to strength.

Barrique matured, with a taste of strawberries and raspberries, this has become a much appreciated wine, a small 'cru', rather precious and, in fact, a collector's item. Very expensive.

Band E

ORVIETO   [DOC / White / Umbria / Lazio]

Like Chianti, Lambrusco and Verdicchio, this was one of the first Italian wines to be exported in large quantities from the 1950s onwards. It takes its name from the town which is at the centre of one of the most important wine-producing areas in central Italy, Orvieto, a very attractive city with an architecturally outstanding cathedral.

It is said that we owe this wine to the first inhabitants of the city, namely the Etruscans, who sensed that the 'tufa' caves with which the area was dotted served as excellent storage facilities.

The Italian poet, Gabriele d'Annunzio, defined it as 'the sun of Italy in a bottle' and it is said that Pope Gregory XVI left a will in which he asked that before burial his body should be washed with Orvieto wine.

It is a white wine from the province of Terni in the Lazio, made mainly with Trebbiano (locally referred to as Procanico), 40-60%, as well as other grapes, such as Verdello (15-25%), Grechetto and Canaiolo, also some Malvasia.

It is produced in thirteen communes in the province of Terni, including of course Orvieto, whence it derives its name, and five communes in the province of Viterbo.

Straw-coloured, dry with a slightly bitter aftertaste in its dry version, it also comes as a semi-dry, semi-sweet and sweet wine; all quite delicate. It is labelled in two ways: as 'Classico', when produced in the original area of production and as 'Superiore', a label which can be applied only to wines sold after the 1 March of the year subsequent to that in which produced. The 'Superiore' must have a minimum alcoholic content of 12° but the minimum for Orvieto is 11.5°.

It is a wine with a long history, to be served chilled and its best combination is, of course, with fish dishes.

Luigi Veronelli reports that Pinturicchio (Bernardino di Betto) liked the Orvieto wines so much that he stipulated, in his contract with the people who were paying for his paintings in the building of the cathedral there, that both he and his workmen should be granted as much Orvieto wine as they could drink.

For the record, there is also a red Orvieto, known as Rosso Orvietano or Orvietano Rosso.

Band A

PARRINA   [DOC / White / Red / Rosé / Toscana]

White. This is produced in an area in a very narrow quarter of south-western Tuscany. The number of producers is as limited as the area of production, which is close to the sea and has ancient origins. It is claimed that Etruscans cultivated the vine there but without going that far, the Spaniards certainly contributed to local viticulture in the seventeenth century. The word 'parra' in Spanish means a pergola of grapes. Only the white is available outside Italy.

Parrina is made with Trebbiano grapes known locally as Procanico in a percentage of 30/50, the balance being made up of Ansonica and/ or Chardonnay (the addition of Chardonnay is recent).

This is a lightly straw-coloured, dry but exceptionally smooth wine, with a persistent and highly perfumed nose and a slightly bitter aftertaste, having a minimum alcoholic content of 11.5°.

Red. This is a ruby red, made with a minimum of 70% Sangiovese and the balance of local non-aromatic grapes. The minimum alcoholic content is 11.5° (12° for the Riserva). It is delicately flavoured, dry and smooth.

Rosé. This is perhaps less available than the previous two, made with the same grapes as the red with a minimum alcoholic content of 11°. It is a brilliantly pink-coloured wine, dry and harmonious, which in its 'Riserva' version cannot be sold for at least two years following 1 November of the year of production, during which period it must spend no less than twelve months in wooden barrels and three months in bottles.

Band C

PASSERINA (*See Offida*)   [DOC / White / Marche]

PASSITO DI PANTELLERIA (*See Moscato di Pantelleria*)

PECORINO (*See Offida*)

PICOLIT – COLLI ORIENTALI DEL FRIULI
                    [DOCG / White / Friuli Venezia (*Giulia*)]

The quantities at source of an unusual wine produced in Friuli Venezia Giulia continue to be low, with the result that it emerges as a fairly expensive commodity. It is often called the prince of Friuli wines. It is a sub-variety of the 'Cialla' (q.v.) group, produced in the area centred around Cialla in the province of Udine.

It is made from the white Picolit (minimum 85%), a grape with low yields and a tendency to 'floral abortion'. It is of golden, intense yellow colour, and has an exceptionally strong nose which reminds the drinker of the acacia flower.

It is available in demi-sweet or sweet versions, both being the type of harmonious yet delicate wine that, as the expression goes, will 'warm the cockles of one's heart'. It is truly a meditation wine. It has a minimum alcoholic content of 15° and must be matured for a minimum of two years. Its residual sugar content is very high, from 8-10 grams per litre.

In recent years, great efforts have been made to 'rehabilitate' it both in quality and, above all, quantity terms.

This fact was acknowledged in November 2005, when the wine 'Picolit' earned a DOCG and is now to be known as 'Colli Orientali del Friuli PICOLIT'.

Band C/D

PIGATO   [White / Liguria]

I have already remarked that Liguria does not produce truly outstanding wines, although this is one of four to which attention is drawn here. It is made with minimum 95% Pigato grapes in the provinces of Savona, Imperia and Genoa, namely in what is known as the western Italian Riviera. Some versions are 100% Pigato grape.

It is a straw-coloured wine of varying intensity with a strong, slightly aromatic nose and a fairly marked, although sometimes, slightly bitter taste of nuts, especially almonds and occasionally of lemon. Some experts claim they can taste the sea in it. . . . .! It has a minimum alcoholic content of 11°.

Pleasant enough, with fish or 'pasta al pesto', on a summer's day, Pigato is not easily found outside the area of production where it is best enjoyed, either by the sea or inland in the Western Riviera. It does not travel too well in any event and does not lend itself to being kept for longer than three years.

Experts tend to prefer it to the other Ligurian white, Vermentino (q.v.); the other two white wines of Liguria (Cinque Terre and Cinque Terre Sciacchetrá, a dry and a sweet) excellent though they are, each in their own way, are not normally available abroad and accordingly are not reviewed here.

The wine industry in Liguria as a whole and especially on its western side has made considerable progress over the past ten years; so much so that in 1999 a Pigato managed to receive the highest accolade from the Gambero *Rosso Guide.*

Band A

COLLI BOLOGNESI – PIGNOLETTO
[DOC / Red / White / Sparkling / Emilia Romagna]

This particular denomination of origin already referred to covers the red and white wine produced over a fairly wide area in the provinces of Bologna and Modena. The grapes used vary as does the vinification.

It is not possible here to provide details of all such wines. I shall therefore confine myself, therefore, to a basic description on the premise that the name of the wine itself will give the reader sufficient information as to what to expect.

Whites. Apart from Pignoletto, which is considered separately, the white wines of the area are made with the Albana grape. Colli Bolognesi Pinot Bianco (minimum 85% Pinot grapes) – also available in a sparkling version,), Colli Bolognesi Chardonnay (minimum 85% Chardonnay grapes), Colli Bolognesi Riesling Italico (minimum 85% Riesling grapes), Colli Bolognesi Sauvignon, which also comes in a superiore version (minimum 85% Sauvignon grapes).

Reds. Colli Bolognesi Barbera (minimum 85% Barbera grapes), Colli Bolognesi Cabernet Sauvignon (minimum 85% Cabernet Sauvignon grapes) Colli Bolognesi Merlot (minimum 85% Merlot grapes).

Pignoletto (*v. Colli Bolognesi*) I am treating this separately from the other Colli Bolognesi wines because I believe that it is the most popular of wines from that region to be found outside of Italy, produced in the same territory as others with the same denomination of origin, with a minimum of 85% Pignoletto grapes. This is an indigenous variety whose origins are in dispute. Consequently, some oenologists who relate it to Grechetto (q.v.) propound the theory that it is none other than a local version of Pinot Bianco.

The additional 15% of the blend is made up of Pinot Bianco, Riesling Italico, and the local Trebbiano which yield a gentle straw-coloured wine with green tinges, dry but not too sharp, in fact quite smooth, considering the dryness, with a pleasant aftertaste and a minimum alcoholic content of 11.5° (12° for the superiore version).

It is also available as a 'passito', with a minimum alcoholic content of 15°. This has a delightful golden colour veering to amber when more mature, delicately perfumed.

The more popular version of Pignoletto, in my view at least, is the sparkling wine, which is said by some to be a competitor of Lambrusco. It has a minimum alcoholic content of 11° and it is available in either a dry or a semi-dry ('amabile') version and is very pleasant indeed.

Bands: For reds and whites B/C

For sparkling and Passito C/D

PINOT GRIGIO
[White / Friuli / Venezia Giulia / Trentino / Alto Adige / Veneto]

Over the past few decades Pinot Grigio, the Italian equivalent of the French Pinot Gris, has become much better known, more sought after and available than Pinot Bianco, both in Italy and, above all, abroad. This must cause some eyebrows to be raised because the area planted with Pinot Bianco grapes in northern Italy is at least two and a half times greater than that planted with Pinot Grigio. An odd situation.

Odd or not, Pinot Grigio appears to have become a very popular and fast-growing wine in the United Kingdom at least, mainly thanks to its popularity with women.

In any event, I find Pinot Grigio an overrated white wine. So much of it is uneven in quality, the flavour is indistinct and one gets a feeling that its acidity has been carefully controlled merely to ensure that it is as inoffensive a wine as possible. Furthermore, the grapes used and their vinification make it a difficult wine to produce to what I would term high standards. This is one situation where, if I had to choose a Pinot Grigio, I would opt for the Pinot Gris of Alsace unless I was certain that what I bought in Friuli, where only a small percentage of overall vineyard space is planted with Pinot Grigio, was of high quality.

But even where the Pinot Grigio of Friuli is concerned, I disagree entirely with the practice of oaking it. This is happening more and more frequently but, is a grave mistake because oaking does not seem to mix well with the particular type of wine one is dealing with: clearly a matter of personal taste, of course.

Regrettably, this oaking is happening everywhere in Italy. When Chardonnay started to acquire popularity in the early 1970s, Italian growers from the north-east thought they would jump on to the bandwagon. When they showed how successful they were at selling it, winegrowers in practically every other Italian region decided to follow suit and a number of local vines were uprooted to make way for Chardonnay, mainly oaked as well.

Pinot Grigio is a wine produced in a number of north-eastern areas of Italy. It is to be found in the hills of eastern Friuli (mainly in the commune of Buttrio), in the Collio (mainly in the communes of Cormons and Gradisca) as well as in the Trentino (Appiano, Caldaro, Merano). The area covered with Pinot Grigio in Friuli is just under 5% of overall plantings. The grape used is the Pinot Gris, (in a minimum quantity of 90%), which gives a yellowish wine with a slight pink tinge, fairly crystal clear, if not brilliant, with a delicate, occasionally fruity nose.

It tastes fresh and dry, fairly pleasant, though occasionally with a slightly bitter aftertaste. Generally, it is a lively wine, sometimes lemony in flavour and usually aromatic. Its alcoholic content is in the range 12-13° (although in the Aquileia area it can start at 10.5° of alcohol) and in some of the communes in the provinces of Udine and Pordenone (the Friuli Grave and Friuli Latisana) it is also available in a minimum alcoholic content of 10.5° for the ordinary version and 11.5° for the 'Superiore'.

The texture of the wine is very similar to that of Alsace, although there are some who argue that the Italian version is less rich in flavour. One should certainly not confuse the two since the French version is richer in substance and spicier in flavour. The Pinot Grigio produced in Friuli differs somewhat from that of Alto Adige, also because a large quantity of the Alto Adige versions is matured in new barriques.

There is also some Pinot Grigio sold under the IGT denomination Veneto or delle Venezie, usually blended with Garganega.

A note of warning as regards the classification of Pinot Grigio. It is only entitled to be termed DOC when it can qualify as falling within the wide description of 'piave' or 'vini del piave' or as a 'friuli grave' or 'grave del friuli'.

The grape is acquiring notoriety abroad. There is now available a

Californian blend of Pinot Grigio/Chardonnay!
Band A/B

POMINO BIANCO   [DOC / White / Toscana]

This is the white version of Pomino made with the grapes of white
Pinot, Chardonnay and Trebbiano, occasionally Sauvignon. It has no
particular specification and in that it differs from the red, for other
grapes can be mixed in.

It comes from the same area as the red, however, has a minimum
alcoholic content of 11°, is dry, delicate and reasonably pleasant. It has
a gentle straw colour, with occasional green shading.
Band A/B

POMINO ROSSO   [DOC / Red / Toscana]

This wine is produced in a limited area (including Rufina) in the
province of Florence, with Sangiovese, Canaiolo, Cabernet Sauvignon,
Cabernet Franc, Merlot and other grapes.

It is similar in taste to other Chianti wines, with a vivid ruby colour
turning to dark red when matured especially after three years, which is
the minimum for it to be called 'Riserva'.

This is a robust, tannic wine when young which becomes much
smoother after two or three years. It has a minimum alcoholic content
of 12° and tastes, at first, of violets with a slightly bitter, almost fizzy,
aftertaste.
Band A/B

PRIMITIVO   [DOC / Red / Puglia]

A descriptive name taken from the grape of the Primitivo variety, it
applies to a number of strong tasty tannic red wines made in the region
of Puglia since at least the seventeenth century. As already noted,
Primitivo is one of the classic wines of Puglia, which is used both for
export and for blending with lighter wines. Very often this blending
emerges as particularly successful, the resultant wine developing
organoleptic characteristics which are probably unique.

It is a staple ingredient for a number of wines originating in those
countries, which import strong southern Italian wine for blending. The
reader might be tempted to believe that the name 'Primitivo' is due to
its coarse, elementary nature: not so. It is so called because the grapes
ripen very early in the hot sun of southern Italy.

The DOC variety is the Primitivo di Manduria made in the
commune of Manduria as well as in adjacent areas such as Grottaglie,
all in the provinces of Taranto and Brindisi.

It is a dark red wine, almost violet in colour which turns to orange
when more mature. It has a unique vinous taste which is difficult to
confuse with other wines, quite pleasant when young, but turning
exceptionally smooth with age. It must be matured for a minimum of
nine months and have an alcoholic content of no less than 14°. It
froths to a lighter, reddish colour and can be aged for up to fifteen
years or even more.

The predominant grape is, of course, the 'Primitivo', hence the name as stated; but varying quantities of Negroamaro and Malvasia, as well as some Bombino can be added.

Non-DOC Primitivo wine is produced in other parts of Puglia, for instance at Gioia del Colle, 17°, Acquaviva, 18°, Turi, 18°, Sava 20°! and is more commonly found in restaurants and 'osterie', not only throughout Puglia, but also in Basilicata, usually sold under the IGT label, especially in its reasonably original Salento versions.

I recall sampling in one of these underground establishments near the railway station in the town of Potenza a Primitivo which must have had an alcoholic content of no less than 17°. Delicious!

Because of the type of wine but, above all, the high alcoholic content, over the past ten years or so it has become quite popular with the Anglo-American and Northern public.

There is a long-running argument as to whether the 'Primitivo' is the father of the Californians' 'Zinfandel' or vice versa; ampelographers appear to be at loggerheads about this. Chauvinistically, I took the view that the 'Zinfandel' was derived from the 'Primitivo' but the discussion is fairly academic; one could perhaps call them brothers or cousins.

Undoubtedly, however, over the past five years or so it has changed from being a wine for blending to a wine for drinking on its own possibly, though not necessarily, with the additions that have already been mentioned.

Some non-DOC varieties of Primitivo are now being bottled as table wines and exported under the label 'Zinfandel', a way of benefiting from the popularity of Californian wines; a mark of the originality, flexibility and adaptability of the Primitivo grape which is emerging as one of Italy's success stories.

Band B/C

PROSECCO (*di Conegliano/Valdobbiadene*)
[DOC / White / White sparkling / Veneto]

Italian restaurants, both abroad and in Italy, and bars throughout Italy have, over the past ten years or so, given increased popularity to a well-established sparkling wine known as Prosecco. This is a convenient short form for what is technically known as Conegliano-Valdobbiadene (alternatively, Conegliano or Valdobbiadene) and is a wine from the Veneto region, particularly the province of Treviso, where the two villages of Conegliano and Valdobbiadene come to the fore, although the wine is also produced in the communes of Cartizze (as to which, see later), Soligo and Pieve di Soligo.

The general area where this wine is produced as dry, medium sweet (or demi-sweet) and sweet has been known since the seventeenth century at least, to which period we can date the first exports of the still wine to Germany and Poland.

When the Charmat-Martinotti method of fermentation was developed, the sparkling wine came to the fore but it should be noted that it starts out in life as a dry white wine, derived from the grape called Prosecco with the addition of other grapes, up to a maximum of

15% (Verdisio and/or Bianchetta, as well as Perera). The sparkling version, however, must be made with a minimum of 90% Prosecco grapes.

It is a straw-coloured wine with a delicate fruity taste, especially in the demi-sweet and sweet versions. There is also a dry version, which has a slight tendency to bitterness, a fault which is gradually being remedied by Italian vintners as they increasingly compete with the much more expensive champagne wines. It is not a full-bodied wine by any means and its alcoholic content starts at 10.5°.

The wine more commonly known, because it is offered usually as an aperitif, is the sparkling version. This is dry with a minimum alcoholic content of 10.5°, but is also available in an extra dry, 'Brut' version with a minimum alcoholic content of 11°.

When produced in a particular, rather limited, sub-area of the commune of Valdobbiadene known as Cartizze, and provided it has a minimum alcoholic content of 11.5°, the sparkling wine is known as Superiore di Cartizze. This is simply a better version of the same wine, usually though not necessarily of a higher quality.

A note of warning, however. What a restaurateur offers you either with his compliments or upon your request as a sparkling pre-meal drink, saying that it is Prosecco, may well not be that. There are now offered in practically every bar in Italy as Prosecco wines, which, in the majority of cases, originate elsewhere than in the Veneto. I was in Caserta (near Naples) quite recently and was regaled with a glass of Prosecco . . . . . from Campania. There are similar locally produced versions to be found even, believe it or not, on Ischia. . . . .

In my view, the term Prosecco has, despite its legal requirement of the DOC regulations, lost some of its specificity in the same way as the noun 'Hoover' has done in this country and is unfortunately often used (or rather, abused), to describe any reasonably dry, sparkling wine which does not qualify for a different, more technical and more genuine, description.

In other words, a good Prosecco is a fine little bubbly which is quite enjoyable and will not give you a headache; but labelled as such without the qualification of the official area from which it emanates, it is not the real thing, although it may be just as good.

Indeed, its gentle straw colouring, delicately fruited flavour and overall amiability have made it a most popular sparkling wine. Exports of it, especially to the USA and the UK, have doubled over the past few years and it is claimed that during the 2004 Christmas holidays more than 45 million bottles of it were sold.

It is a wine that lays no claim to compete with Champagne and, indeed, is in no sense comparable to it; but it has a friendly nature that makes it almost universally acceptable as an aperitif. However, make sure that it is served very well chilled.

I have noticed over the past few years, however, that some of the Prosecco which is exported and labelled 'dry' emerges as semi-dry. I do not think that it is merely a question of my taste buds not working satisfactorily; on the contrary, I believe that the vinification process has been adapted to produce a wine which is more in keeping with the taste of the Anglo-American/Scandinavian public. This does not detract from the value of the product as such, but it may not be entirely acceptable to those who prefer this type of sparkling wine to be on the dry side. If you should share my view, then I suggest that if the Prosecco is to be drunk as an aperitif you might consider adopting the practice of some Italian barmen to pour it onto a small quantity of 'campari'. Apart from the resultant colour being quite pleasant, the bitters will sharpen the taste of the Prosecco.

Band A/B

RAMANDOLO   [DOCG / White / Friuli Venezia Giulia]

The only DOCG white, sweet wine in Friuli Venezia Giulia is not at all well known, apart from being also fairly scarce.

It is produced in a well-defined area of the commune of Nimis in the province of Udine with Verduzzo grapes in a minimum quantity of 90%; the remainder being made up of non-aromatic other grapes. The vines grow at 1,250 feet above sea level, on steep slopes.

It is of a golden, intense yellow colour with a characteristic nose, full-bodied, fairly tannic with what one can only term a woody apricoty taste, despite the pleasantly sweet background. It is unusual in the sense that it has a minimum alcoholic content of 15°. It is sometimes referred to as the Italian Sauternes, but its overall sweetness seems to me less aggressive.

Band D

RECIOTO AMARONE   [DOC / Red / Veneto]

The ancestor of the more commonly known, nowadays, Amarone. It has been produced, they say, for at least 2,000 years in the communes of Negrar, Marano, S.Ambrogio, San Pietro in Caiano and Fumane, using the same grapes that go into the Valpolicella Amarone (q.v.).

It is the result of the 'appassimento' process, a dark red wine with a red froth, a fine delicate nose and a sweet harmonious taste. Its alcoholic content ranges from 13° to 14° and because it is produced with carefully selected grapes and also because of the sometimes cumbersome 'appassimento' procedure, it is not a cheap wine.

Sweetness is obtained by an incomplete fermentation of the must. It is not a wine that has found great success abroad although more modern growers in the locality are trying to 'revive' it. It is comparable to port and is fairly versatile in the sense that it emerges as extremely pleasant both at room temperature and if chilled.

Band C/D

RECIOTO DI SOAVE   [DOCG / White / Veneto]

Soave is a delightful little village in the province of Verona; one of eleven communes, of which the more important are Monteforte d'Alpone and Colognola ai Colli, which produce this demi-sweet or sweet white DOCG wine.

It is made with grapes of Garganega (up to a maximum of 70%) to which may be added those of white Pinot, Chardonnay, and Trebbiano for the balance. These follow the 'appassimento' route to provide an intensely golden amber-coloured wine, very fruity, with body, demi-sweet or sweet, often with an oaky taste.

The minimum (there appears to be no maximum. . . . .) alcoholic content is 14° and it can only be marketed when it is at least one year old. When it comes from a very limited and well-defined area, it can be termed 'classico'.

For the linguist, the name 'Recioto' comes from the local term 'recie', that is to say the especially selected bunches of grapes which are believed to be the best and which appear on the outer sides and the top of the vine. This is a fine dessert wine, one of the white glories of the Veneto region.

There is also a variety known as Acinatico. The name comes from the Latin 'acinaticum', a wine of some antiquity; known to the Longobards and mentioned by Cassiodorus in one of his letters.
Band C/D

REFOSCO DAL PEDUNCOLO ROSSO
[Red / Friuli Venezia Giulia / DOC – Grave del Friuli]

This red wine (the name means the 'Refosco' grape with the red stalk) originates in the eastern part of Friuli in a number of municipalities in the provinces of Udine and Gorizia, many close to the Slovenian frontier. The wine is claimed to have been around in Roman times, Pliny the Elder referring to it in his *Naturalis Historia* as 'pucinum'.

In this area is to be found the small town of Cormons, an attractive little place that can be considered the wine capital of Friuli, not only because of its 'Enoteca' where regular sampling of the local wines are offered, but also because its 'co-operative' of producers comprises 210 families of viticulturists who together produce 20,000 hectolitres of wine per year.

The Refosco is made with the grape of the same name (minimum 85%), is of a dark violet-like red colour, has a very characteristic nose of a fruity and spicy nature and a dry, warm but slightly bitterish taste.

Its minimum alcoholic content is 12° and it must be matured for at least three years before being sold. Indeed, its fairly high quality and, above all, tannic content ensure that it reaches its peak well past the minimum maturing period of three years. I feel that it is probably best at between six and eight years and in some versions, it may even last longer.
Band B

REGALEALI
[IGT / Red / White / Sicilia]

Red. Made with Perricone, Nerello Mascalese and also with a variety known as Tasca, which is often identified with Malvasia but is a rather different clone.

Regaleali Rosso consists of 90% 'Nero d'Avola', the remaining 10% being made up of a number of other grapes with a predominance of Perricone.

White. Made from a blend of 40% Inzolia and 60% Sauvignon, a pleasant well-structured wine.

Band A/B

RIBOLLA (or Ribolla Gialla)   [IGT / White / Friulia Venezia Giulia]

This is a well-known local wine made only with Ribolla grapes usually, but sometimes with the permitted addition of up to 15% of white grapes from the same area.

It is straw-coloured veering occasionally to greenish, highly scented, dry, aromatic and fresh-tasting. The minimum alcoholic content is 11°. If matured for two years and provided the alcoholic content has risen to 12° it can be termed 'Riserva'.

This wine is not particularly well known; and yet, the grape from which it originates has a long history. It started out in life – at least, such seems to be the consensus of opinion amongst ampelographers – as the rebula from the Greek island of Kephalonia. The Venetians, who controlled the Greek Islands for many years indeed, later imported it into Yugoslavia whence it found its way to Friuli.

Band A/B

RIESLING   [White / Trentino Alto Adige / Friuli Veneza Giulia]

There is much Riesling produced in these two areas from either what I believe is an indigenous grape, despite the German name, namely the Riesling Italico (Welschriesling) or the German Riesling (or Riesling Renano (Rhenis)). In Trentino it is often crossed with Sylvaner.

Generally, it is a white wine with a minimum alcoholic content of 11° but more often 12° or 13°, straw-coloured with a delicate and pleasant nose and a dry taste, full-bodied and, in my opinion at least, not differing too dramatically from one area to the other. The Renano Riesling very often produces a slightly more aromatic wine but apart from that, it is a fine wine: cynically, one could say that a Riesling is a Riesling wherever it is produced but wine connoisseurs would consider this a blasphemous statement; particularly upset would be those of the Val Venosta which grow the vine at reasonably high altitudes and have to work hard on them. Of course, this is not to decry Rieslings, which are excellent wines in their own right.

The Collio Riesling made from Riesling Italico is much appreciated and one comes across wines which are a blend of both the Riesling Italico and the Riesling Renano.

For the record, there is also a Riesling del Piave made exclusively with Riesling Italico and in Lombardia the local Riesling is a blend of Italico and Renano.

Band A/B

ROERO (*v. also Arneis*)   [DOCG / Red / Piemonte]

This version of the Roero is produced with Nebbiolo grapes in a percentage of between 95% and 98%, the remainder allowed being Arneis grapes (2%-5%).

It has a strong ruby colour turning to amber when mature. It has a fruity, fragrant nose and will mature well. It has good body, dry and a rather persistent aftertaste and is slightly tannic. It may be oaked. It has a minimum alcoholic content of 11.5°; this rises to 12° in its 'Superiore' version.

Together with its white version (v. Arneis) in November 2004 it received the accolade of the DOCG designation. It is produced in a number of communes in the province of Cuneo (nineteen of them, according to the regulations) but given that the area in question is dedicated to wine culture, vinification is allowed outside the zone of production in an additional twenty communes always in the province of Cuneo.

Band C

ROSSESE DI DOLCEACQUA (*or Dolceacqua*)

[DOC / Red / Liguria]

The only DOC wine produced on the western side of the region in the area surrounding the ancient, typically medieval village of Dolceacqua in the province of Imperia.

It is an unusual red, first because it is the only wine produced from the Rossese grape in this area (otherwise known as Rossese di Ventimiglia); second, because it has a very intense and rather difficult to describe nose.

It is ruby red, veering to orange as it ages. A warm wine, where the tannins are not at all marked. It has a minimum alcoholic content of 12° but, as usual, with a year's maturing and a minimum of 13° it can be termed 'Superiore'.

It is produced also in the area around Ventimiglia and San Remo on the hills going up to the French border. An interesting, though by no means outstanding, wine, made mainly with native Rossese grapes (95%); the remainder is not specified.

The Rossese di Dolceacqua is produced in fairly limited quantities and as a result is not easy to find. Its quality is also quite variable. A good one is a worthwhile red, but in my view there is not much of it around.

Band B

ROSSO CONERO

[DOC / Red / Marche]

This wine, which grows on the hills in the province of Ancona, has a long history. It takes its name from the Conero mountain which is quite visible above the vineyards, whose name is said to derive from the great number of 'arbutus unedo' (strawberry trees) which grow abundantly in the area.

Pliny the Elder, writing in the first century AC his *Naturalis Historia*, when recording the wines that were produced in Italy, identifies those of Ancona for this area.

The wine itself is made with Montepulciano grapes (85%) with additions of Sangiovese. It is a full-bodied, brilliant ruby red, pleasantly harmonious wine with an extremely likeable nose and a minimum alcoholic content of 11.5° which when sold with a minimum of 12.5°

and matured for a period of two years may be termed 'Riserva'.
Band A/B

ROSSO DI MONTALCINO   [DOC / Red / Toscana]

The younger brother of the Brunello di Montalcino (q.v.) is produced
in the territory of Montalcino in the province of Siena, made with the
same Sangiovese grape (100%).

It is a brilliantly intense ruby-coloured red with a strong vinous taste,
very dry and slightly tannic. It must be matured for a minimum of
twelve months and has a minimum alcoholic content of 12°, though
the most available versions usually run to 13°.

It is a fine red wine, much more genuine and less expensive than its
famous brother and, in that sense, better value for money. The wine
has been around for some time but it has kept improving from the date
it obtained its DOC classification in 1983.
Band B/C

ROSSO PICENO   [DOC / Red / Marche]

Not to be confused with Rosso Conero, this comes almost from the
same area, namely, from the provinces of Ancona, Macerata and Ascoli
Piceno; an area embracing more than seventy communes over 2,000 sq.
kms for Ascoli Piceno alone, said to produce more than half of the
total wine yield of the Marche. It is made with Montepulciano grape
(maximum 70%) and Sangiovese (maximum 50%) with the addition of
other red non-aromatic local grapes.

Although the DOC qualification is reasonably recent, the origins of
the wine are quite ancient. Indeed, a Piceno wine is documented in
dates prior to the Roman occupation. (The Piceni people were in the
area long before the Romans.) The principal reference to it is owed to
Polybius, the Greek historian of the Roman world.

Rosso Piceno is a ruby red wine of varying intensity with a marked
nose and a balanced taste, which is available in two versions, depending
on the production zone. Its minimum alcoholic content is 11.5°.

In the Northern area of production the 'Novello' predominates,
which is only slightly less alcoholic. A very smooth fragrant young wine.

In the more southerly part of the production area we have the
'Superiore', a more substantial wine with a minimum alcoholic content
of 12°. It cannot be sold until the 1 November of the year subsequent
to that in which its grapes are gathered. A dark red wine, scented, sapid
and not too dry, it is one of the best products of the locality.
Band: B

SAGRANTINO DI MONTEFALCO*   [DOCG / Red / Umbria]

The wine was formerly known as Sacrantino di Montefalco, from the
area of Montefalco which was part of the bishopric of Spoleto from the
thirteenth to the nineteenth centuries.

It is believed to have found its origin in a sweet wine now known as
Sagrantino Passito, a DOCG wine made from ripe grapes.

The adjective 'sacro' in Italian means 'sacred' and the earlier name of the Sacrantino wines is said to be due to the fact that it was first produced by monks in the area and used initially for church purposes.

Whether the Sagrantino grape is derived from the Itriola variety described by Pliny the Elder is debatable; its 'sacred' origin, however, does not seem to be much in doubt.

The DOCG classification describes it as Montefalco Sagrantino but the older Sacrantino di Montefalco is still used in the relative specification. The locals refer to it simply as Sagrantino.

Until the late 1970s/early 1980s it was still known as Sagrantino di Montefalco and was made with two varieties of grapes, namely the Sagrantino and the Sangiovese, having an alcoholic content of between 13° and 15°. It had a red dark colour and originated mainly from villages in the province of Perugia, namely Montefalco, Gualdo Tadino and Giano.

The potential of the Sagrantino grape, with or without Sangiovese, soon began to be appreciated and a more popular version came about, namely a dry red with a delicate vinous scent and average body, as well as a glorious ruby red colour, turning to garnet with age. It tastes mainly of violets and blackberries.

Nowadays, most producers use exclusively 100% Sagrantino grapes, as indeed the DOCG regulations prescribe. Most are hand-picked and are vinified by the gravity system.

It is now sold with a minimum alcoholic content of 12° and it is a DOCG wine which must be matured for a minimum of eighteen months. If the alcoholic content is raised to a minimum of 12.5° and it is matured for longer than thirty months, it can then be described as 'Riserva'. Of these, at least twelve months must be in wooden barrels, but the oaking is not too marked.

It is the pride of Umbria, the 'green heart of Italy', and has now become one of Italy's most distinctive reds, also because it lends itself to considerable ageing. Some varieties bottled in 1985 are coming onto the market now and they are said to be excellent.

The original sweet wine is still there, having a delightful garnet red colour, full-bodied: an excellent 'dessert' wine in its 'passito' form. An outstanding replacement for port, for no other reason that it has no added alcohol and it is less likely to give anyone a headache. However, this sweet version of Sagrantino di Montefalco is becoming more and more scarce and, inevitably, expensive.

There is also a Montefalco DOC red (q.v.), made with the same grapes, as well as a Montefalco white, made from Grechetto and Trebbiano grapes.

* The description Montefalco Sagrantino is now invariably used by the Gambero Rosso Guide and by many Italian supermarkets, as well as most other wine guides. A first class red, which obtained 'official' recognition in 1979 and since then has gone from strength to strength.
Band C

SALICE SALENTINO (*formerly known as Salento*)
[DOC / Red / White / Rosé / Puglia]

Salice Salentino has always been known to be a fine wine but it was perhaps less favoured in Italy than it is nowadays, especially since the 1980s. It is also making a strong comeback abroad. In its modern version it was first produced as Salice in 1954, graduating to a DOC in 1970. It takes its name from the commune of Salice Salentino, a place well-known since about the year 1000.

A strong, full-bodied, very dry and yet smooth wine of more or less intense ruby colour, turning brick red with ageing. It will mature quite gracefully, reaching maturity at about five years and improving until at least ten.

It is exceptionally fruity. The local producers' own tasting notes say that it tastes of plums. That cannot be denied but I suggest that in the better versions one detects a fairly intense note of blackberries and, possibly, blackcurrants.

It is produced in a number of communes (Salice Salentino, Copertino, Squinzano in the provinces of Lecce and Brindisi) mainly from Negroamaro (80%) grapes with the remainder split between Malvasia (Nera di Lecce, Nera di Brindisi) and Primitivo.

It has a minimum alcoholic content of 12° (the 'Riserva' must have 12.5°) rising to 14° and sometimes even 14.5°.

It is what one would term a strong wine, robust yet harmonious which is also available (though not abroad) in a 'novello' version, much smoother and fruitier. Experts consider it eminently suited to game dishes and to roasts generally, but I think it is more versatile than that. Its flavour is, in my view, unusual: as observed, its fruity nature is quite marked.

Salice Salentino is also produced in a white version, mainly from the Verdeca, Aleatico and Moscato grape, less well known than its red brother.

The rosé type is a fine wine. Little white Salice is exported but the rosé is beginning to prove its worth.

Over the past decade a number of non-indigenous grapes have been introduced into the area, such as Cabernet Sauvignon, Chardonnay, Merlot, Montepulciano, and Sauvignon, the relative issuing wines being sold under either a generic name or an IGT description.

Band B/C

SAN SEVERO
[DOC / White / Puglia]

San Severo and its surrounding area are in the province of Foggia. One finds there a very pleasant white wine made with the Bombino (white) and Trebbiano (Toscano) grapes to which are added some white Malvasia and Verdeca.

It is a friendly, straw-coloured wine, vinous and at times slightly scented with a dry, fresh nose and a minimum alcoholic content of 11°.

A sparkling version is also available as well as a red and a rosé.

Band A

SANGIOVESE DI ROMAGNA   [DOC / Red / Emilia Romagna]

A very pleasant violet-scented and tasting, occasionally slightly tannic with a bitterish aftertaste, dry wine produced on the hills in the provinces of Bologna, Forli, Rimini and Ravenna, usually better than the other IGT or table wines coming onto the market under the name Sangiovese.

It is made from a minimum of 85% Sangiovese to which other unspecified grapes can be added, and has been vinified locally since the seventeenth century. It has a minimum alcoholic content of 11.5° and if matured for two years can be termed 'Riserva'. If the Sangiovese originates from a specified, limited area and has a minimum alcoholic content of 12° it can be termed 'Superiore'.

It is often sold as a 'Novello', or new wine. Like the more mature one, this has a ruby red colour with violet tinges, a fruity nose and a friendly, not too dry taste, veering at times to almonds. The new wine must have a minimum alcoholic content of 11°.

Sangiovese is a pleasant wine available abroad mainly in the 'Riserva' version with an alcoholic content of 13°, often replacing the Montepulciano d'Abruzzo as a table wine in Italian restaurants. Increasingly, non-DOC Sangiovese wines are becoming available which originate in other Italian regions, e.g. from Tuscany, from Puglia and from Sicily. A mark of the versatility of the grape.

Band A/B

SANGIOVESE DI TOSCANA *(and elsewhere)*
                          [IGT / Red / Toscana & various regions]

One should not omit to mention again the growing popularity of the Sangiovese grape, which has resulted in a number of wines coming onto the market made wholly or partly with it, as remarked.

That of Toscana is on sale in the UK, and other regions are beginning to produce what may be described as reliable, though not outstanding, reds with an average alcoholic content of no less than 12.5°, rising to 13.5°. There is also available in the UK a *Sangiovese* from Apulia sold under the label of a piedmontese vintner!

These are mostly drinkable wines, if they are not kept for too long; they will usually go off in about one year. Some versions are also emerging blended with Cabernet Sauvignon, and these will last well into their fifth year.

Band A/B

SASSELLA *(see Valtellina Superiore)*

SASSICAIA *(a 'Super Tuscan')*   [DOC / Red / Toscana]

Little did the poet Giosué Carducci realize how his popular description of the long road lined by cypresses that runs from San Guido to Bolgheri would become significant to all lovers of well-known, high quality Italian wines.

In his poem *Davanti a San Guido*, known to practically all Italian schoolchildren, he describes the cypresses as tall and dignified, but he could not possibly dream that the area around Bolgheri would become almost a mecca for all lovers of custom wines.

Sassicaia started out in life as one of the 'new' Italian wines, namely a blend of Italian and French grapes; it is but one of several such wines that represent a determined attempt, on the part of Italian vintners, to keep up with the times, as some say, to diversify, as others maintain or to ignore the Italian ampelographic variety and tradition, as a more extreme view would suggest. It is the first of these new wines to qualify for a DOC being now known as Sassicaia-Bolgheri San Guido.

It is made with a minimum 80% of Cabernet Sauvignon grapes grafted from the vines of Chateau Lafite in the early 1940s, plus other local grapes. Its colour is ruby red, its acidity well balanced, it has a vinous, elegant nose, good body and a full, dryish, harmonious taste of currants. Minimum alcoholic content 12°. Its first commercially produced vintage dates back to 1968.

It is not too clear where the name of this wine originated although the consensus appears to be that it was derived from the stony nature of the soil in the area ('sasso' meaning stone in Italian) which is also thought to facilitate the growth of the French vines used, the gravelly nature of the land corresponding to the French area of Graves.

As is the case with Tignanello, Solaia and Ornellaia, the price of this wine, as well as the others, puts it outside the reach of the ordinary drinker. In fact, it can truly be said that it has become a scarce commodity, reaching almost iconic status thanks also to the efforts of the present incumbent of a family that owned land in the area for over 200 years, namely Nicoló Incisa della Rocchetta.

But the estate, the 'Tenuta San Guido' is not resting on its laurels since it launched in 2000 a new wine, the first to be released since the 1968 Sassicaia, made with 45% Merlot, 45% Cabernet Sauvignon and 10% Sangiovese, all fermented separately in stainless steel vats and subsequently aged in oak barrels.

Band E

Note – As I have observed, Bolgheri was not until recently an area of Tuscany known for its wines. The emergence of Sassicaia has given the name Bolgheri a certain kudos. As a result, there are now available red wines called 'Bolgheri' which originate from the area: they could be termed the cousins of Sassicaia and are fairly acceptable, good-bodied wines which are substantially cheaper than the equivalent 'Super Tuscan', though by no means inexpensive.

SAUVIGNON TRENTINO [DOC / White / Trentino / Alto Adige]

This is a straw-coloured wine with a tendency to greenish. It has a pleasant scent and a dry tasty aroma characteristic of the grape from which it originates. It has a minimum alcoholic content of 11° but if matured for two years and with a content of 11.5° it can be termed 'Riserva'. The varieties available are of a higher alcoholic content of about 12.5°.

Band A/B

SCHIOPPETTINO   [DOC / Red / Friuli Venezia Giulia]

This is a ruby-coloured wine, occasionally veering to violet, with a minimum alcoholic content of 11°. It has a strong nose, is fruity and yet dry, pleasant and quite smooth. The fruits can be easily identified as blackberries and raspberries. It is also a reasonably tannic wine.

It is made from Ribolla Nera grapes, known locally as 'Schioppettino'. It is a wine that is not too popular abroad, although much appreciated in the area of production; well structured but by no means outstanding. The grape variety first appeared in the late-thirteenth century but had a chequered history. It was only in the mid-1970s that it was revived on a commercial scale allowing it to gain DOC classification in 1992. The name is a bit of a mouthful but, for those who are interested in the Italian language, it is said to originate from the fact that the particular fruits of the grape have a tendency to make a popping noise when eaten or pressed for must.

Band B

SFURSAT (or Sforzato) see Valtellina

SOAVE   [DOCG / DOC / White / Veneto]

A first-class wine from the Veneto region grown in the province of Verona (communes of Soave, Monteforte d'Alpone, etc.) derived from the Garganega, Trebbiano, Pinot Bianco and Chardonnay grapes. It is well known throughout the world. It has a yellow/greenish, clear colour, delicate scent, a dry, slightly bitter taste, but quite velvety.

With a minimum alcoholic content of 10.5°, it may be labelled 'Superiore' if above 11.5°, and 'Classico' if it comes from the original production area. Recently, Soave Superiore has become a DOCG wine.

It is a well-balanced wine which was much appreciated by the Romans. In modern times, it has become successful as a very suitable accompaniment to soups, hors d'oeuvres, eggs and seafood generally, probably because of its velvety taste and its medium body.

A fine wine, which derives its name from the village of Soave, a delightful place in which to sample Veronese wines. Indeed, this small town is at the heart of the wine-producing area west of Verona.

Soave is produced in great quantity. Some statistics suggest that the total production of all kinds of Soave (normal, 'Superiore' and 'Classico') exceeds 45m litres every year, which is a massive figure comparable to the production of Asti wines.

I must say, however, that I have not always been able to enthuse about Soave generally, although it is fair to say that in its Classico version, that is to say the wine produced from the hills of Soave and those surrounding its practically adjacent (but not so attractive) 'brother' village of Monteforte d'Alpone, it is indeed a fine wine which, surprisingly for a white from this area, will also age fairly well. However, the 'Classico' version is expensive.

There has recently developed a tendency to oak some Soave Classico wines which have now become available outside Italy.

Band B/C

SOLAIA (*a Super Tuscan*)   [Red / Toscana]

Another of the 'new' wines from the House of Antinori, this is, in terms of grape content, the reverse of Tignanello (q.v.) as it comes from Cabernet Sauvignon with small added quantities of Sangiovese.

It has also proved an exceptionally successful, high-calibre wine; its only fault is that it is too expensive.

Band E

SOLOPACA   [DOC / Red / White / Campania]

A fairly scarce wine, much appreciated by the locals but hardly known abroad, this DOC product is made in the province of Benevento in the communes of Cerreto Sannita, Melizzano and, of course, Solopaca in the general geographical area which is known by the all-embracing term of 'Sannio'.

Red. The red is made with the Aglianico, Olivella, Piedirosso and Sangiovese grapes and other non-aromatic red grapes (in a quantity not exceeding 30%) available in the area. The locals are very fond of this extremely drinkable, pleasant ruby-coloured wine with a rather intense nose. The wine is dry, smooth and has a minimum alcoholic content of 11.5°. It can be termed 'Superiore' if it is matured for a minimum of one year and has an alcoholic content of at least 12.5°.

The colour tends to become less intense with the passage of time; the wine will not stand long ageing and should, in my opinion, be drunk by its fifth year.

White. The white version of Solopaca is produced in the same area as the red with a mixture of grapes (Biancolella, Coda di Volpe, Falanghina, Malvasia Toscana and of Candia, the latter referred to by the locals as Cerreto from the name of the locality where it is mainly grown as well as Trebbiano Toscano, together with other white grapes in non-prescribed quantities). It is a straw-coloured, gentle, dry, smooth wine with a minimum alcoholic content of 11°.

Neither wine is well known outside its area of production and is exceptionally difficult to find outside Italy; the same may be said for the even more scarce rosé.

Band B/C

SPANNA (*v Nebbiolo*)

SQUINZANO   [DOC / Red / Rosé / Puglia]

Squinzano Rosso. Supermarkets have made this wine fairly popular in the UK and elsewhere. It originates in the province of Lecce and takes its name from the old Roman town in an up-and-coming wine-producing area (Copertino (q.v.) nearby) and is made, as is to be expected in this area, from Negroamaro and Malvasia grapes to which is added some Sangiovese. It is of a ruby colour veering to orange when aged, has a vinous nose, is tasty, full-bodied and yet has a strange smoothness.

Its minimum alcoholic content is 12.5° but with the usual two years maturing and a minimum of 13° it can be termed 'Riserva'.

Squinzano Rosato. This is its rosé brother, of colours veering from light ruby to light cherry, delicately perfumed and smooth, quite pleasant and eminently drinkable. It tends to be on the strong side with a minimum alcoholic content of 12.5° rising to 13.5°.

Band A

SYLVANER (*or Silvaner*)   [White / Trentino Alto Adige]

This is made with grapes of the same name (90%) and is grown in the area of Bressanone in northern Tirol. The grapes grow sometimes at fairly high altitudes, as much as nearly 750 m above sea level in an area where the sun is not too generous. The locals have learnt to overcome this lack of light by tilting, so to say, the vines at a sharper angle than is customary in the remainder of the region.

Despite this handicap and the fact that the yields are reasonably modest, there is merit in this type of wine. It has a minimum alcoholic content of 10° rising (seldom) to 12.5°, is fresh-tasting and vivid, of a straw yellow colour with shades of green. The only fault, if such it be because on the other hand it helps preserve the wine, is the acidity of the Sylvaner which some may find not to their taste.

Band B

TAURASI   [DOCG / Red / Campania]

A DOCG wine, the red glory of the region of Campania. It is produced in the province of Avellino (mainly in the villages of Taurasi, Mirabella, Gesualdo, San Mango sul Calore and Sant'Angelo all'Esca), in an area squeezed betewwn Campania and Puglia.

It is made with the principal grape of the area, namely Aglianico with the addition of other grapes such as, for example, the Piedirosso. It has a deep ruby red colour which, like many other Italian strong reds (e.g. Barolo) tends easily to brick red and/or orange when mature. It tastes essentially of cherries, is quite tannic and starts with a minimum alcoholic content of 12° rising to 15°. It must by law be matured for a minimum of three years, at which point it becomes quite drinkable; it reaches its peak after five to seven years and is one of the few Italian reds which are suitable for long ageing (up to fifteen years or more). On 28 October 2003, I uncorked a bottle of Taurasi (dated 1970 content 0.720lt. (*sic*) alcoholic content 12°) of the well-known firm of Michele Mastroberardino of Atripalda (Avellino), a long-established (1878) producer. The cork was crumbling but the wine still drinkable.

When offered with a minimum alcoholic content of 12.5° and matured for four years, it can be described as '*Riserva*'. One of our authorities on wine, Luigi Veronelli, considers that Taurasi is the best wine to accompany wild boar dishes.

It is truly an outstanding wine.

Band C/D

TERLANER [White /Trentino Alto Adige]

Much wine is grown in the hills in the province of Bolzano, especially at Terlano, from which the wine takes its name, and Termeno, but more particularly in the well-known villages of Andriano, Nalles, Appiano and Caldaro.

This wine was initially made exclusively with the Terlaner grape but nowadays this is blended and there are a number of combinations. The most common one is that of Pinot Bianco and/or Chardonnay to a minimum of 50% (with the balance made up of Riesling and Sauvignon, Sylvaner and Muller Thurgau).

Terlaner is a straw-coloured, often white/greenish wine with a very delicate perfume and a dry, full fruity flavour; differing from other local wines, it is not too acid but it leaves a slightly bitter aftertaste. Minimum alcoholic content 11.5°.

Band B

TEROLDEGO ROTALIANO
[DOC / Red / Rosé / Trentino/Alto Adige]

Locals call this the prince of the wines of 'Trentino' and there is no doubt that it represents the backbone of the production of red wine in this area; in its rosé version it is called 'Rosato'.

This is a wine much appreciated by the German-speaking communities both locally as well as in Austria, Germany and Switzerland, as is evidenced by the fact that it would appear that the name of the grape itself is derived from the German, Tiroler Gold.

It is made with Teroldego grapes which grow exclusively in the province of Trento and is available in both red and rosé versions. The variety yields a fairly sweet grape with plenty of colour in the skins.

Red. This is a wine with a deep ruby colour, balanced acidity, dry, only slightly tannic, and a faint bitter almondy aftertaste. Its bouquet however is very fruity and reminds one of violets and raspberries.

It has a minimum alcoholic content of 11.5°, but it is strong and round. It matures at three years and keeps improving until six, when it is probably at its best. It should be said, however, that it can and indeed is drunk when fairly young and it doubles quite effectively – price apart – as a very successful and easily drinkable table wine.

Rosé. Teroldego Rotaliano Rosato (Kretzer). This is one of the best Italian rosé wines, although it is not too common.

It is of a rather strong, rosy colour, a fruity nose and, like the red version, with an almondy taste and aftertaste. It is a velvety wine which is usually drunk when young.

Experts have claimed that it is the alluvial lands on the side of the River Noci, which, coupled with a subsoil of sand and bones, give Teroldego its characteristic flavour.

Band B

THE SUPER TUSCANS (*not an official designation, merely a consumer attribution*) v – also Ornellaia and Sassicaia

These have already been mentioned. I do not know who invented the expression 'Super Tuscans' but it must have been someone with a great flair for public relations and advertising, for it has stuck and it has raised a number of wines to a level which, but for the resources behind them, they might possibly never have reached. (The expression has caught on: we now have 'Super Venetian' wines and, more recently, 'Super Whites'!)

The only thing that I consider 'super' about these wines is their price; nevertheless, I propose analysing some of them briefly, firstly because of the importance that they have acquired as a mark of the ability of Italian winemakers to keep up to date with the requirements of an ever-more exacting market; secondly, because they are, in their own right, outstanding wines, which show the resourcefulness of Italian producers in competing on the international market.

There are now over two dozen wines which are claiming the label 'Super Tuscan' and inevitably, more will be added to this non-legally (yet!) recognized denomination with the passage of time. One of the latest is San Martino, an IGT wine, resulting from a blend of Sangiovese and Sangioveto grapes.

This is a full-bodied, reasonably tannic and exceptionally fragrant dry red wine of 13° alcohol and is much more accessible price-wise.

Little did Giosué Carducci, one of our best-known poets, realize that the area of Tuscany which he cited in one of the poems that most Italian schoolboys are made to memorize, *Davanti a San Guido*, would in all likelihood become better known for experimentation with the vines of Bordeaux. New wines seem to emerge every year around Castagneto Carducci and Bolgheri (see in 2003, for example, the Montepergoli 2001), close to the sea.

Two final notes on the Super Tuscans. In the first place, it should be recorded that most of the major producers of Tuscan wines have in fact over the years been experimenting with and creating these particular new types of wine.

Second, the reader might like to know that excellent though they are, there is no consensus of opinion as to the value of the relationship between their reputation and the prices charged for them. Put differently, a few wine experts would appear to have started to become somewhat disenchanted with them and more than once one reads the comment that they are not good value for money.

It has been suggested that the proximity of the growing area to the sea is a favourable contributory factor to the success of these wines.

TIGNANELLO (a 'Super Tuscan') [IGT / Red / Toscana]

I have already commented on this, one of the fine 'new' Italian wines created by Antinori; or rather, by his winemaker Giacomo Tachis, a Piedmontese. Effectively, they brought up-to-date a nineteenth-century practice of blending Cabernet Sauvignon with Sangiovese and have consistently proved its merits since it was first introduced in 1971, having been bottled the year before, at a time when its success was hardly anticipated.

A full-bodied strong, flavourful, harmonious but very expensive wine.

Band E

TOCAI   [White / Dry / Friuli Venezia Giulia-Veneto]

The Tocai of Friuli is produced throughout the region from the Tocai grape. The reader should not be tempted to believe that there is any connection either with Hungary or Alsace: this is 100% an Italian grape. Thus one has a Tocai of the Colli Orientali, a Tocai del Collio, a Tocai Friuli Annia, a Tocai Aquileia, and a Tocai Friuli Isonzo.

Only a few of these wines are available abroad and they follow a fairly standard form, namely they are made with the Tocai grape, are straw-coloured with lemony reflexes, have a pleasant nose, are dry and harmonious wines with a minimum alcoholic content of 11.5° which when rising to 12° can, for a wine matured for two years, be termed 'Riserva'.

Pleasant enough, of course; by no means exceptional. In recent years, the slight animosity that has always existed between the producers of this area of Italy and the Hungarians, proud of their well-known, sweet wine, Tokaji, has become more intense. The matter was referred to the European Commission some time ago and in December 2004 it was determined, apparently, that the Hungarians were right. The Italian producers of Tocai point out that not only are the two wines quite different (a dry wine of 12° alcohol on one side, a very sweet dessert wine of 14° alcohol on the other), not only do they have different colours (a pale straw in the Italian version, a much darker gold in the Hungarian wine) but the local stream, the 'Rio di Tocai' is, according to those of Friuli, the best possible proof of its ancient origin.

Not good enough for the European Commission which in any event has also agreed with the Australians that they may safely label their wine Tocai!

In June 2005 it was suggested that, to comply with the decision of the European Court, the wine could be relabelled Toccai. Maybe: to me, the proposal sounds wrong bearing in mind that the word 'toccai' is in Italian the first person singular of the past definite of the verb 'toccare' which means to touch.

I am not sure how long the denomination of origin will last but the wine will undoubtedly continue to be appreciated, more particularly with what the locals consider almost an essential adjunct, the speciality of the area, the 'prosciutto di San Daniele'.

There is also a Tocai from the Veneto region, known as Tocai di San Martino della Battaglia . It is made with 100% Tocai 'friulano' grapes and is of a lemony yellow, veering to golden as it matures, with a good nose, a round flavour, and a bitterish aftertaste. Minimum alcoholic content is 12°. It is produced mainly on the southern shores of Lake Garda.

Band A/B

TORBATO
[White / Sardegna]

This wine is produced in the commune of Alghero (Sassari province). It is straw-coloured when mature but when fresh, it is greenish with a gently aromatic nose, sapid and harmonious with a slightly bitter aftertaste.

The minimum alcoholic content is 11° but it can rise to 15° and it is derived from the grape of the same name. From the same grapes when dried a 'Passito' is available of golden colour, very aromatic and sweet with an alcoholic content of between 15° and 17°.

Band A/B

TORGIANO (BIANCO)
[DOC / White / Umbria]

This wine originates in the territory of Torgiano in the province of Perugia and is made with Trebbiano Toscano, Grechetto and other white grapes (not exceeding 15%). It is lightly coloured, straw yellow, with a pleasant smell of flowers, very dry and lightly fruity taste. The aftertaste is slightly acidy, but not offensively so. Its minimum alcoholic content is 10.5° but one finds it more often at 11.5°/12°.

Band B

TORGIANO (ROSSO)
[DOC / DOCG / Red / Umbria]

This is its proper name although many restaurants in the UK offer it as Rubesco Torgiano, a name which is also used in Italy. A wine of some standing, it has become much better known over the past few decades even outside its area of origin.

It derives its name from the medieval 'Turris Giani' in Torgiano and is the result of a blend of Sangiovese, Canaiolo, Trebbiano, Ciliegiolo and Montepulciano grapes. It is of a brilliant red colour, good body and delicate dry taste. Its minimum alcoholic content is 12.5° and in 'Riserva' versions it must be matured for no less than three years.

A solid, reliable red which seems to prove itself quite successful with foreign buyers, mainly because of its consistency in quality. The 'Riserva' version is now a DOCG wine.

DOCG Band C/D
DOC Band B

TRAMINER (*Gewürztraminer*)
[White / Trentino / Alto Adige]

Of all the white wines of the region, this is probably the best known abroad, after the *Pinots*. It is usually marketed in the German style (Rhenish) bottle and is made with the Traminer grape, stated by some to be indigenous to the area and by others to originate in Alsace. In its more popular version it is called *Traminer Aromatico* which is merely another way of underlining the exceptionally pleasing, fruity aroma of the wine.

To be drunk not too cold (at about 10°C), it has a colour veering from straw yellow to golden, a very marked, almost intense nose and a full, pleasant, either dry or semi-sweet taste. It has a minimum alcoholic content of 11.5° but it is very often available in 12.5° to 13.5° and ages reasonably well, not losing its original perfume, which tends to become more refined. Inevitably, the straw colour deepens.

It originates in the district of Termeno (Tramin in German). In the UK it is probably much less well-known that the Gewürztraminer from Alsace but it should be noted that it can stand the comparison quite well. Indeed, without being too chauvinistic, I suggest that it is a slightly more full-bodied and more elegant wine than its French/German counterpart. This is due to the fact that the Traminer grape (aromatic or Gewürztraminer) although probably of German origin has acclimatized very well in north-east Italy, having been available in south Tyrol for very many years indeed. It is true that only recently have Italian producers begun to exploit it in the same manner as the French do; it must be recorded that a number of connoisseurs of wine still maintain that only very few Italian Gewürztraminer wines reach the standard of scent, spiciness and lushness of the Gewürztraminer of Alsace.

Having said this for the sake of the record, I would suggest that those who subscribe to the view that the Traminer of Alsace is better than the Italian, should try some of the 2003 vintage Traminer that reached the market in 2005. Some have been oaked but despite my strictures on oaking, I have to admit that there are cases were the results are outstanding.

Band B/C

TREBBIANO D'ABRUZZO   [DOC / White / Abruzzo]

The white brother of the well-known Montepulciano d'Abruzzo (q.v.) is produced in the same area, namely in all the Abruzzo provinces, although that coming from hills facing the sea seems to emerge as a much better version. It does not get the recognition it deserves and it has been said that, as a result, it runs the risk of becoming the 'Cinderella of wines'. This may be taking it a little bit too far but there is an element of truth in the statement, although it should not be forgotten that this particular wine was well known to the Romans. Indeed, Pliny remarks that the wine may have been imported to the present area of production from a vine known as Trebulianum originated in Campania.

Nor should one forget that, generally speaking, wines from the Abruzzo area of Italy (reds and whites) enjoyed a good reputation with the Romans, as the Latin poet Ovid records.

It is made with the Trebbiano d'Abruzzo grape, otherwise known as Bombino Bianco as well as with the more common Trebbiano from Toscana (85%), the remainder being taken up by other grapes within the area. It is a pleasantly perfumed wine of straw colour with a delicate dry sapid taste, having a minimum alcoholic content of 11°. It is becoming very popular.

Band A

TRENTINO PINOT   [DOC / Red / White / Trentino / Alto Adige]

The DOC covers both the Pinot Nero and the Pinot Grigio and Bianco. The Bianco and the Grigio are not too dissimilar from the other wines of the area but the Pinot Nero, also known as

Blauburgunder, is worthy of note.

It is produced from the grape of the same name, which is fairly extensively cultivated in the region. It is a very bright ruby red turning to brick coloured tints when mature. It has an intense aroma, is moderately dry, slightly bitter, suitably tannic, with a lingering aftertaste which is somewhat difficult to define.

Its minimum alcoholic content is 11.5° but it can rise to 13° and once it goes above 12° if matured for two years it can be termed 'Riserva'. It grows principally in the areas of Merano, Appiano, Caldaro, Terlano, Mezzo Corona and Trento.

Band B

TRENTO   [DOC / White / Rosé / Trentino Alto Adige]

The DOC Trento (established in 1993) covers two types of sparkling wines, (white and the rosé) made with Chardonnay and/or white Pinot and/or Pinot Noir and/or Meunier.

The area of production extends to 1,200 hectares where some 3,000 small producers supply in the main the twenty larger marketing establishments.

Vines are grown on calcareous soil hills between 200 and 800 metres above sea level, often sloping. The wine has a minimum alcoholic content of 9° for the standard version and 10° for the 'Riserva' (only available in the white version) which must be matured in bottles for at least three years. It is golden in colour, rather fine, tasty, often pleasantly fruity, though slightly acid. The rosé is delicate and pleasant.

Band C

VALDADIGE (ETSCHTALER)
[DOC / Red /White / Trentino / Alto Adige]

A general DOC description for wines produced in the territories of thirty communes in the provinces of Bolzano and Trento and, incidentally, in that of Rivoli Veronese in the province of Verona, most of ancient lineage.

The vineyards run alongside both sides of the River Adige and the resultant wines are quite varied. There is a white, a red, a rosé, a Chardonnay, a Pinot Bianco, a Pinot Grigio, a Carbernet Franc, a Cabernet Sauvignon.

The grapes used are the obvious ones for the area as well as Garganega from Veneto, the local Enantio (a variety of Lambrusco) and the Schiava. Specifications vary, save for Chardonnay, Pinot Bianco, and Pinot Grigio which must have a minimum 85% of grapes of that name.

The Pinot Bianco is known in German as Weissburgunder. The descriptions that have already been given for these types of wines apply also to those from the Valdadige.

The Pinot Noir from this area is known locally as Blauburgunder, a ruby red, smooth, dry, pleasantly aromatic though slightly bitter wine with a minimum alcoholic content of 11.5°. The Valdadige DOC covers fifteen different types of wine.

Band B

VALDICHIANA   [DOC / White / Toscana]

A delicately scented white wine originating in a number of districts in
the provinces of Arezzo and Siena. It is a blended wine (Trebbiano
minimum 20%, plus Chardonnay, Pinot (Bianco and Grigio) and
Grechetto for the balance but with the possibility of adding other white
grapes).

It is a lightly straw-coloured wine with green tinges, and a slightly
bitter almond aftertaste. It has a minimum alcoholic content of 10° but
the version available in the UK is 11.5°. It is available locally also in a
sparkling version.

A pleasant enough wine although one cannot really enthuse about it;
but Pliny the Elder certainly did. Somewhat chauvinistically I should
record that in the nineteenth century French producers from Burgundy
and Champagne had recourse to many of the wines of the Val di
Chiana, after their own vineyards were ravaged by phylloxera.

Band A/B

VALGELLA (See *Valtellina Superiore*)

VALPOLICELLA – AMARONE   [DOC / Red / Veneto]

Valpolicella. This is a well-known Italian red from the Veneto region.
It is of a light ruby colour veering to garnet red with age. Overall, a
delicate mellow wine, dry with not-too-much body and a taste which is
often described as that of bitter almonds. It is produced in the
communes of Fiumane, Negrar, Marano, San Ambrogio, San Pietro in
Cariano and Pescantina.

It is made with a mixture of grapes starting with the Corvina (40-
70%), Rondinella (20-40%) and Molinara (5-25%), as well as other
grapes of different kinds. It must have a minimum alcoholic content of
11°, more commonly 12° and it also comes in a 'Superiore' variety
which, apart from having a minimum alcoholic content of 12°, must be
matured for at least one year.

It is not a wine that lends itself to ageing and – perhaps I am being
unkind – it is not that exciting as a red, for quite often it emerges as
lacking in taste.

Amarone. Valpolicella is by no means a new wine; 'newer', however
and most successful with the Anglo-American public is its version
known as Amarone which is made with the same grapes but dried in
the autumn sun. This is known as 'appassimento' (the process of
withering). The grapes shrivel, so that they can concentrate their sugar
content, by resting on either fruit crates or bamboo racks, or being
hung from wires in buildings where the air can circulate, for varying
periods of time (between three and six months). When the wine is
wholly made by this method it is called 'passito'. The term does not
apply to Amarone where only partially dried grapes are used in varying
percentages, depending on the vintner.

The wine is stored in oak barrels for varying periods of time but, given that Slavonian and especially French oak is becoming more expensive, some producers are experimenting with local woods (cherry and chestnut, mainly). It must be matured for at least two years from 1 December of the vintage year and is normally sold with an minimum alcoholic content of 14°, rising to 15° or even 16°: it is such high alcoholic content which has made it so popular with Northern buyers. It is claimed that Amarone is the successor, perhaps not in name, but certainly in approach, to what was known to the Romans as 'acinaticum'. The wine, however, is only fifty years old since the name 'Amarone' was first used in 1953 when the first bottles were sold to the public of a wine that had been produced three years previously to celebrate the eightieth birthday of Alberto Bolla of the well-known producers Bolla of Verona (established in 1883). As a result of its success Alberto Bolla became known affectionately as 'the grandfather of Amarone'.

Amarone is also known as Recioto Amarone della Valpolicella, but beware, since Recioto della Valpolicella is a sweet wine (q.v.). It is a strong, very dry, full-bodied impressive red, which has proved extremely successful with the British public. It is quite flavoured, fruity, sapid, with a very pleasant aftertaste of almonds. The nose is of plums and cherries. Unusually for a wine that lends itself to maturity, it is not very tannic.

Over the past five to ten years much Valpolicella wine has been treated to the 'ripasso' processing. Very often the wine is given a period in barrels, on the lees of the much stronger and more flavourful Amarone. This feature is highlighted on the label of the bottle which, in addition to the usual wording, also has RIPASSO in block capitals.
Band D/E

VALTELLINA
[DOCG / Red / Lombardia]

The name covers an area on the right-hand shore of the River Adda and, to a lesser degree, on its left, in the province of Sondrio, which produces from the local grape Chiavennasca (another name for Nebbiolo) in a minimum quantity of 80%, with the addition of other local grapes, e.g. Brugnola, a fine, strongly-coloured, dry red wine, with a delicate nose, dry and tannic, with a minimum alcoholic content of 11° and six months' compulsory maturing. This is a DOCG wine of high quality.

Outstanding in the area, as a result of the 'appassimento' process, is the Sfursat (or Sforzato) of a much darker red colour, a very fruity, long-lasting nose, much body and harmony.

A quality product which has a minimum alcoholic content of 14° (but is often found at 14.5°) and must be matured for no less than two years, it lends itself to considerable ageing, reaches its peak between eight and ten years, but will continue quite happily up to fifteen years. There are some who maintain that it vies with Amarone; the latter, the champion red of Veneto, the former of Lombardia, which I find it easier to drink at a meal than the Amarone; the Sfursat being certainly smoother.

The Valtellina region lies close to the Alps and to Switzerland, the most northern area where Nebbiolo vines will still grow.

Band C/D

VALTELLINA SUPERIORE   [DOCG / Red / Lombardia]

On the shores of the River Adda in the province of Sondrio in a well-defined area including the communes of Chiuro, Teglio and Montagna five outstanding reds are produced with fairly typical characteristics, all qualifying for DOCG classification. All five are derived from the local grape called Chiavennasca (a Nebbiolo) with a minimum 90% to which are added other local red grapes, e.g. Brugnola, as well as some Pinot noir and Merlot.

They are dark red, full-bodied wines with a persistent subtle nose and a dry and slightly tannic taste. Each in a different way is a harmonic and characteristic wine having a minimum alcoholic content of 12° (usually sold at 13°) and a compulsory maturing period of two years, one of which at least in oak barrels. When they are labelled 'Riserva' they must be matured for a minimum of three years.

These are first-class wines that will age gracefully, less well-known abroad than they should be, and, depending on the locality in which they are grown, are named as follows:

Grumello the gentlest of the group
Inferno a strong body wine
Maroggia (pleasantly full bodied)
Sassella a refined wine
Valgella the most delicate

The Valtellina valley was well known for its reds even in Pliny's days, the wines themselves being described by Leonardo da Vinci as 'very powerful indeed'. Today, production is substantial and can boast more than 4,000 vintners. Some of these wines are also bottled in neighbouring Switzerland.

Band C/D

VELLETRI   [DOC / White / Lazio]

The Velletri wine is produced in the municipalities of Velletri and Lariano in the province of Rome, as well as partly in the commune of Cisterna in the province of Latina. It is derived from Malvasia Bianca di Candia (maximum 70%) and Trebbiano (minimum 30%) blended with other grapes (maximum 20%).

It comes in a white version which is more or less straw coloured with a very pleasant, delicate, fruity nose and a smooth taste. Of medium body, it is available either as dry, semi-dry or sweet. It is also available as a sparkling wine, but only in a dry version. The minimum alcoholic content is 11° but for the dry wine, if it rises to 11.5°, it can be termed 'Superiore'.

Band B

VELLETRI   [DOC / Red / Lazio]

A wine which also comes in a white version is produced in the area

covered by the towns of Velletri and Lariano which are in Rome
province and partly in the area of Cisterna, which is in the province of
Latina.

This is an unexpectedly good, drinkable wine, one of the few reds
produced successfully in the region of Lazio. It is made with Sangiovese
(maximum 45%), Montepulciano (maximum 50%), Cesanese (minimum 10%) and occasionally other grapes such as Bombino, Merlot and
Ciliegiolo, in varying proportions.

It has a strong ruby colour, veering to dark red as it matures, an
intense vinous nose, a pleasant dry or not-so-dry, smooth taste and a
minimum alcoholic content of 11.5°. When matured for the minimum
period of two years and having an alcoholic content of 12.5° it can be
labelled 'Riserva'.

It is a pleasant red which comes into its own at three or four years. It
ages well in the sense that it gains in smoothness but I would not
expect it to last well much beyond six or seven years.
Band B

VERDICCHIO   [DOC / White / Marche]

This was, with Frascati, one of the most widely available Italian whites
in the United Kingdom in the 1950s and 1960s, thanks also to the
fancy Roman-style bottle. The subsequent quarter century or so years
saw a steady decline in popularity for this wine which has now begun
to pick up. At the same time as its image has improved, so has its
quality.

Many, especially the French, consider it a superior white wine to be
combined with fish. It would be unfair to contradict this view although
I could never enthuse about Verdicchio wines generally. Nevertheless, it
is a good product which comes in two varieties:

Verdicchio dei Castelli di Jesi. This is grown almost exclusively in
the provinces of Ancona and Macerata in the Marche, the region of
central Italy on the Adriatic which, so to say, fronts Yugoslavia.

It takes its name from the commune of Jesi, on the hills traversed by
the river Esino, where most of it is produced from Verdicchio grapes
(minimum 85% plus Trebbiano and Malvasia). The Verdicchio grape is
the glory of the Marche and was known since Roman days, so much so
that there is an old story that when the Carthaginian army led by
Hannibal was crossing the region, there was great rejoicing in Rome at
the thought that Hannibal's soldiers might be so tempted by the local
wine that they would end up drunk. (It is also known as Trebbiano
Verde and many ampelographers consider it to be no more than a
Trebbiano di Soave.)

The Roman connection is also underlined by the fact that one of the
principal areas of production of the Verdicchio di Jesi is Cupramonta-
na. According to tradition, the name derives from a temple erected on
the hill to the Roman goddess Cupra, a building which was restored by
the Emperor Hadrian in 127 BC. It is said that in the religious rites in
honour of the goddess Cupra the Verdicchio wine played a large part.

The wine has a light straw colour and is very clear: it has a delicate, rather faint aroma but quite a dry, bitter-ish and slightly lemony, sometimes almondy, acidic taste, which persists. Some writers say it also displays notes of peach, apple and acacia blossoms!

There is in the wine some green shading at times and it comes in a dry or semi-dry version. The minimum alcoholic content of this Verdicchio is 11.5° rising to 12.5° for the 'Riserva'. It should be drunk slightly chilled, not too cold. It is suitable for only moderate ageing, though some modern versions claim to reach perfection after seven years.

In addition, there is a sparkling version and a 'Passito' which is a very tasty, sweet wine with a minimum alcoholic content of 15°.

The dry wine itself can, as with most Italian wines, be called 'Classico' if produced in the original area of production, 'Superiore' with a minimum alcoholic content of 12° and 'Riserva' with a minimum alcoholic content of 12.5°.

Verdicchio di Matelica. This takes its name from the principal village in the area where the wine is made (an area which extends right down to Fabriano in the province of Ancona) with Verdicchio grapes to which are added Trebbiano and Malvasia. The resultant wine is brilliantly coloured in very gentle straw yellow. It has a typical delicate scent and a dry, harmonious taste with a slightly bitter aftertaste.

Its minimum alcoholic content is 11.5° rising to 12.5° for the 'Riserva' and like its brother at Jesi, it comes also in sparkling and 'Passito' versions, with similar characteristics to the Verdicchio dei Castelli di Jesi.

In fact, at the risk of being termed a philistine, I must admit that I find it very difficult to distinguish the two, although experts and purists argue that the Verdicchio di Matelica is to be preferred.

I have noticed over the past few years a tendency for both varieties of Verdicchio to have a higher alcoholic content, quite commonly 13°.

This no doubt follows from improved vinification techniques and also from the need for the wines to be able to withstand storage for longer periods. Nowadays, five to seven years storage is not unusual for a Verdicchio at 13° alcohol.

Band A/B

VERDUZZO DEL PIAVE   [White / Friuli / Venezia Giulia]

This is a white wine produced in the provinces of Treviso and Udine from the Verduzzo grape which also produces the Verduzzo di Ramandolo, in its dry, though slightly 'petillant' version as well as in its very sweet version, the latter of which having recently become more available abroad.

It comes in two versions, Verduzzo Trevigiano and Verduzzo Friulano with similar characteristics. They are both available in a straw-coloured or an amber-coloured version of more or less intense tonality, with a tendency to veer towards a greenish colour. They have a delicate rather characteristic nose and a dryish but pleasant taste. The minimum alcoholic content is 11°.

Band B

VERMENTINO DI GALLURA   [DOCG / White / Sardegna]

The first Italian white to achieve DOCG status. It is a fine, flavourful, reasonably potent white wine grown almost exclusively from the grapes of Vermentino which, by law, have to represent a minimum of 95%. There may be added to them small quantities of other local non-aromatic white wines.

Vermentino has been produced for some time in the north-eastern region of Sardinia, known as the Gallura and more especially in a territory consisting of twenty-one communes in the province of Sassari, as well as two (Budoni and San Teodoro) in the province of Nuoro. It grows on hard, granite-based poor soil, amongst shrubs of myrtle and juniper.

It is a pleasant, straw-coloured wine with slight green tinges having an intense, though delicate, nose and a pleasant alcoholic taste of gooseberries with a slightly bitter aftertaste, which occasionally reminds the drinker of almonds. Some writers claim they can taste bananas and pineapple in it.

It has a minimum alcoholic content of 12° which rises to 13° for the 'Superiore' variety; some versions have 13.5° alcohol. When young, it is quite often very slightly fizzy. In my view, it has only one fault, namely its acidity.

This is not particularly high in the absolute sense (0.65%) but it is of a nature that makes it an exceptionally difficult wine to combine with some foods and especially with fruit. Nevertheless, it is a very fine, smooth white wine which is becoming better known.

There is also a sparkling Vermentino made in other parts of Sardinia. For this variety, the required minimum of Vermentino grape is lower, i.e. 85% and the minimum alcoholic content is 10.5°. One sad note, at least as far as I am concerned. I begin to detect a trend towards oaking this fine wine. I can only hope that it is a passing phase.
Band C

VERMENTINO DI SARDEGNA   [DOC / White / Sardegna]

Although they both originate in the same island, this should not be confused with the Vermentino di Gallura (q.v.). According to specification, the latter must be made with no less than 95% Vermentino grapes whereas for the former a minimum of 85% is prescribed.

Furthermore, Vermentino di Gallura can only be produced in the region known as such, which is situated in the north-eastern part of Sardinia, whereas the more liberally described Vermentino di Sardegna is produced throughout the island.

It is an exceptionally pale white wine which sometimes emerges as very lightly straw-coloured, with gentle greenish reflexes. It is a brilliant wine with a typical delicate nose, usually dry but also semi-dry, a fresh, summer wine with a slight acid aftertaste.

Its minimum alcoholic content is prescribed as 10.5° but it is normally available at 11.5°/12.5°. There is also a sparkling version.
Band B

VERMENTINO (*di Liguria*)   [White / Liguria]

This is one of a very few drinkable white wines from Liguria made with a minimum of 85% Vermentino grapes. The grape grows practically throughout the region and this wine is made both east and west of Genoa. It is straw-coloured with greenish shading, a fruity delicate nose and a dry, sapid, harmonious taste. Almost typically a summer wine, less interesting perhaps than Pigato (q.v.).
  It has a minimum alcoholic content of 10.5° but is more often sold at 11.5°. Like Pigato, it is usually found only in the area of production and reaches its peak at about two to three years.

Band A

VERMUT (VERMOUTH)   [Red / White – Piemonte]

This is one of a handful of Italian wines with a German name, the only one in fact not originating in the Trentino-Alto-Adige-Südtirol area (the others being Blauburgunder (Pinot Noir), Sudtiroler, Casteller, Etschtaler, Kaltereresse, Gewurztraminer).
  I hesitated before adding Vermouth to the list of wines. I was swayed ultimately by the fact that this is one of the most interesting and typical luxury Italian wines. It is almost certain that once the distillation of wine became established, the temptation could not be resisted of adding to it herbs, honey, or other flavours. It is said that Hippocrates, the Greek doctor who lived in the fifth century BC, used to add herbs, especially artemesia (wormwood), to wine to produce a drink that had digestive and stimulating properties. So true is this that right up to the Middle Ages in Italy herb wines were generally referred to as 'vino hippocratico' (or 'ippocrasso').
  The Romans, as they did in other fields, improved on the concept since they added to the wine myrtle, rosemary, and thyme essentially to aid digestion. The resultant wine was known to them as 'absinthiatum' (or 'absinthianum') vinum.
  When in the Middle Ages, the Venetians, the universal traders of the period, brought back to Europe the spices of the Orient, wine was mixed with cinnamon, cardamom, myrrh, rhubarb, cloves, and so on.
  The practices, however, were piecemeal and uneven and we had to wait until the eighteenth century for an Italian from Piemonte, one Alessio, to standardize the drink which took its name from the German term 'vermuth', meaning artemisia.
  The Italians themselves called it initially vermouth, and then reduced the noun to vermout. Vermouth is referred to in a book entitled *Oenologia Toscana*, published in 1773 by C. Villifranchi, but it had to wait until the end of the eighteenth century when Antonio Benedetto Carpano made it its own by selling it in his Turin shop.
  Vermouth started out in life as having an amber/orange colour and known as red vermouth; with the passage of time it was almost overtaken by what we now call Vermouth Bianco having golden yellow, clear colour.
  Originally it was made with white muscat grapes in the area of Canelli, fermentation including the skins. (With the passage of time

cheaper wines have been used originating from Romagna, Puglia, Sardegna and Sicilia.) To such wines are added alcohol, sugar, caramel and a variety of herbs which form part of the recipe of individual producers.

In addition to those which I have mentioned above, there can be found in Vermouth absinthe, coca, hyssop, marjoram, salvia, roman camomile, saffron, aniseed, coriander, fennel, vanilla, gentian, angelica, china and so on.

Most varieties of Vermouth have an average alcoholic content of 16/17°, starting at a minimum of 14° and rising to just under 20°. They are not really tannic, their acidity is fairly standard: their sugar content varies a lot.

Band C/D

VERNACCIA DI ORISTANO   [DOC / White / Sardegna]

Sardegna, due to its history, is largely planted with Spanish grape varieties and therefore produces wines more Spanish in style than Italian. Excellent red wines – especially from the Cannonau grape or the Carignano – are an island speciality, to the point that a red from Sulcis in the south-west gained the Trophy for the best Italian wine out of hundreds at the prestigious International Wine Challenge a few years ago.

Modern production techniques, introduced by a number of the island's quality producers, can now offer consistency of red wine flavour in place of rather hit or miss experiences in the past. And red quality predominance on the island is echoed by the fact that Sardegna's greatest sweet wine also uses red Cannonau, this time dried in the sun on straw mats placed around the vineyard, drying the berries and concentrating the grape sugar. The name? Anghelu Ruju (Red Angel) (q.v.).

But white wines are more of a mixed bunch because many producers succumbed to temptation and planted on the too-fertile flatlands in the south, gaining quantity and losing quality. A few wineries are now offering excellent quality dessert wines from Moscato grapes – production of which should be a natural in these surroundings.

A very good white is wine made from grapes (the Vernaccia) in all likelihood introduced into Sardinia from Spain towards the end of the fourteenth century. It is called di Oristano in order not to confuse it with other Vernacce which are available both in Sardinia and in other parts of Italy.

Sardegna was effectively under Spanish rule, as part of the Kingdom of Naples, since the sixteenth century. The association of Sardegna with Spain was always very close, the island being nearer Spain than either Naples or its sister island of Sicily. Many Spaniards had settled in Sardegna, a feudal society which was very similar to the one whence they had migrated; this is reflected not only in the importation of vines from Spain but also in a great similarity in the names of the various places. To give but a small example, Cannonau, one of the best Sardinian wines, produced in the area of Jerzu, is to be found abundantly in the village of Cardedu. Visitors to Cataluña may have noticed that not too far from its capital, Barcelona, there is a village called Cardedeu.

Whilst undeniably many Sardinian grapes are of Spanish origin, they can be said to have acclimatized so well that in many respects their character has changed.

Vernaccia is a generous strongly alcoholic white, golden or amber-coloured wine with a delicate nose and an aftertaste of almonds. Its minimum alcoholic content is 15° and it can rise to 18°. When matured for a minimum of three years it is defined as 'Superiore', after four years as 'Riserva'. Some versions are aged for many years in oak barrels.

It is produced in the province of Cagliari in a number of villages in the valley of the river Tirso (Oristano, Baratili San Pietro, Cabras, Santa Giusta, Simaxis, Solana).

It is also available in a sweet version.

The dry Vernaccia is excellent as an aperitif and may be even preferred as an after-dinner drink. The locals drink it throughout meals, but that may be a trifle excessive unless one is used to drinking, with the meal, wines of a fairly alcoholic content. It is best served at about 14/15°, but some like it very slightly chilled

There is little to choose between it and a 'fino'; the Vernaccia is probably smoother and warmer and, ultimately, although organoleptically they may not differ very much, emerges as slightly less dry than a 'fino'.

The locals recommend it for mature cheese and desserts. It is probably more versatile than they think. Unfortunately, the number of producers of this wine is reducing, there being at present no more than four who can make it available on anything like a commercial scale. Tastes are changing in Italy as elsewhere; indeed, I have heard it said that the flavour of the Vernaccia di Oristano reminds one of oxidized wine. That may be: I like it very much.

Band B/C

VERNACCIA DI SAN GIMIGNANO (*sometimes called Vernaccia di Pietrafitta*)   [DOCG / White / Toscana]

Like the town from which it takes its name, this wine has a very long history. It was already well known in the thirteenth century and is mentioned by Dante (*Divine Comedy*, Canto XIII).

The reader may know that visitors to Tuscany seldom fail to go to the village of San Gimignano, characterized by what one could term the first skyscrapers in the world. Known as 'tower houses' they were built in about 1200. According to extant records, about seventy-six of them were erected but only thirteen stand today, some over 175 ft high.

I suggest that it is an extremely pleasant experience to walk through the pedestrianized 'high street' of San Gimignano: it is flanked by bars where the local wines, especially the Vernaccia of course, can be sampled, together with 'nibbles' of very high quality. It is a very popular wine, both in Italy and abroad.

Francesco Redi, a famous Tuscan poet of the seventeenth century (who was also a scientist of repute because to him are ascribed the first scientific study into spermatozoan generation and the setting out for the first time of the theory of infection), known chiefly for his 'Bacco in Toscana' (Bacchus in Tuscany), compiled in 1685, wrote in one of his poems, (his *Ditirambo*) about the God, Bacchus, who extols the virtues of the Vernaccia wine and inveighs against anybody who does not like it. . . . .

His words are often found on the reverse label of bottles of Vernaccia di San Gimignano. For the record they are as follows:

Se v'è alcuno a cui non piaccia
la Vernaccia
vendemmiata in Pietrafitta,
interdetto, maledetto
fugga via dal mio cospetto

Which freely translated reads:

Let anyone who doesn't like
the Vernaccia
grown in Pietrafitta,
be damned, banned
and removed from my presence

Perhaps in recognition of the great seniority of this wine it was the first Italian wine (regardless of colour) to receive the accolade of the DOC.

It is made within the municipality of San Gimignano in the province of Siena from grapes bearing the same name (90%) and the addition, in respect of the remainder, of other local white grapes. The area of production is comparatively small (around 2000 acres).

When young, it is gently straw-coloured, turning to bright gold as it ages. It has a fine penetrating, characteristic nose and a dry well-balanced taste with a slightly bitter aftertaste.

Its minimum alcoholic content is 11° but when matured for no less than fourteen months 'according to traditional methods' with an extra four months spent in bottles, it can be termed 'Riserva'.

Lastly, one should record that there is considerable doubt as to the origin of the Vernaccia grape. Modern ampelographers, however, seem to be agreed on two matters, namely in the first place that the Vernaccia di San Gimignano has nothing to do with other Vernaccia grapes such as that of Serrapetrona or that of Oristano and, secondly, that it is more likely to be a clone of the Trebbiano variety which has acclimatized particularly well in its area of production in Toscana, namely the Val d'Elsa.

Band B/C

VERNACCIA DI SERRAPETRONA   [DOCG / Red / Marche]

An outstanding dry and sweet wine made in the commune of

Serrapetrona and others in the province of Macerata with the Vernaccia grape (minimum 85%) and the addition of local ones.

It has a fine, scented nose and is purple coloured, sparkling with a very persistent foam and a minimum alcoholic content of 11.5°. Despite the slightly bitter aftertaste it is an extremely pleasant dessert wine, the result of a local form of 'appassimento', and is much underrated. In recognition of its quality it was upgraded to DOCG in 2005.

Band C

VESUVIO   [DOC / Red / White / Rosé / Campania]

The dark ashen colour soil on the slopes of Mount Vesuvio produces a number of wines, red, white and rosé which are well known locally but not quite recognized abroad. Probably the most common is the Lacrima Christi del Vesuvio which comes in white, red and rosé versions.

The white is made with Codadivolpe and Verdaca with optional additions of Falanghina and Greco and it is a straw-coloured, slightly acidic, dry and reasonably pleasant wine, having a minimum alcoholic content of 11°.

The red, made with Piedirosso grapes as well as Aglianico, is a reasonably pleasant ruby, medium-bodied wine with a vinous nose and a dry harmonious taste. It has a minimum alcoholic content of 12° and is also produced in a sparkling version.

The rosé has a minimum alcoholic content of 10.5°, and is more or less tinted, dry to the palate, with a pleasant, vinous aroma.

Band B

VIN SANTO DEL CHIANTI (*Vin Santo del Chianti Classico*)
                                        [DOC / White / Toscana]

'Vin Santo' means 'holy wine' and is a fairly generic description for sweet, highly alcoholic liqueur-type wines made in many parts of Italy. For instance, there is the Vino Santo del Trentino (Trento) of Gambellara (Vicenza), of Montefiascone (Lazio), of Orvieto (Umbria), Pugliese (throughout Puglia), Trevigiano (Treviso), Veronese (Verona).

Indeed, it is true to say that this kind of wine is, like Muscat, almost an ancillary to wine production so that given the right type of grapes, wherever the grape is distilled, a sweet version can emerge.

What we are dealing with under this heading, however, are the two types of Vin Santo that are classics as far as Italy is concerned, which originate in the Chianti district and are entitled to the DOC label.

They are both made with Trebbiano and/or Malvasia grapes (minimum 70%) as well as other recommended or authorized varieties (e.g. Colombano) which are carefully selected and subjected to the *appassimento* process, then turned into must between 1 December and 31 March of the year following the vintage.

Both wines go from straw colour to golden amber, getting darker as they mature, have a very marked, fruity, intense and typical nose and are exceptionally pleasant, almost velvety to the palate.

There are only minor differences between the two. The Vin Santo del Chianti is available in four versions, namely dry, semi-dry, semi-sweet and sweet.

The Vin Santo del Chianti Classico is available only in the dry and semi-dry versions. The former has a minimum alcoholic content of 15.5°, the latter of 16°. Both have to be compulsorily matured in small barrels for three years and if they wish to have the 'Riserva' label, for four.

Both are available in an 'occhio di pernice' version. This type of Vin Santo comes from the Sangiovese grape (minimum 50%) as well as from other red grapes. It has a colour that goes from gentle to dark pink and a minimum alcoholic content of 17°. Otherwise, the process does not differ materially from the white Vin Santo nor, in my opinion, does the taste.

In the same way as there are sub-areas for the production of the ordinary dry red Chianti, the Vin Santo can also come from the Colli Aretini, Colli Fiorentini, Colli Senesi, Colline Pisane, Montalbano, Montespertoli and Rufina areas.

There is also a Vin Santo di Montepulciano which I do not believe is available in the UK but is mentioned for the sake of the record. This is made in the same area as the Vino Nobile di Montepulciano DOCG (q.v.) with Malvasia, Grechetto and Trebbiano grapes (minimum 70%). It is similar in colour to the Chianti Vin Santo but the nose is much more marked and fruitier. Minimum 70% from Trebbiano and Malvasia grapes. It must be matured for no less than three years but, if it wishes to be labelled as 'Riserva', that period rises to five.

It, too, is available in an 'occhio di pernice' version which is made with Sangiovese grapes (minimum 50%) as well as others. This is a different type of Vin Santo; the colour is changed, for it veers between amber and topaz with a reddish tinge turning brown as it ages. It has a complex fruity nose and a very marked sweet aftertaste. Minimum alcoholic content 18°, minimum maturing eight years. A much rarer and more expensive commodity.

The Trebbiano Toscano and the Malvasia grape are to be found throughout Tuscany. So you have the Vin Santo from Carmignano in the province of Prato, the Vin Santo of Empoli, of the Colli Apuani, of Capalbio, of Montecarlo (in the province of Lucca), of Elba, of Massa, of Siena, of Montescudaio, in the province of Pisa, of Montalcino, of San Gimignano, of Montepulciano.

Depending on where it is made, and on the vines popular or successful in the area, other grapes are added; Sangiovese occasionally, Grechetto in Montepulciano and Vernaccia in San Gimignano.

The minimum alcoholic content varies but as a generalization it starts at 15.5°, it averages 16°, but in some cases, as for the Vin Santo di Montepulciano, is even higher at 17°.

The minimum maturing period varies, depending on the quality of the wine. Nowhere can this be less than three years but, in many cases, it can be four (for the 'Riserva' type), five or even, for a special variety of Montepulciano, which has a minimum alcoholic content of 18°, eight years. I mention this for the sake of the record: wine of this kind is not only scarce, but is also very expensive: it is, of course, something special.

Most types of Vin Santo mature well and many reach their peak at ten years, but over the past few years there has been a tendency to sell the wine when it is still fairly young. This has contributed to its becoming slightly less expensive. One of the results is that the popularity of this dessert wine has spread. Italian restaurateurs sometimes offer it as a complimentary drink at the end of the meal usually, though not necessarily, accompanied by biscuits, especially of the Tuscan variety known as 'Cantuccini'.

I mentioned at the beginning the Vino Santo of other areas. I should also record that the description 'Vinsanto' is applied in many regions of Italy to certain types of sweet wines. The use of these descriptions is being reviewed. Giving effect to EEC Regulation 753/2002, the Italian government issued a Ministerial Decree on 3 July 2004 the consequence of which is that the traditional ways of describing wines which are identified in Schedule III to that Decree are reserved exclusively for DOC and IGT wines which are also identified there.

The net result is that the description 'Vinsanto' will only continue to apply to IGT, DOC and DOCG wines which traditionally have been called 'Vin Santo' (and this is clearly the case for the 'Vin Santo' of Toscana, but it will also apply to others) and it will no longer be lawful to use it, as is done at the moment, generally on a number of liqueur-type wines.

Two small matters worth mentioning. Firstly, there is also a dry version of the Vin Santo, mainly consumed locally.

Secondly, the expression 'Vin Santo' probably came about in the fourteenth century because it was used in church during the celebration of the Mass. But there is another story attached to it. Long before the Vin Santo was so called, there was produced in the locality a 'Vin Pretto' i.e. a 'genuine wine' (by which presumably the locals meant that there would be no 'additives' and 'sophistication'). When, on the occasion of the Ecumenical Council that was held in Florence in 1349, the Greek patriarch Bessarion was offered some of this 'Vin Pretto', he is alleged to have remarked chauvinistically: 'this is the wine of Xantos' presumably because it tasted like the sweet wine of his homeland Thrace. The locals misunderstood that and thereafter called their fine product Vin Santo.

Believe what you will. . . . . .

Band C/D

VINO NOBILE DI MONTEPULCIANO
[DOCG / DOC / Red / Toscana]

A DOCG wine whose origins can be traced back to the fourteenth century, though some believe we owe it to the Etruscans. It is called 'noble' presumably because of its high quality but also in all likelihood because, historically, its production in a fairly well confined area in the commune of Montepulciano (in the province of Siena) was entrusted to ancient noble families in the locality.

It is derived essentially from Sangiovese grape (known locally as Prugnolo gentile) in a minimum percentage of 70%, plus Canaiolo (max 10%); other grapes may also be used (e.g. Mammolo). These are recommended, authorized grapes for the particular area and can only be added in a quantity not exceeding 20% and on the further understanding that of this additional 20% white grapes should not exceed 10%.

The detailed specification covering the wine shows the great concern for the genuineness of DOC and, in this case, DOCG wines, the Nobile di Montepulciano qualifying for the DOCG appellation in 1980 soon after Brunello di Montalcino.

It is ruby-coloured, with a minimum alcoholic content of 12.5%. In some varieties the colour is garnet rather than ruby with tints of purple. It is a delicately perfumed wine, dry with a fairly persistent, elegant aftertaste. It must be kept for at least two years after 1 January of the year subsequent to that in which it is made and it is not uncommon for it to be matured in casks for two-and-a-half years and six months in bottles. In some varieties the colour is garnet rather than ruby with tints of purple, often tasting of violets, dry and pleasant. It is somewhat uneven when young, but settles down quite successfully with the passage of time.

It should not be confused with the Montepulciano d'Abruzzo, which comes from a different region (Abruzzo is on the eastern coast of Italy) and takes its name from the grape, grown there as well as extensively in south-eastern Italy. The Vino Nobile takes its name from a town, the red of Abruzzo comes from a grape thus named.

The Tuscans are exceptionally proud of their Vino Nobile di Montepulciano: there is in fact a local saying 'Montepulciano d'ogni vino è re', namely 'Montepulciano is king of all wines', echoing the words used by the poet Francesco Redi, whom we have already mentioned when dealing with Chianti.

There is another red version, the DOC Rosso di Montepulciano. This is a very pleasant, intensely vinous, dry and reasonably tannic wine having a minimum alcoholic content of 11° and made in the main with Sangiovese and Canaiolo Nero grapes. It is a very recent addition to the range since the DOC was established in late 1998. Its production area in the province of Siena overlaps that of the Vino Nobile di Montepulciano but obviously the controls (yield per hectare, alcoholic content, ageing and so on) are less stringent.

DOCG Band B/C

DOC Band A/B

ZAGAROLO [DOC / Lazio / White]

A wine dating back to the sixteenth century, much appreciated locally but seldom exported, Zagarolo is produced in the territory of Gallicano and, partly, in that of Zagarolo. It is a blend of no less than 70% Malvasia, up to 30% Trebbiano and up to 10% of Bellone and Bombino.

A gently straw-coloured delicate, fairly pleasant, dry wine, occasionally semi-dry, it has a minimum alcoholic content of 11.5°. When produced with no less than 12.5° it can, in common with most other wines referred to in this work, be called 'Superiore'. It does not lend itself to any kind of maturing and it is normally consumed with the year.

APPENDICES

APPENDIX

APPENDIX 1

LIST OF ALL WINES REVIEWED IN THIS BOOK

(numbers shown refer to pages)

257

LIST OF OFFICIALLY RECOGNIZED WINES IN ITALY

(Those with an asterisk have not been reviewed in this book although they might be mentioned in passing. All DOCG and DOC wines are listed. Only 16 IGT table wines reviewed are included.)

DOCG Wines

Albana di Romagna White – Emilia Romagna
Arneis (Roero) White Piemonte
Asti or Asti Spumante – Moscato d'Asti White/Sparkling Piemonte
Barbaresco Red Piemonte
Bardolino Red Veneto
Barolo Red Piemonte
Brachetto d'Acqui Red Piemonte (or Acqui)
Brunello di Montalcino Red Toscana
Carmignano Red Toscana
Chianti Red Toscana
Chianti Classico Red Toscana
Conero Red Marche
Fiano di Avellino White Campania
Franciacorta White/Sparkling Lombardia
Gattinara Red Piemonte
Gavi – Cortese di Gavi White Piemonte
Ghemme Red Piemonte
Greco di Tufo White Campania
Montepulciano d'Abruzzo – Colline Teramane Red Abruzzo
Ramandolo White Friuli Venezia Giulia
Recioto di Soave White Veneto
Sagrantino di Montefalco Red Umbria
Sforzato (or Sfursat) see Valtellina
Soave Superiore White Veneto
Taurasi Red Campania
Torgiano Rosso Riserva Red Umbria
Valtellina Superiore Red Lombardia
Vermentino di Gallura White Sardegna
Vernaccia di San Gimignano White Toscana

Vernaccia di Serrapetrona Red Marche
Vino Nobile di Montepulciano

DOC Wines

*Aglianico del Taburno e Taburno
Aglianico del Vulture
*Albugnano
Alcamo
*Aleatico di Gradoli
*Aleatico di Puglia
*Alezio
Alghero
*Alto Adige (Südtiroler)
*Alta Langa
Ansonica Costa dell'Argentario
*Aprilia
*Arborea
*Arcole
Arneis (or Roero)
*Assisi
*Atina
Aversa Asprinio (or Asprinio di Aversa)
*Bagnoli di Sopra
Barbera (d'Alba & d'Asti)
Barbera dell'Oltrepó Pavese
Barbera del Monferrato
Barco Reale di Carmignano o Rosato di Carmignano
Bardolino
*Bianchello del Metauro
*Bianco Capena
*Bianco della Valdinievole
*Bianco dell'Empolese
Bianco di Custoza
*Bianco di Pitigliano
*Bianco Pisano di San Torpé
Biferno
*Bivongi
*Boca
Bolgheri e Bolgheri Sassicaia (see Sassicaia)
*Bosco Eliceo
*Botticino
*Bramaterra
*Breganze
Brindisi
Cabernet Trentino
*Cacc'e mmitte di Lucera
*Cagnina di Romagna
Caldaro

*Campi Flegrei
*Campidano di Terralba
*Canavese
*Candia dei Colli Apuani
Cannonau
*Capalbio
*Capri
*Capriano del Colle
*Carema
Carignano del Sulcis
Carmignano (Barco Reale di Carmignano)
*Carso
Castel del Monte
*Castel San Lorenzo
*Casteller
*Castelli Romani
*Cellatica
Cerasuolo di Vittoria
*Cerveteri
Cesanese del Piglio or Piglio
*Cesanese di Affile
*Cesanese di Olevano Romano
Chardonnay Trentino (Trentino Chardonnay)
*Cilento
*Cinque Terre e Cinque Terre Sciacchetrá
*Circeo
Ciró
*Cisterna d'Asti
*Colli Albani
*Colli Altotiberini
*Colli Amerini
*Colli Berici
Colli Bolognesi
Colli Bolognesi Classico Pignoletto
*Colli del Trasimeno
*Colli della Sabina
*Colli dell'Etruria Centrale
Colli di Conegliano
*Colli di Faenza
*Colli di Imola
*Colli di Luni
*Colli di Parma
*Colli di Rimini
*Colli di Scandiano e di Canossa
*Colli Etruschi Viterbesi
Colli Euganei
Colli Lanuvini
*Colli Maceratesi
*Colli Martani

*Colli Orientali del Friuli
*Colli Perugini
*Colli Pesaresi
*Colli Piacentini
*Colli Romagna Centrale
*Colli Tortonesi
*Collina Torinese
*Colline di Levanto
*Colline Lucchesi
*Colline Novaresi
*Colline Saluzzesi
*Collio Goriziano
Conegliano-Valdobbiadene
*Contea di Sclafani
Contessa Entellina
*Controguerra
Copertino
*Cori
Cortese (dell'Alto Monferrato)
*Corti Benedettine del Padovano
*Cortona
*Costa d'Amalfi
*Coste della Sesia
*Delia Nivolelli
Dolcetto (d'Acqui, d'Alba, d'Asti, delle Langhe Monregalesi.
   di Diano d'Alba & di Dogliani)
Dolcetto di Ovada
*Donnici
Elba
Eloro Sicilia
Erbaluce di Caluso (otherwise known as Caluso)
Esino
Est! Est! Est! di Montefiascone
Etna
Falerio (dei Colli Ascolani)
Falerno (del Massico)
*Fara
*Faro
Frascati
Freisa (d'Asti & di Chieri)
*Friuli Annia
*Friuli Aquileia
Friuli Grave (Grave del Friuli)
*Friuli Isonzo
*Friuli Latisana
*Gabiano
*Galatina
*Galluccio
Gambellara

*Garda Bresciano
Garda Colli Mantovani
*Genazzano
*Gioia del Colle
*Giró di Cagliari
*Golfo del Tigullio
*Gravina
*Greco di Bianco
Grignolino d'Asti & del Monferrato Casalese
*Guardia Sanframondi
Ischia
Ischia
Lacrima Christi del Vesuvio (see Vesuvio)
*Lacrima di Morro d'Alba
Lago di Caldaro (Kalterersee) (see Caldaro)
Lambrusco (di Sorbara, Grasparossa di Castelvetro &
    Salamino di Santa Croce)
*Lambrusco Mantovano
*Lamezia
Langhe-Langhe Favorita
*Lessini Durello
*Lessona
*Leverano
Lison-Pramaggiore
*Lizzano
*Loazzolo
Locorotondo
Lugana
Malvasia delle Lipari
Malvasia di Bosa
*Malvasia di Cagliari
Malvasia di Casorzo (otherwise known as Casorzo)
Malvasia di Castelnuovo don Bosco
Mandrolisai
*Marino
Marsala
*Martina (Martina Franca)
*Matino
*Melissa
Menfi
*Merlara
Merlot
*Molise
Monferrato
Monica di Cagliari
Monica di Sardegna
*Monreale
Montecarlo
*Montecompatri-Colonna

*Montecucco
Montefalco
*Montello e Colli Asolani
Montepulciano d'Abruzzo
*Monteregio di Massa Marittima
*Montescudaio
*Monti Lessini
Morellino di Scansano
Moscadello di Montalcino
*Moscato di Cagliari
Moscato di Noto
Moscato di Pantelleria
Moscato Passito
*Moscato di Sardegna
*Moscato di Siracusa
*Moscato di Sorso-Sennori
Moscato di Trani
*Nardó
*Nasco di Cagliari
Nebbiolo
Nero d'Avola
*Nettuno
*Nuragus di Cagliari
Offida
Oltrepó Pavese
*Orcia
Ormeasco (otherwise known as Pornassio)
*Orta Nova
Orvieto
*Ostuni
*Pagadebit di Romagna
Parrina
*Penisola Sorrentina
*Pentro d'Isernia
*Piemonte
Piglio
*Pinerolese
*Pollino
Pomino
Primitivo
Prosecco (di Conegliano/Valdobbiadene)
Recioto Amarone
*Reggiano
*Reno
*Riesi
*Riviera del Brenta
*Riviera Ligure di Ponente
Roero
*Romagna Albana Spumante

Rossese di Dolceacqua
*Rosso Canosa
Rosso Conero
*Rosso di Cerignola
Rosso di Montalcino
*Rosso di Montepulciano
*Rosso Orvietano
*Rosso Piceno
*Rubino di Cantavenna
*Ruché di Castagnole Monferrato
Salaparuta (corvo)
Salice Salentino (formerly known as Salento)
*Sambuca di Sicilia
*San Colombano
*San Gimignano
*San Martino della Battaglia
San Severo
*San Vito di Luzzi
Sangiovese di Romagna
*Sannio
*Santa Margherita di Belice
*Sant'Agata dei Goti
*Sant'Anna di Isola Capo Rizzuto
*Sant'Antimo
*Sardegna Semidano
Sassella
Sassicaia – (now Bolgheri Saisicaia)
Sauvignon Trentino
*Savuto
*Scanzo
*Scavigna
*Sciacca
Schioppettino
*Sizzano
Soave
Solopaca
*Sovana
Squinzano
Taburno
*Tarquinia
Teroldego Rotaliano
*Tene dell'Alta Val d'Agri
Terre di Franciacorta
Terreni di San Severino
*Torcolato
Torgiano Bianco
Trebbiano d'Abruzzo
*Trebbiano di Romagna
Trentino

*Trento
*Valcalepio
Valdadige (Etschtaler)
*Val d'Arbia
Valdichiana
*Val di Cornia
*Valle d'Aosta (Vallée d'Aoste)
*Val Polcèvera
Valpolicella
*Valsusa
Velletri
*Verbicaro
Verdicchio (dei Castelli di Jesi & Matelica)
*Verduno Pelaverga
Vermentino di Sardegna
Vernaccia di Oristano
Vernaccia di Serrapetrona
Vesuvio
*Vicenza
*Vignanello
Vin Santo del Chianti (V S del Chianti Classico & di
  Montepulciano)
*Vini del Piave
Zagarolo

List of IGT & Other Wines

Aleatico di Portoferraio IGT Red Elba-Toscana
Anghelu Ruju Red Sardegna
Ansonica White Elba-Toscana
Barolo Chinato Red Piemonte
Cabernet Red Friuli Venezia Giulia
Chardonnay IGT White Trentino Alto Adige Friuli Venezia
  Giula
Chiaretto del Garda IGT Rosé Veneto
Copertino IGT Red Puglia
Corvo IGT Red/White Sicilia
Custoza (or Bianco di Custoza) White Veneto
Falanghina White Campania
Garda (Garda Classico – Garda Colli Mantovani)
  White/Red Lombardia/Veneto
Grecanico IGT White Sicilia
Grechetto IGT White Umbria
Inzolia White Sicilia
Lagrein Red,/Rosé Trentino Alto Adige
Marchese di Villa Marina Red Sardegna
Marzemino Red Trentino/Alto Adige
Masseto (see Ornellaia)
Montevetrano Red Campania

Moscato Rosa (Rosenmuskateller) Rosé Friuli-Venezia
　　Giulia Trentino/Alto Adige
Negroamaro Red Puglia
Ornellaia – a 'Super Tuscan' Red Toscana
Picolit White Friuli Venezia Giulia
Pigato White Liguria
Pinot Grigio White Friuli/VeneziaGiulia Trentino/Alto
　　Adige Veneto
Refosco dal Peduncolo Rosso Red Friuli Venezia Giulia
Regaleali IGT Red/white Sicilia
Ribolla (or Ribolla Gialla) IGT White Friulia Venezia Giulia
Riesling White Trentino Alto Adige Friuli Veneza Giulia
Rosso di Montalcino Red Toscana
Sangiovese di Toscana and elsewhere IGT Red Toscana
　　& various regions
Solaia – a 'Super Tuscan' Red Toscana
Sylvaner (or Silvaner) White Trentino Alto Adige
Terlaner White Trentino Alto Adige
Tignanello – a 'Super Tuscan' IGT Red Toscana
Tocai White dry Friuli Venezia Giulia Veneto
Torbato White Sardegna
Traminer (Gewurztraminer) White Trentino/Alto Adige
Verduzzo del Piave White Friuli/Venezia Giulia
Vermentino (di Liguria) White Liguria

APPENDIX 3

ANNUAL ITALIAN PRODUCTION OF WINE 1986-2005

1986	77,093,300	**1996**	58,543,000
1987	75,830,900	**1997**	50,563,000
1988	61,010,300	**1998**	57,140,000
1989	60,326,800	**1999**	58,073,000
1990	54,927,000	**2000**	54,088,000
1991	59,787,600	**2001**	52,293,000
1992	68,686,100	**2002**	44,604,000
1993	62,672,000	**2003**	44,086,000
1994	59,290,000	**2004**	53,135,000
1995	56,201,000	**2005**	50,566,000

PRINCIPAL WINE PRODUCING COUNTRIES

Countries	2001	2002	2003	2004
France	53,389,000	50,353	46,360	57,386
Italy	50,093,000	44,604	44,086	53,000
Spain	30,500,000	33,478	41,843	42,988
United States	19,200,000	20,300	19,500	20,109
Argentina	15,835,000	12,695	13,225	15,464
Australia	10,163,000	11,509	10,194	13,811
China	10,800,000	11,200	11,600	11,700
Germany	8,891,000	9,885	8,191	10,047
South Africa	6,471,000	7,189	8,853	9,279
Portugal	7,789,000	6,677	7,340	7,481
Chile	5,658,000	5,623	6,682	6,301
Romania	5,090,000	5,461	5,555	6,166
Russia	3,430,000	4,060	4,530	5,120
Hungary	5,406,000	3,333	3,880	4,340
Greece	3,477,000	3,085	3,799	4,295
Moldavia	1,400,000	2,251	3,215	3,026
Brazil	2,968,000	3,212	2,620	3,925
Austria	2,531,000	2,599	2,526	2,735
Ukraine		2,430	2,380	2,000
Bulgaria	2,260,000	1,982	2,314	1,949
Croatia		2,095	1,768	1,561
Yugoslavia	2,100,000	1,620	1,734	1,740

Amounts in Hectolitres
Source: Office International de la Vigne et de Vin, Paris, France

AVERAGE ANNUAL WINE CONSUMPTION PER CAPITA

(litres/per person/per annum)
(as at 31.12.2002)

Country	Amount
Luxembourg	66.1
France	48.5
Italy*	47.5
Portugal	42.0
Switzerland	40.9
Argentina	34.6
Greece	33.8
Uruguay	33.3
Denmark	32.6
Spain	30.6
Austria	29.8
Finland	26.3
Germany	23.6
Belgium	23.0
Romania	23.0
Malta	22.3
Bulgaria	21.3
Australia	20.4
United Kingdom	20.1
United States of America	9.5

Source: *Drink Pocket Book 2006*, AC Nielsen, Henley-on-Thames

The above table showing the position as at 31 December 2002 I have provided for record purposes only. The figures appear to fluctuate depending on the source. The latest available to me were produced on the occasion of the largest wine fair in the world, VinExpo, by a firm of researchers known as IWSR.

They made a study of 114 countries, 28 of which being wine producers and they came up with some rather startling information as far as Britain is concerned.

According to them, from 2001 to 2005 retail wine sales in Britain rose by 25%; similarly, consumption there has been rising every year since 1980 (it is falling in France and Italy. . .). According to such study, in 2005 residents in the British Isles drank 1.7 billion bottles equal to some 36 per adult. Disagreeing with the 2002 figures already mentioned, they found that the heaviest drinkers in the world were the Danes with 51 bottles a year each, closely followed by the Germans with 49 bottles each.

Whilst they record that Britain comes fifth amongst the world's biggest consumers (in order, France, Italy, the USA and Germany) they attribute the increase in wine popularity in Britain to a number of factors such as greater affluence, a form of social snobbery, the aggressive sales techniques of UK supermarkets and the habits acquired whilst holidaying abroad. All these factors are, of course, true but I would proffer a slightly different explanation, namely that because of the higher alcoholic content of wine, a number of people find it easier to get drunk more quickly and maybe even more cheaply. That may be unfair, but it is undoubted that wine has a faster effect on the body in terms of reducing inhibitions, hence the old Roman saying 'in vino veritas' namely that after people have been drinking wine they show themselves in their true light.

IN CONCLUSION

And that is it. When my publisher first suggested I write a book about Italian wines, I know that what he had in mind was an elementary text. I believe what I have written is exactly that, except that in my enthusiasm for the subject, I have perhaps gone beyond my initial brief!

In retrospect, this may not have been such a bad idea - first, because I had great fun writing the book, and second, because I am convinced that given the ever-increasing availability of quality Italian wines, those who discover them may well wish to know more about particular wines and about the Italian wine scene in general.

Thus, if I have succeeded in stimulating greater interest in the subject, at whatever level (and not just the wines which please me!), then I shall consider myself both fortunate and satisfied.

Salute!